Bonnie,

Thank you for being such a dear and special friend,

Earlene

1/11/10

The Case of the Missing Person

The Case of the Missing Person

How Finding Jesus of Nazareth Can Transform Communities and Individuals Today

R. Earle Rabb

WIPF & STOCK · Eugene, Oregon

THE CASE OF THE MISSING PERSON
How Finding Jesus of Nazareth Can Transform Communities and Individuals Today

Wipf & Stock
An Imprint of Wipf and Stock Publishers
199 W. 8th Ave., Suite 3
Eugene, OR 97401
www.wipfandstock.com

ISBN 13: 978-1-60608-996-5

Manufactured in the U.S.A.

For my beloved Ann and my wonderful family

Contents

Acknowledgments

It is unusual for a book to be forty years in the making. This book is, indeed, the culmination of a long process of personal and professional growth and struggle. Because the book is the result of many years of research, preaching, and teaching, many people have influenced and shaped the end product, even when they might disagree with some of my conclusions.

As every author is keenly aware, writing a book is never simply a solitary task. As I submitted my manuscript to the publisher I realized how much I owe to others. Many people ought to be thanked, far more than can be named in this brief space. I am deeply indebted to thousands of individuals who have gone before me and on whose shoulders I stand.

I begin with my wife, Ann, who originally suggested the idea for this book. She has patiently endured my writing schedule and my preoccupation with this project.

I also want to thank the fellows of the Jesus Seminar for their scholarly research into the life and teachings of Jesus of Nazareth. These are scholars of great intellect and warm hearts, who have shared their insights with one another and with the general public. I am indebted to many from whose books, articles, and lectures I have learned. I especially want to pay tribute to one of my seminary professors, the late Dr. Robert Funk, who founded the Jesus Seminar in 1985 and led it for the first twenty-three years of its existence. He was a brilliant and terrifying presence in the classroom, and we seminary students were in awe (and fear) of him. He taught us to think critically and carefully about the faith we held dear to our hearts.

I am grateful also to the thousands of lay people in the five churches I served over a forty-three year career as a United Methodist pastor. They have accepted me as I am, have listened to many sermons, and have interacted with me in various classes I have taught. Through it all they have helped me grow into the person I have become, for better or for worse.

In many ways, they have been examples to me of what it means to be followers of Jesus.

I also pay tribute to my colleagues in ministry. Their friendship and encouragement through the years has carried me along the road of life. I want to especially mention Reverend Paul W. Wagner, a minister of vision and openness. He was my hero in my youth, a model of what I wanted to be as a minister. It was my privilege to conclude my active ministry in the very church he founded as a young minister.

In addition, I want to thank my editor, Tara McDonald-Tiner, for her invaluable help in the preparation of the manuscript. Her suggestions and guidance made the process of writing a joy and a pleasure. I am also grateful to my editor at Wipf and Stock Publishers, Christian Amondson, and my copyeditor, Susan Carlson Wood, for their valuable assistance in bringing this project to completion.

As I wrote this book, I often wondered in whose debt I was for a phrase or idea appearing in my manuscript. Was it something I heard in a lecture or a sermon? Was it something I read in a book or journal? Did it arise out of a conversation with a colleague or a lay person? I don't know if I ever could answer these questions, but I do know I am deeply dependent on many people, and I am grateful for each one who has touched my life.

Introduction

When I was growing up in the 1950s a clever saying was making the rounds:

> My mind is made up; don't confuse me with facts.

Hopefully you are more open-minded than the attitude expressed in this saying, especially regarding your religious beliefs. In this book I am asking you to be open to first exploring the question of what Jesus of Nazareth was trying to accomplish in his public activity, and then asking what this might mean for us today. This book is divided into two parts, and I want to now introduce you to each one.

PART I: THE SEARCH FOR A MISSING PERSON: JESUS OF NAZARETH

The late Senator Daniel Patrick Moynihan once said, "Everyone is entitled to his or her own opinion. No one, however, is entitled to his or her own facts." In this regard, when it comes to Jesus, every individual, church, and denomination is entitled to their own opinion (or beliefs) about Jesus. Some of these beliefs are the following:

> Jesus is (or is not) the divine Son of God.
> Jesus is (or is not) the Second Person of the Trinity.
> Jesus is (or is not) the Savior of the world.
> Jesus died for the forgiveness of sins of those who believe in him.
> Jesus is the only means by which a person can enter into heaven.

These and similar statements about Jesus are opinions, or beliefs. They are not factual statements with evidence proving the case one way or the other. Simply because a large number of people (such as a church or a denomination) hold a particular belief about Jesus, the belief (or opinion) does not turn into a fact. Beliefs are not facts. The wide variety of beliefs about Jesus, even among his devoted followers, confirms the truth that these are opinions about Jesus, not factual statements about Jesus. Certainly, each person is entitled to his or her own opinions (or beliefs) about Jesus.

In this book I will *not* be focusing on opinions or beliefs about Jesus. I will set those aside for the duration of this book. Nor will I be exploring what Jesus came to mean to the church through the centuries following his life.

My aim in part 1 of this book is to find the missing person Jesus of Nazareth. It may come as a surprise to the reader to learn that Jesus of Nazareth is in reality a missing historical person, probably the most famous missing person in history. However, as I will describe in chapter 1, the fact of the matter is that Jesus of Nazareth is a missing person. It will take some real detective work to find this missing person. Further, when we find him we may be surprised again by what we discover about him. It will be an exciting detective story, and I invite you to join me in this search for Jesus of Nazareth.

Like a detective, we will first examine the historical facts related to Jesus of Nazareth to learn what he really said and did, and then through this process reconstruct a picture of Jesus congruent with that evidence. This process is in keeping with the second part of Senator Moynihan's statement, "No one is entitled to his or her own facts."

An honest faith calls us to search for the truth of the evidence and use God-given reason in creating our faith. If one is to follow Jesus then it should be done right; honest to Jesus's own intentions and how he saw himself. We will want to know what *he* had in mind when he established his mission in Galilee almost 2,000 years ago.

Millions of people regard Jesus as one of the most remarkable people to have ever lived upon our earth. He obviously made an impact on people's lives in his own day, and this impact continues into our day. Many people throughout the ages have proclaimed Jesus of Nazareth as Lord and Savior. The astounding fact, however, is the wide diversity of beliefs and practices this faith has produced, everything from radical right conservatism to fundamentalism to Christian humanism to liberal left-wing movements. All of these groups, and multitudes more, appeal to the same Jesus as the source of their faith and actions. There is widespread disagreement, though, about what his life means to people today. There are numerous competing denominations, theologies, and interpretations of his life and its meaning. Clearly, they can't all be right. Yet behind all these various understandings of Jesus there was a specific person who lived upon this earth, one who left a powerful legacy behind him.

Knowledge of what Jesus of Nazareth said and did, then, is important in that it can provide the content of one's faith and keep that faith grounded in historical reality. This helps to avoid creating a Jesus in one's own imagination or image. So the question arises, who was Jesus?

Until about one hundred years ago the answer to that question seemed rather obvious in the Western world. Just read the New Testament and the answer is clear: Jesus Christ is the Lord and Savior of the world who died on a cross to save people from their sins, and if you accept him as your Lord and Savior, you will enter into heaven when you die.

Most Christians still hold to that understanding of Jesus. It is the view the Apostle Paul began to proclaim about twenty years after Jesus died, and is the view that prevailed during the writing of the New Testament over the next seventy-five years or so. It is the understanding of Jesus expressed in the traditional creeds of the churches, and continues to be the view of the majority of the churches, whether they be Roman Catholic, mainline Protestant, or evangelical churches. This traditional view appears to be the only correct way of acknowledging Jesus.

Over the past one hundred years, however, biblical scholars have discovered there were many other understandings of Jesus, even among his earliest followers. Paul's interpretation of Jesus was not the only way to understand Jesus, and was not necessarily the viewpoint of the very first followers of Jesus. Paul, who never met Jesus, developed his own particular understanding of Jesus, differing in many ways from the view of Jesus held by the first-generation followers who were with him during his ministry in Galilee.

What is the difference between Paul's understanding of Jesus and the viewpoint of the first followers of Jesus who had been with him in his ministry? Why don't we know more about those first followers of Jesus? Why didn't their understanding of Jesus make its way into the New Testament? Why did Paul's point of view prevail when the church assembled the New Testament from the hundreds of available tracts?

This book will explore these questions, seeking to learn more about Jesus by examining the impact he had on those around him. One of the ways to learn about any historical figure is by examining the legacy that person left. This is especially true in the case of Jesus. He did not leave any written words or accounts of his teachings or deeds. Only the reports of those whose lives were directly affected by him are available for research. There is no way to get to Jesus except through the writings of those who were affected by him. In order to understand this person whose life made such an impact on so many people, it is necessary to examine carefully the writings they left for us.

More than ever before in history, the tools to accomplish this task are available and accessible. First, biblical scholars have developed the techniques to explore the New Testament in a more thorough and complete manner. Second, archeological discoveries in the last one hundred years have unearthed previously unavailable ancient manuscripts that have been helpful in filling in the picture of the life of Jesus and his early followers. Third, there is a much clearer understanding of the historical situation in Israel, especially Galilee, during the lifetime of Jesus. This critical mass of discoveries, research tools, technology, experience, and information has created an opportunity to arrive at a more honest, faithful depiction of Jesus. In fact, other than the early first-century followers of Jesus who knew him personally, we have the possibility of understanding Jesus better than any generation in history. Living in this day provides a new and unique opportunity to finding Jesus of Nazareth, and that is good news to be embraced.

In this book, I will be using the best available scholarly information to discern the facts of the life of the historical person Jesus of Nazareth. Putting those facts together, I will share with the reader my understanding of what Jesus was seeking to achieve during his life on this earth. I realize facts alone are not enough on which to base one's religious faith. Whatever we believe about Jesus, however, should be congruent with the facts, at least as much as we can discover them. Christians especially should never be afraid of factual information that leads to truth.

Liberal or conservative, readers undoubtedly will come across some information that will cause them discomfort. Preconceived notions and ideas about Jesus may be disturbed. I hope you will welcome that. If the evidence supports your point of view, wonderful. If the evidence weighs in against your point of view, what then? Are you willing to open your mind and heart to an uncomfortable truth?

Thousands of books have been written asking who Jesus was. Was he the one and only Son of God? Was he God in human form? Lord and Savior of the world? A prophet? A teacher of wisdom? A miracle worker? A revolutionary? Or something else entirely?

Many arguments and debates have arisen out of the search for the answer to the question, who was Jesus? Like an incandescent light bulb, these arguments and debates have created more heat than light, with no definitive answer emerging. The debate about Jesus rages on, each person or group digging in their heels, sticking to their own particular point of view.

I believe the simple reason the debate continues, even in our day, is that people are asking the wrong question. It is time to move beyond the fruitless arguments and debates about Jesus by learning to ask the right question. Rather than ask, who was Jesus? much more will be accomplished with the question, what was Jesus's original intention? In other words, what was Jesus seeking to accomplish with his public ministry on this earth? The only way to answer that question is to let Jesus's words and deeds speak for themselves. We owe him that. What he said and what he did are infinitely more important than what Christians through the centuries have believed about him. His words and deeds are the building blocks for developing an understanding of Jesus and what he was trying to accomplish with his life. Rather than impose our own preconceived ideas upon Jesus, by exploring these words and deeds, we can discover his original intention and find the missing person Jesus of Nazareth.

It is clear Jesus had a purpose and sense of mission as he lived his life upon this earth. He did not wander aimlessly around Galilee with no goal or vision in mind. By paying attention to what Jesus actually said and did we can discern what he had in mind as he conducted his mission on this earth. His words and deeds form a unified intention on his part, revealing what he was seeking to accomplish. This book will explore the available evidence regarding these words and deeds, thereby enabling us to answer with a high degree of confidence the question of Jesus's original purpose.

Many people today are being drawn to the original message of Jesus apart from the image of Jesus proclaimed by the traditional church. There is a hunger for the values Jesus proclaimed and practiced, as more and more people sense the emptiness of a life of consumerism and self-centeredness. This book will help everyone, religious or not, discover Jesus's original purpose and find the missing person Jesus of Nazareth.

PART II: BUILDING THE BELOVED COMMUNITY

The search for Jesus of Nazareth is simply an intellectual exercise unless the results of that search make a difference to us in our modern world.

Part 2 examines the ramifications of Jesus's life and teachings for individuals and faith communities today.

This section of the book begins with an exploration of what it means to be a contemporary follower of Jesus. In the gospel accounts, Jesus repeatedly called on people to "follow" him. This is an action word, and thus the focus of chapter 11 will be on actions rather than beliefs.

Next comes an examination of the relationship between the individual and the community. We human beings form our communities from two basic needs: the need for self-development and the need for belonging. We often have difficulty recognizing the paradox of these two different needs. As a result, the two are often seen as antagonists, making them incompatible with one another. This means we will seek to satisfy one at the expense of the other. In this chapter I will explore how we can give equal attention to both individual and community needs.

The closing two chapters of the book deal with practical matters of interest to individuals and to faith communities. What would it mean to emulate the words and deeds of Jesus in modern society? The emphasis will be on how to build Jesus's Beloved Community in our towns and cities. This section will provide guidance on the process of community organizing, answering many of the questions an individual or faith community might have regarding this challenging and exciting endeavor.

The Bible translation I will use most often is the 1989 New Revised Standard Version (NRSV). This version was compiled by biblical scholars, is written in contemporary English, and is based upon the most recent knowledge in biblical studies. Whenever I cite a reference from the *Gospel of Thomas* I will use the Scholars Version found in the book *The Complete Gospels*.

Throughout this book when I refer to dates I will use the letters BCE or CE. The letters follow the commonly accepted practice of dating the modern calendar from the date of Jesus's birth. Dates prior to his birth are indicated by the letters BCE (Before the Common Era), while dates after Jesus's birth are noted by the letters CE (Common Era).

This book uniquely combines the scholarly research related to Jesus of Nazareth with practical guidance for building his Beloved Community in our world today. My aim is to speak to both the religious and the nonreligious who are interested in discovering how a new understanding of Jesus can enable the building of community life today.

I will not be using footnotes because this book is written for a general audience, and I hope it will be helpful to people who would not be comfortable with a more scholarly approach to the issues raised in the book. For those who want to know more, I have included a bibliography. I have learned much from the scholars and authors whose works are listed in the bibliography, and it is my hope the listing of their works will serve as a thank you for their endeavors.

I also will not discuss the various disagreements among scholars regarding their understandings of the details of the life of Jesus. Where I believe there is a general consensus among scholars, I will say so. Where there is ongoing disagreement on specific details, I will say so, and I will leave those issues open to further research and discussion. Any future resolutions of ongoing scholarly disagreements will not affect the basic goal of this book: to discover the missing person Jesus of Nazareth and his original intention, and to apply that discovery to the building of community life today.

Part One

The Search for a Missing Person: Jesus of Nazareth

1

A Detective Is on the Case

A FAMOUS PERSON FROM history is missing! That person is Jesus of Nazareth. You may ask, "How can that be? Isn't Jesus one of the best-known persons in history? Doesn't almost everyone know about Jesus?" That is certainly the common perception, yet the truth is, Jesus of Nazareth is missing. Let me show you how he is missing.

First, start with the most famous creed of the church, the Apostles' Creed. Here is what it states about Jesus:

> I believe in . . .
> Jesus Christ his [God's] only Son our Lord:
> who was conceived by the Holy Spirit,
> born of the Virgin Mary,
> suffered under Pontius Pilate,
> was crucified, dead, and buried;

What is missing? Jesus of Nazareth. In this creed, recited on a weekly basis in churches around the world, there is nothing but a comma between his birth and his death. All we know is that he was born and he died. There is nothing of his life in the creed, neither his teachings nor his deeds. It is as if what he said and what he did have no significance. The most famous person in history, and he is reduced to a comma!

Jesus of Nazareth is a missing person from the creeds of the church. But what about the New Testament? Surely we can find him there. What about the letters of Paul? He focuses all his attention on Jesus Christ. Surely he must tell us quite a bit about the life and teachings of Jesus.

Actually, no, he doesn't. He focuses on the death of Christ on the cross and God's raising him from the dead. He writes almost nothing about the life and teachings of Jesus. Thus, Jesus of Nazareth is a missing person in the letters of Paul.

Surely the book of Acts or the letters and writings in the rest of the New Testament mention Jesus many, many times. Yes, they do, but they also show no interest in the human life of Jesus—what he said and what he did. Jesus of Nazareth is missing from these writings in the New Testament as well.

This brings us to the four gospels of the New Testament. Certainly he is not a missing person in the four gospels. They are exclusively about Jesus—what he said and what he did. Here at least we can say we have the missing person Jesus of Nazareth.

He may not be missing from the four gospels, but he is most definitely hidden within them. Biblical research has shown there are different understandings of Jesus within the four gospels, as well as numerous contradictions and inconsistencies about what he said and what he did. This may come as a surprise to some, and it may even seem discouraging. But let me show you what I mean.

Who is the real Jesus of Nazareth? The Jesus who never equated himself with God and identified with the least, the lowest, and the lost of his society (Matthew, Mark, and Luke), or the Jesus who boldly proclaimed, "I am the way, and the truth, and the life. No one comes to the Father except through me" (John 14:6). The Jesus who told numerous parables (Matthew, Mark, and Luke), or the Jesus who never told a single parable (John)? The Jesus who prayed to God in the Garden of Gethsemane, "Father, if it be possible, deliver this cup from me" and cried out upon the cross, "My God, my God, why have you forsaken me?" or the Jesus who stated, "I and the Father are one." These, and other confusing inconsistencies in the gospel accounts, make it difficult to find the historical person Jesus of Nazareth in the New Testament.

Also, if Jesus had been, in the popular view of Jesus today, a teacher traveling around dispensing spiritual truths, telling people how to get into heaven, why did the Jewish religious leaders in Jerusalem and the Roman rulers conspire to execute him as a traitor to the country? What was it about his words and deeds that led the Roman authorities to be suspicious of him and mark him as a "trouble maker"? The Romans would have been glad to have a person calming down the people by having them focus on life after death. They would have simply ignored him and let him go on his merry way. Yet they executed him in a manner (public crucifixion on a cross) reserved for those who are viewed as threatening the peace of the Roman Empire. Why would they do that?

So finding Jesus and discovering his purpose for his public ministry is not as easy as it might at first have seemed. Jesus of Nazareth is indeed a missing person. He is missing from the creeds of the church, the letters of Paul, the other writings in the New Testament, and he is hidden within the four gospels. To find this missing person will take some real detective work. It is not an easy task, but it can be done, and it is important that it be done. If we are interested in Jesus at all, honesty and integrity call us to find *him*, not some figment of our imagination.

The detective work required to find Jesus of Nazareth may seem daunting. Fortunately we are not alone in this endeavor. There are experts in the field who can help us sift through the New Testament material with a realistic chance of discovering the Jesus of Nazareth, and in discovering him, find his purpose on this earth as he saw it. They will help find the missing person Jesus of Nazareth, and it will be an exciting and crucial piece of detective work.

A good detective always begins the attempt to solve a case by examining the evidence. Several necessary steps are involved in the search for answers. The first step is to sift through the evidence to determine its validity and relative importance. This entails an examination of the accuracy of the various pieces of evidence. Pieces of evidence may turn out to be of lesser or greater importance in the particular case. The second step is to put the pieces of evidence together, following the factual evidence wherever it may lead. The final step is to seek to arrive at some conclusions about the case at hand and to make the case in a court of law. The goal is to present the case in a manner that will enable the jurors to make a decision "beyond all reasonable doubt," the threshold for arriving at a conclusion in a court of law. It is not expected the evidence will necessarily produce a verdict beyond all doubt, but simply beyond "reasonable doubt."

Likewise, in the search for the truth about Jesus, it is vital to begin with the evidence: what Jesus said and what Jesus did. This involves the examination of the various pieces of evidence to determine their relative validity and importance. It is also necessary to put the pieces of evidence together, following the factual evidence about Jesus wherever it may lead. The last step is to arrive at some conclusions about Jesus's original intention as he saw it and to present those conclusions to you, the reader, hopefully enabling you to arrive at your own conclusions. As in a court of law, the evidence is not expected to produce a result beyond all doubt, but hopefully beyond "a reasonable doubt." Absolute certainty is not possible. However, as we follow the evidence, we can arrive at a conclusion that goes beyond a reasonable doubt. Ultimately, through this process, a reliably accurate and faithful picture of Jesus of Nazareth can be discovered.

A basic principle of detective work is the more evidence and information you have the more likely you will be able to discover the truth about any situation. For the detective, there is never too much information or too much evidence. The same is true in the historical search for Jesus. The more information and evidence we have about Jesus, the better the results of our inquiry. Fortunately, through the work of the biblical scholars and researchers we have more information and evidence about the world of Jesus and the life of Jesus than any period since the first century. That information and evidence give us a great deal of confidence that we can find Jesus of Nazareth and the original purpose of his mission in Galilee.

The evidence about Jesus is found primarily in the New Testament, and most especially in the four gospels. However, the extraction from the biblical materials of authentic evidence about the life and ministry of Jesus is not an easy process. Most people need help interpreting the research necessary to discover the Jesus who lived upon this earth. Biblical scholars have carefully studied and researched that information and have shared it in their writings. We will depend upon those scholars to assist us in our search for the missing person Jesus of Nazareth. Many of their works are listed in the bibliography at the end of this book.

Let me make it clear the issue is not whether the scholars are conservative or liberal. The issue is whether they are competent or incompetent biblical scholars. Are they using the best research methods available? Are they using the best available information and evidence? Are they doing research in concert with other biblical scholars? The portrait of Jesus and his mission can only be as good as the quality of the evidence and information that is utilized.

HOW TO EXAMINE THE EVIDENCE

As a reader of this book, you are doing inquiry into the life of a historical person, Jesus of Nazareth. This involves seeking to discover evidence from history and then reconstructing that evidence into a cohesive picture. Historical research is a disciplined skill. For example, in detective work one gathers evidence, as much of it as he or she can find, then tries to see the big picture, to see the importance of certain pieces of the puzzle and how those pieces fit in with the other available evidence. Likewise, historical evidence does not come prepackaged and complete. It comes in bits and pieces and must be put together in a careful and imaginative manner, faithful to the facts. The core of historical research is intellectual integrity. One is either engaged in an honest examination and appraisal of the evidence, or one isn't. In examining the evidence about Jesus one must be willing to approach the evidence with intellectual honesty.

All historical research involves reconstruction, the fitting together of the evidence in order to develop a picture of what is most likely to have happened. In reality, *everyone* does historical reconstruction. It is impossible to look at the "facts" without adding one's own interpretation of those facts. Some people claim they just take the Bible as it is. They are failing to acknowledge, however, the reality that they are taking bits and pieces of the Bible and putting those pieces together to arrive at certain conclusions about Jesus and Christianity. Competent biblical scholars, on the other hand, are self-aware enough to honestly acknowledge they are doing reconstruction of the bits and pieces of historical evidence to develop their image of Jesus. What is required is that the image of Jesus emerging from the reconstruction of the bits and pieces of historical evidence be congruent with the evidence. Otherwise, the image is simply a figment of one's imagination.

Historical research is not an effort to come up with a "once and for all" final truth, but only plausible truth based upon the available evidence. All historical knowledge is tentative and partial. Partial knowledge, however, is not the same as ignorance. One can have accurate knowledge without having absolute, final answers. It is possible through careful historical research to produce useful knowledge, even though it is imperfect and subject to correction through further examination.

It should also be noted that no one comes to the quest for Jesus of Nazareth with a blank slate. We come with our own background, biases, preconceptions, and experiences. This will influence our endeavor, and none of us can escape our own skin. We have no objective platform on which to stand to do our historical research. That awareness should bring a degree of humility to our efforts. It does not, however, prevent us from finding useful knowledge from the past and putting the knowledge together into a reconstruction of the image of Jesus.

Certainly religious faith is not based only on evidence and facts. There is an emotional and passionate content to one's faith. Human beings have two basic ways of knowing, the rational and the emotional. We each have a head and a heart, and one is useless without the other. The two operate together. This means the heart of faith must be within the realm of reason, while the mind is enlisted to serve the heart. As you join me in this examination of the evidence about Jesus, I ask only that you have an open mind, enabling you to adjust your heartfelt beliefs on the basis of new evidence. In this way your faith will be congruent with the facts about Jesus of Nazareth. Finally, religious or not, one should never be afraid of the truth. By necessity, a detective must look at the evidence as carefully as possible, even if such examinations lead to unexpected conclusions. Let the facts lead where they may. As the pieces of evidence are put together and a reconstruction made on the basis of that evidence, the result provides the confidence that one's beliefs and actions are based on the best information available about Jesus.

THE SEARCH FOR THE MISSING PERSON JESUS OF NAZARETH

When you have a health issue you want a physician, or a team of physicians, with the latest and best information, knowledge, and skills to take care of your health. When you need your car serviced or repaired, you want automobile technicians with the best knowledge and tools to properly maintain your vehicle. If you have a plumbing problem in your home, you want the best plumber available. When it comes to taking care of our bodies, our vehicles, our homes, we want the people with the latest and best knowledge, tools, and techniques to provide the help we need.

Likewise, when it comes to understanding Jesus and his original intentions in his adult life, it only makes sense to get the help of those with the best knowledge and information about the Jesus who lived upon this earth. In the last twenty-five years there has been a burst of research by biblical scholars into the life of Jesus of Nazareth. This research has been carried out by a wide variety of scholars and has provided a rich picture of Jesus. Not all the scholars agree with one another on that picture, but the fullness of the picture is beyond debate. Many "Jesus" books have been published and are now easily accessible to the public. This allows people to participate in historical Jesus research through the writings of the biblical scholars.

One of the most significant steps in historical Jesus research was taken in 1985 with the founding of the Jesus Seminar by Dr. Robert Funk. Its 125 scholars have undertaken a study of the words and the deeds attributed to Jesus in the four New Testament gospels and other early Christian writings. The scholars meet twice a year, discussing and voting on the historical authenticity of the words and deeds of Jesus. They have published their results, and many of the scholars have written books highlighting the results of their research into the life of Jesus.

One advantage of the Jesus Seminar is that the work is done in a spirit of collegiality where the scholars discuss, debate, argue, and learn from one another. The Seminar members are trained biblical scholars, competent in the biblical languages. They use the tested methods of historical scholarship accepted and used for centuries.

When the Jesus Seminar began to examine the sayings of Jesus, they had a collection of over five hundred sayings, in many different settings. It quickly became clear not all the sayings attributed to Jesus actually originated with Jesus. On what basis would one separate sayings that came from Jesus from those that did not? A commonly used method is to begin with an image of Jesus and then select sayings supporting that image. A better method, however, involves first setting the criteria for determining which sayings came from Jesus. Once the criteria, or rules of evidence, have been determined, then the group of scholars can come together to discuss each saying and express a consensus by voting on each saying. This is exactly what the Jesus Seminar has done, and the results provide the best evidence for discovering what Jesus actually said and did.

First, the scholars examined each of the sayings attributed to Jesus in an open spirit of debate and discussion, followed by a vote on each of the individual sayings. They then color-coded the results as follows:

red:	Jesus actually said it.
pink:	Jesus probably said it, or something like it.
grey:	Jesus probably did not say it.
black:	Jesus surely did not say it.

The results of their work have been published in the book *The Five Gospels*. They then followed the same procedure regarding the deeds attributed to Jesus, and published those results in *The Acts of Jesus*. The scholars do not claim that their decisions about the relative authenticity of the words and deeds attributed to Jesus are absolute and final. The decisions on each saying and deed are subject to further review and can be altered as new information becomes available. However, based on present knowledge, and using the sayings and deeds designated red or pink (Jesus said or did it or probably said or did it), an accurate picture of Jesus can be attained. These New Testament scholars show a remarkable degree of consensus regarding what are considered to be the sayings and deeds originating with Jesus.

Numerous other scholars have worked independently in their studies of Jesus, many making outstanding contributions to the research. In this exploration into the mission of Jesus, I am primarily using the works of the members of the Jesus Seminar, supplemented by the conclusions of other biblical scholars who have worked in this field.

This exploration, however, is not an attempt to develop a biography of Jesus. It is an attempt to know the historical truth about Jesus. As with detective work, the search involves a review of the facts of the life and mission of Jesus. According to Jesus himself, what was his original intention? What was he seeking to accomplish for the people among whom he carried out his ministry? These are the questions to be pursued in this book. This will involve the detective work of examining the available evidence in order to find the missing person Jesus of Nazareth and recover his original intention.

There are three items of importance to examine in finding this missing person Jesus of Nazareth:

A. The historical evidence: the events in Israel, especially in Galilee, just before, during, and after the lifetime of Jesus
B. The written evidence: the development and compilation of the New Testament materials related to the life of Jesus
C. The words and deeds originating with Jesus found in the earliest written source materials, within the New Testament and beyond the New Testament

Please join me as we now begin our detective work of examining the evidence for the missing person Jesus of Nazareth.

2

Examining the World of Jesus

In the search for a missing person, the detective begins with an examination of the last place the person was seen. This involves a careful exploration of the scene and any clues it might hold regarding the missing person. In the case of the search for the missing person Jesus of Nazareth, this entails a careful look at the place and time in which he lived his entire life. That place and time was the northern province of Galilee in the nation of Israel (a vassal state of the Roman Empire) in the first century of the Common Era. What was going on in that place at that time, providing clues leading to the finding of this famous missing person? This is where we begin our search.

The last one hundred years have opened up a new window of opportunity to find Jesus of Nazareth. The scholarly tools in the areas of archeological and historical research have advanced greatly, enabling our generation to have access to the vital evidence needed to discover Jesus and his original purpose in his mission in Galilee. So we start with the world in which he lived; Jesus lived in a certain place at a certain time. The people he interacted with were real people, and the events happening around him impacted what he said and did.

THE WORLD OF JESUS

Jesus lived in the first three decades of the first century, in the northern province of Israel, known as Galilee. It was an area some twenty-five miles across. He traveled primarily in this small region, from the little village of Nazareth in central Galilee to the larger town of Capernaum on the shore of the Sea of Galilee. It was a rural area, somewhat isolated from the rest of the nation. The southern province of Israel, Judea, was the home of the capital, the city of Jerusalem. In between was the province of Samaria. The people from Galilee were considered by the Judeans to be less educated and less sophisticated than those from Judea.

The topography of Galilee fostered its marginal status. It was surrounded by mountains, with the Sea of Galilee on one side and the Mediterranean Sea on the other. In the period leading up to Jesus's birth, it lacked any sizable cities, primarily because the major trade routes were located in neighboring areas. Excavations, surveys, and ancient sources indicate that at the time of Jesus Galilee was overwhelmingly composed of small, humble Jewish villages, hamlets, and market towns.

Galilee, however, was filled with lush farmland. It had an abundance of water, fertile soil, and pleasant temperatures. The small farms scattered around Galilee were able to produce outstanding crops. There was also a wide variety of flowers and plants growing throughout the region.

The world of Jesus was very different from our world today, and we can't assume his life in ancient Galilee was similar to our life today. The issues he and others faced in that time and place were not the same issues we face today. To understand Jesus's original intention in his mission in Galilee we must intentionally step back in time to his world.

THE GREEKS

The search begins with Alexander the Great. He played an important role in setting the stage upon which the message and mission of Jesus would be spread throughout the Mediterranean world. In 332 BCE Alexander claimed Israel as a part of his conquest of the known world of that day. Enamored of Greek culture, he sought to impose that culture (Hellenism) throughout the world: Greek art and architecture, theater and athletics, philosophy and mythology, the city-state form of government, and perhaps most importantly, the Greek language. Greek became the common tongue of the world, thus allowing for the expansion of international commerce as merchants from various countries could now communicate easily with one another.

When Alexander conquered Israel, the nation had a strong Hebrew tradition based upon the land, the Law, and the Hebrew Scriptures. The major impact of Alexander's conquest on Israel was that she now became a blend of Hebrew tradition and Greek culture, a blend that would continue into the time of Jesus.

Following Alexander's death in 324 BCE, his Greek empire was divided into several parts. Israel came under the control of his general Ptolemy. Over the next century and a half, Israel was ruled by several Greek dynasties, becoming a vassal state under the control of outsiders who ruled with an iron fist. Greek technology and culture continued to be interjected into Israel, and the Greek mentality became more deeply ingrained into the life of Israel.

JEWISH INDEPENDENCE

A growing Jewish resistance to the rule of Israel by the Greeks developed over these years. In 164 BCE Judas Maccabeus, along with his brothers, led a successful rebellion against the Greek rulers, and Israel became an independent state under his leadership. He not only ousted the foreign leaders, he also overthrew the high priests of the temple in Jerusalem, whom he considered to be corrupt. For the next one hundred years, Israel was an independent nation, as Judas Maccabeus and his descendants exercised both political and religious rule over Israel.

THE ROMAN EMPIRE

The major historical fact about Israel in Jesus's time was the rule of the nation by the Roman government. Roman rule in Israel began in 63 BCE when Pompey claimed Israel as a province of the Roman Empire. After one hundred years of independence, Israel was once again under the control of foreign rulers. Israel was an important territory to the Romans, due to the fact it was located between two key Roman provinces: Egypt, the breadbasket of the Roman Empire, and Syria, the eastern fortress of the empire.

Roman rule drastically affected everyone's life in Israel. In order to understand the life of Jesus, it is necessary to be aware of the impact of the Roman Empire on the people under its rule, especially the impact of Roman rule on the people of Galilee in northern Israel.

The Romans used pure military might to intimidate conquered people into obedience and compliance with Roman rule. Any threat to their imperial rule was quickly dealt with through military power. Public crucifixion of those considered to be a problem was just one means by which the Romans exerted their power over the people.

One method the Romans employed to rule over outlying provinces like Israel was through client kings, local figures who ruled in their place and on their behalf. These client kings were responsible for keeping the peace, funneling taxes and tributes to Rome, and promoting the Roman cultural climate. They could relate to the local population better than any Roman official, and they would therefore be able to anticipate and deal with local problems and tensions. In Jesus's time, Pilate in Judea and Herod Antipas in Galilee were two such client kings in Israel.

The Romans also ruled through collaboration with the aristocratic members of the conquered nation. For example, they appointed client rulers and authority figures from the elite of the society, thereby turning the wealthy against their own people. This was an effective "divide and conquer" strategy.

Collaborating members of Israel's population included the aristocratic families, as well as the priests of the temple in Jerusalem. They co-operated with the Roman rulers to preserve their own positions of power, prestige, and privilege. Pleasing Rome for their mutual benefit became a way of life for the elites of Israel and the temple priesthood, at the expense of the poor of the nation. They well understood the advantages of loyalty to the Roman rulers.

The Roman Empire was big, powerful, and rich. For the wealthy aristocrats and the temple priests, it was a time of comfort and wealth. Very little changed for them. For the vast majority of the people, however, it was a time of hardship, poverty, and cruelty. Under Roman rule, life for the poor changed dramatically for the worse.

HEROD THE GREAT

In 40 BCE the Roman emperor Caesar Augustus named Herod the Great to be the client ruler over Israel. He became one of Rome's most trusted client kings. Herod was a Jew only by birth, the child of converts to Judaism. That did not prevent him, however, from petitioning the Roman Senate to name him king of the Jews, a title they granted him. He was the king of Israel in name only, but was never in any sense accepted by the Jews as a Jewish king. Nevertheless, in Herod the Romans had a reliable client king and friend who ruled over Israel for thirty-six years. He was devoted to the Roman rulers who had installed him as "King of the Jews." The Romans expected Herod to fulfill two main duties: keep the peace and collect taxes and tribute money for Rome. He accomplished both tasks quite successfully for the Roman government.

Herod ruled ruthlessly, eliminating any opponents and rewarding those who would cooperate with him. He became one of antiquity's most prolific builders, as he initiated a major building program of luxurious palaces, fortresses, and massive government buildings. He also constructed a major seaport city, naming it after his emperor, calling it Caesarea. Further, as a way of placating the temple priests, he reconstructed the dilapidated Jewish temple in Jerusalem into a building of magnificent splendor. The Jerusalem temple again became the center of Jewish worship, sacrifices, and festivals. His building projects reflected his love of luxury and opulence.

Of course, all these building projects cost money, so Herod kept increasing taxes on the populace. To appease the wealthy and keep them on his side, he mainly increased taxes on the poor, who had no voice or political influence. Over the years of his reign, the plight of the poor became increasingly difficult, with many of them losing their farms through indebtedness and confiscation by the Romans and the Jewish elite.

Under the oppressive rule of Herod the Great, life for the Jewish peasant farmers in Galilee was bad. But it would get worse.

HEROD ANTIPAS

Herod the Great died in 4 BCE and there was great rejoicing throughout the nation of Israel, especially in the northern region of Galilee. There was also widespread political unrest, as well as a growing desire among the peasants for a messiah to arise and lead Israel in a victorious holy war against the Roman Empire.

Following Herod's death, the Romans divided Israel into three provinces. In Galilee, where Jesus lived, Herod Antipas, son of Herod the Great, became the ruler. He is the ruler who had John the Baptist executed. He ruled over Galilee for forty-three years (4 BCE–39 CE), during Jesus's entire lifetime. We cannot understand Jesus and the purpose of his mission in Galilee without having a clear picture of the nature of Antipas's rule and how it affected the people of Galilee.

Since Antipas was not responsible for Israel's southern region, Judea, he could focus his attention solely on Galilee, treating it as his own private fiefdom. Like his father, he built lavish new buildings and cities in his territory. Among his building projects was the reconstruction of the city of Sepphoris, a city that had been destroyed in an uprising following the death of his father. Though Sepphoris was located only four miles from Nazareth, it is not mentioned in the New Testament. It did, however, play an important role in first-century Galilee as a regional administrative and political center. Excavations reveal the construction of a gleaming marble theater and surrounding public buildings that were architectural marvels.

Herod Antipas also constructed a new seaport along the southwest shore of the Sea of Galilee and named it in honor of Emperor Tiberias. He designated the city the region's new capital, enabling him to have even tighter administrative control over all of Galilee. These two cities, Tiberias and Sepphoris, dominated the region and were powerful symbols of the new Roman control of culture, economics, and indeed the whole way of life in Galilee. Tiberias enabled Antipas to control the commercial fishing in the Sea of Galilee, while Sepphoris made it possible for him to oversee commercial farming for his own benefit.

The population of Galilee increased during this time (while Jesus was growing up), as did agricultural production. Much of the wealth generated by the farms, however, went into the hands of the few Galilean elites who lived in the cities or large towns and were connected with Antipas. The gap between the wealth of the elite and the poverty of the peasants increased dramatically, and Antipas's costly construction brought higher taxes to the poor of Galilee. His unfair economic policies had an enormously negative impact on the lives of the village farmers of Galilee as their situation continued to deteriorate. Excavations and surveys have shown that the peasants in the villages were coming under increasing economic strain during the time of Jesus. The establishment of Roman rule and the Roman economy into Galilee transferred any income and power from the peasants to the Roman rulers and their collaborators from the elite of Israel.

As will be seen in later chapters, the economic impact of Antipas's policies and building projects is clearly visible in the words and deeds of Jesus. He roundly condemned the accumulation of wealth, while at the same time he spoke gently and kindly regarding the plight of the poor.

THE CITIES WERE FOR THE RICH

During the time of Jesus there were only two classes of people in Galilee. The large majority of the population (about 95 percent) were very poor, while the remaining 5 percent were from the wealthy class. There was no middle class as we know it today.

The gap between the upper class and the lower class was enormous, in terms of both economics and power. The wealthy upper class wielded great decision-making influence in the society, while the impoverished had no voice, no representation, no power, and no influence.

In recent years, excellent archeological work has been carried out in Israel, deepening our understanding of the world of Jesus in Galilee. One important discovery reveals the cities were occupied primarily by the wealthy and those who served them.

At the time of Jesus there were only two major cities in Galilee, the Roman cities of Sepphoris and Tiberias. Excavations have yielded evidence of a sophisticated lifestyle in both cities. These two urban centers had many amenities not available in the villages: sanitation, a wide variety of shops, Roman public baths, theaters, athletic fields, gymnasiums, libraries, paved streets, aqueducts providing a clean water supply, and luxurious homes and villas. The two cities also had walls and gates for security, as well as protection provided by the presence of Roman soldiers.

The residents of the cities were the Roman administrators, the Jewish elites, Roman soldiers, and those who provided for them. They lived the "lifestyle of the rich and the famous."

THE VILLAGES WERE FOR THE POOR

According to the Jewish historian Josephus, Galilee had about two hundred rural villages, hamlets, and small towns scattered throughout the countryside. Recent excavations have uncovered the remnants of about seventy-five of these villages in the hills and valleys of Galilee. None of these villages had the amenities of the two large urban cities. Archeological discoveries indicate the villages had dusty, unpaved streets and humble homes made of unhewn stone with dirt floors. There were no sanitation facilities available in the villages, and no wall to protect them from invading armies. The villages were too small to have a large marketplace or shops.

Though they varied slightly in size, a typical village would be composed of ten to twenty families, with a population of one hundred to two hundred residents. The villagers were mostly peasant farmers living not on their farms, but in the village. They went out each day to tend to their small ancestral family farm that had been passed down through the generations. They raised enough food for their families, while having a small amount left over to provide funds for maintaining their farm equipment, their work animals, and other necessities of life. As had been the custom in Israel for many years, from their meager income they also paid the annual temple tax and the priestly tithes. For the majority of the rural farm families, it was an annual effort to simply have enough to survive until the next year. Life was difficult and precarious, depending always on the quality of the harvest in any given year.

Since it was not feasible for each farmer to have his own well, the one amenity each village had was a common well. The villagers shared responsibility for care of the village well. The well served as a gathering place for the villagers and often became the center of village life. Since the small villages could not afford to build a synagogue, their religious and civic gatherings were often held around the common well.

Jesus himself came from one of these small peasant villages, Nazareth. He conducted his entire mission in the small villages of Galilee, among people whose lifestyles and situations he knew and understood. There is no evidence in the New Testament that Jesus ever visited the large cities of Sepphoris or Tiberias, where the wealthy lived.

VILLAGE LIFE IN GALILEE

The expensive and lavish building projects initiated by Herod Antipas required a massive amount of money. The only way to raise the funds was through increased taxes on the Jewish population in Galilee. The peasants were already paying taxes (a half-shekel per year for each adult male) and tithes (10 percent of one's annual income) to the temple and the priesthood in Jerusalem. These taxes and tithes paid for the upkeep of the temple, as well as the elegant homes and opulent lifestyle of the temple priests. In addition to these Jewish taxes and tithes, the peasants also had to make an annual tribute payment to the Roman Empire. Now, in the time of Jesus, Antipas imposed a new level of taxation on the peasants, meaning the Galilean peasants now had three layers of taxes, tithes, and tribute placed upon them. This combination of required payments made life increasingly difficult and precarious for the rural poor of Galilee.

The priests of the Jerusalem temple as well as the Roman administrators and Jewish aristocracy were getting richer, while the peasant farmers of Galilee were becoming poorer. It is not hard to understand why the tax collectors (both religious and secular) were among the most despised people in Galilee at the time of Jesus.

Excavations and ancient written material combine to indicate the devastating effect the arrival of Roman rule about sixty years before the birth of Jesus had upon the peasant farmers of Galilee. Debt became an increasingly difficult problem for the farmers, especially during the rule of Herod Antipas. If a peasant was unable to buy seed for the next harvest or food to feed his family, he would be forced to borrow from a fellow villager against future harvests. The villagers, however, quickly used up each other's small amount of surplus funds. They then had to seek loans from the wealthy Roman and Jewish aristocrats of the cities. The interest rates for these loans were high (25 to 100 percent) and it took just one or two bad harvests for a peasant to be so deeply in debt he had no way to repay the loan. Since the only collateral the peasant had available to use to obtain the loans was his land, the end result was the foreclosure and loss of his farm to the wealthy creditor.

This meant he no longer owned his ancestral home that had been passed down through the generations. This was a devastating blow to the farmer. He was now condemned to live as a tenant farmer or sharecropper, sometimes, bitterly, on land he once owned. Even worse, if he could not become a tenant farmer or sharecropper, he became a day laborer. In that case, he lined up in the village each morning with other day laborers, hoping for work he could do for that day. There was no guarantee of work, and he might go many days without any income, especially in the off-season for crops. Many peasants during Jesus's time were sinking deeper and deeper into poverty, not knowing where their next meal was coming from, or how they would feed their family. This brought debilitating hunger and malnutrition. Some peasant farmers became so destitute they had to resort to begging. If they had children they could not feed, they might be forced to send them away to become beggars, or they would sell the children into slavery.

What followed was the deterioration of village life. Based on the economic principles found in the Torah, these small villages had a long-standing tradition of mutual support and care for one another. Villages were usually close-knit units, with the elders generally governing the village life. However, as peasant families sank deeper and deeper into debt, and chronic hunger and malnutrition became endemic, serious tensions developed between the villagers. In order to feed their own starving families, they began to demand repayment of the small neighborly loans they had made to each other. The villagers became resentful and suspicious of each other and turned against one another in village conflicts.

The arrival of the Roman armies and administrators, and the collaboration of the temple priests and the Jewish elite, had transformed these close-knit little villages into communities of desperate and frightened individuals. In place of their traditional Jewish spirit of community cooperation and mutual responsibility, divisiveness and mistrust became rampant in the villages of Galilee.

Political agitation against the Roman rulers and the urban aristocrats was inevitable, especially among the poor in the northern province of Galilee. It was not without reason the Jewish aristocrats and the Roman rulers viewed Galilee as a center of sedition and rebellion. Bands of rebels roamed the rolling hills and mountains of Galilee, and from time to time during Antipas's rule a peasant rebellion would break out. Whenever that occurred, the heavily armed and massive Roman army would swoop in and crush the rebellion, resulting in enormous bloodshed and loss of life among the Jewish peasants. Rebellion proved to be both futile and suicidal.

SUMMARY

This is the social context in which Jesus initiated his mission in Galilee in 27 or 28 CE. At that point in time, the Romans had controlled Israel for about ninety years, with Antipas ruling the province of Galilee for over thirty years. Due to its location, Galilee served as a defensive bulwark against possible enemy invasions and was of strategic importance to the Roman Empire. There was, therefore, a strong military presence in Galilee, as the Romans maintained their dominance through intimidation, power, and violence.

Life for the peasant villagers was difficult, and was deteriorating rapidly year by year. As a resident of one of those small villages, Jesus well understood the struggling situation the rural peasants were facing. They were sinking deeper and deeper into debt, many had lost their farms, others were on the verge of losing their farms, and all of them were in dire economic straits. Furthermore, village life had fallen apart as bitterness, resentment, and mistrust thrived, while families competed with each other for scarce resources, struggling to survive in any way they could.

In that situation, at that moment in history, the burning question facing the village peasants of Galilee was, What should be done about the Roman rulers who are making life unbearable for us? Should it be rebellion? Should it be acquiescence? Or is there another way?

JESUS HAD AN ANSWER

Jesus came to the villagers of Galilee with an answer for them. He had grown up among them during this period of major economic upheaval, and he had seen what it was doing to the traditional Hebrew village life throughout Galilee. As he came to their villages, he offered neither rebellion nor acquiescence as a way to deal with the oppressive Roman rule. Rather, he provided them with an alternate vision of life for their villages, life lived as God intended it to be lived. He summed up his vision and program in the phrase "kingdom of God." It was not an abstract philosophical or even spiritual concept, but a new way of ordering their village life that would empower the peasants to live together creatively in the midst of the brutal Roman rulers and their Jewish collaborators. Jesus's message and program resonated with the peasants of Galilee, and when it is seen for what it is, still resonates down to our own day.

Sadly, through the centuries his message and program have largely been lost and overlooked by traditional Christianity. With the help of modern scholarly research methods, however, we have the opportunity today to rediscover what Jesus was really trying to do with his mission in Galilee. As we shall see, he demonstrated the reality of his vision and plan in both his words and deeds.

So our detective work of necessity begins with understanding the social situation in first-century Galilee. One cannot understand Jesus's words and deeds without being aware of what was happening in his world. Jesus did not speak and act in a historical vacuum. He lived at a specific time in a specific place, interacting with real people who were going through a very difficult experience. Roman rule had a dramatically negative impact on the lives of the village peasants of Galilee. To find this missing person Jesus of Nazareth, one must begin with his world.

It is the goal of this book to recover Jesus's original purpose and program, and to make it available to you, the reader.

3

Examining the Four New Testament Gospels

IN ADDITION TO THE historical evidence regarding the social context of the world of Jesus in first-century Galilee, there is also written evidence to be examined as the search for Jesus of Nazareth continues. Following the practice of a good detective, this chapter will carefully sift through the written evidence in the four New Testament gospels.

THE FOUR NEW TESTAMENT GOSPELS

The written evidence providing the most complete accounting of the life and teachings of Jesus is found in the four gospels of the New Testament: Matthew, Mark, Luke, and John. But what kind of documents are the four gospels? They are first of all historical documents dealing with a historical figure. They can, therefore, be examined like any other historical documents. In order to gather accurate information about the Jesus who lived and conducted his mission in first-century Galilee, it is necessary to carefully investigate the material in the four gospels. This does not diminish the importance of the four gospels, but it does provide the opportunity to examine the evidence related to Jesus. No person of faith should be afraid of honest historical research.

The first thing to do is to inquire about the word *gospel*. The word simply means "good news." As soon as you include the word *good* in the phrase "good news," you know the person is writing from a particular point of view. Thus, a gospel is not a neutral report of what happened, nor does it claim to be. It is written by those who perceive the news they are conveying to be "good." The second word, *news*, indicates the writer believes the message is important, and worth communicating to others. It is seen as "news." So the gospels are what they say they are—good news.

The writers of the gospels are properly called "evangelists" rather than "reporters" or "historians." They were not primarily interested in simply reporting historical events and verbatim words from the past. They were interested in expressing their understanding of the "good news" about Jesus of Nazareth.

The four New Testament gospels are all narrative gospels—that is, they tell a story about Jesus. They relate his words and deeds, as well as events that happened to him. Not all gospels are narrative gospels. In later chapters we shall examine another early type of gospel—sayings gospels consisting entirely of sayings attributed to Jesus, with no story line about events from Jesus's life.

Up until about one hundred years ago most Christians assumed the Gospels provide a completely reliable account of the words and deeds of Jesus. Today many Christians still operate on that assumption. The evidence discovered by biblical scholars in recent years, however, calls that assumption into question. This in turn requires one to take a deeper look at the four gospels and what they tell us about Jesus.

SIX KEY GOSPEL FACTS

Facts are stubborn things. They help keep us grounded in reality, as well as preventing us from jumping to false conclusions. In examining the four New Testament gospels there are six important facts to keep in mind.

1. Dating of the Gospels

The beginning point for understanding the four gospels is the dating of the writing of each of the gospels. In recent years biblical scholars have arrived at a consensus on the approximate dates when each of the four gospels were written. All reputable biblical scholars acknowledge the four New Testament gospels were originally written in Greek, a language neither Jesus nor his disciples spoke. Jesus and his original disciples spoke Aramaic, a Hebrew dialect, meaning the four gospel accounts of his teachings are a translation from the language spoken by Jesus and his followers.

The earliest date any of the four gospels could have been written is around the year 70 CE. The reason is simple: they mention the destruction of the Jewish temple in Jerusalem, an event that occurred in 70 CE when the Roman army was responding to a Jewish rebellion. The historical assumption is that any event must occur prior to a written document describing the event. Therefore, the gospels were written no earlier than 70 CE.

The first of the four gospels to be written was the Gospel of Mark. It was written soon after the year 70 CE (forty years after the death of Jesus) and provides the basic narrative story of the ministry of Jesus. It begins with Jesus as an adult being baptized by John the Baptist, recounts the events and teachings of his mission in Galilee, describes his arrest, trial, and death by crucifixion in Jerusalem, and concludes with the discovery of the empty tomb by three women. It does not include a story of his birth or childhood, nor does it include a genealogy of Jesus's ancestors. Also, no resurrection appearances are mentioned in the Gospel of Mark.

Amazingly, Mark does not tell much about Jesus himself. He does not indicate whether Jesus was married, nor does he relate anything about Jesus's appearance or his personality. He gives no information about the length of Jesus's ministry, nor his age at death, and no description of his background or his general outlook on life. Mark was clearly not interested in writing a biography of Jesus, as we think of biographies today. About fifteen years later (fifty-five years after the death of Jesus) Matthew and Luke independently composed their two gospels. They used two major sources in the writing of their gospels. The first source was the Gospel of Mark, which they used for their basic story outline. Matthew reproduces about ninety percent of Mark, while Luke includes about fifty percent of Mark's gospel. They each felt free to omit, edit, and change the order and wording of Mark to fit their own particular version of the story. Clearly neither Matthew or Luke regarded Mark as the inspired word of God, and neither treated Mark's text as something that could not be altered or changed.

Matthew and Luke also used another common source for the composition of their respective gospel accounts, the Sayings Gospel Q, which we will explore in the next chapter. Each one also added his own unique story of the birth of Jesus. In addition, both added their own individual stories of resurrection appearances at the conclusion of their gospel. All of Matthew's resurrection stories occur in Galilee, while Luke's resurrection stories occur in and around Jerusalem.

Finally, another fifteen years or so later (about seventy years after Jesus's death) a quite different version of the story, the Gospel of John, was written. His gospel begins with creation, continues with the ministry of Jesus, both in Galilee and in Jerusalem, and concludes with his own version of the death and resurrection of Jesus. Like Mark, he does not have a story about the birth of Jesus.

2. Eyewitnesses

None of the gospels were written by eyewitnesses to the events, nor do the authors claim to be eyewitnesses. Significantly, none of the gospels were written in Israel, nor were any of the writers from Israel. Matthew, for example, writes in an erudite and scholarly Greek, more in keeping with an educated writer, not someone from a village in Galilee. Like Paul, none of the authors of the four gospels had ever met Jesus.

The only writer of the gospels who describes his process of writing is Luke, who also wrote the book of Acts, a description of the early history of the church. He introduces his two writings with these words to Theophilus, a Roman official:

> Since many have undertaken to set down an orderly account of the events that have been fulfilled among us, just as they were handed on to us by those who from the beginning were eyewitnesses and servants of the word, I too decided, after investigating everything carefully from the very first, to write an orderly account for you, most excellent Theophilus, so that you may know the truth concerning the things about which you have been instructed. (Luke 1:1–4)

Luke's introduction offers several important pieces of information. First, he indicates there are many other accounts of the life of Jesus and of the early church, some by eyewitnesses and some by "ministers of the word." Second, he acknowledges that he is not an eyewitness to the events. Third, he does not claim any divine inspiration for his writings. He simply states he is using the accounts of others to "write an orderly account" of the life of Jesus and the early church.

3. Paul's Perspective

All four gospels were written after Paul wrote his epistles and after his death at the hand of Emperor Nero in 64 CE. Paul wrote his letters in the 50s of the first century, starting about twenty years following Jesus's crucifixion. The four gospels were written by followers of Paul who each in his own way shared Paul's understanding of the Christian faith. Mark was written in 70 CE and is a primary carrier of the message Paul proclaimed, projected back onto the life of Jesus. Both Matthew and Luke then passed on Mark's core message. To an even greater extent, the Gospel of John reflects Paul's exalted understanding of Jesus. The four gospels, as well as the books of the rest of the New Testament (with the notable exception of the Letter of James), were written in keeping with Paul's perspective. What we have in the four gospels are four different perspectives on one particular understanding of Jesus. Most Christians assume this was the only Christian message ever preached and there was no other message. However, such was not the case, as will be seen in the next section of this chapter. There were actually a wide variety of expressions of the Christian faith over the first two hundred years of Christianity.

4. Other Points of View

In the early years of the Christian faith many arguments developed over which of the many different versions of Christianity was the one true expression of the faith. During this time various groups in the early Christian movement wrote accounts of the life and teachings of Jesus. It was not until around the year 180 CE that Irenaeus, the Bishop of Lyon, declared the version of Christianity espoused by the church in Rome to be the only true faith. He insisted that all other churches and Christians must agree with the teachings of that particular church.

Also around this time Irenaeus established the four gospels of Matthew, Mark, Luke, and John, and only these four, to be the accepted accounts of the story of Jesus. All other gospel accounts of the life and teachings of Jesus were considered heretical and were banned from the churches. Either through intentional destruction or neglect, many of these other gospels were lost to history. It is only within the last one hundred years or so that some of these gospels have been recovered and are now available to us.

Irenaeus explains his reason for selecting four as the number of authentic gospels, and it is an interesting reason:

> It is not possible that the gospels can be either more or fewer in number than they are. For, since there are four zones of the world in which we lived, and four principal winds, while the Church is scattered throughout all the world, and the 'pillar and ground' of the Church is the gospel and the spirit of life, it is fitting that she should have four pillars, breathing our immortality on every side,

and vivifying men afresh. (*Against Heresies* 1.11.8, quoted in Freke and Gandy, *Laughing Jesus*, 69)

As strange as his reasoning may be for choosing four as the number of gospels to be considered sacred Scripture, we can be grateful he did include at least these four gospels as authoritative. This provides the opportunity to examine and compare the four gospels, thus enabling us to arrive at a more accurate picture of the historical Jesus than if a lesser number of gospels were available to read and study. We should remember, however, as Luke reminded us, there were many other versions of the gospel story, most of them lost to history.

5. Anonymous

Each of the authors of the four gospels is anonymous. None of them identify themselves by name. The names of the writers of the four gospels were supplied by Bishop Irenaeus. To give these four gospel accounts greater authenticity, he provided the unknown authors with the names of two of Paul's companions (Mark and Luke) and two of Jesus's disciples (Matthew and John). While it is common practice to refer to the gospels using the names provided by Irenaeus, it should be remembered no one knows the actual names of the authors of the four gospels in the New Testament. As we noted, none of them were eyewitnesses to the events they describe.

6. The Historical Writing Style

It was common practice in that day for those who were writing about heroic figures (Alexander the Great, Julius Caesar, Augustus, etc.) to have the literary license to embellish their accounts. They had the freedom to mix fact and fiction. They could attribute words to a person they felt the individual might have said in a certain situation. Writers of history in antiquity were also storytellers. They had the freedom to write their histories with imagination, providing words and deeds as they thought appropriate.

In that culture there were no copyrights, intellectual property rights, no sense that words could "belong" to someone, so every writer felt free to change, edit, interpret, and even misconstrue words attributed to a person. There was no ownership of words. It was an oral culture rather than a written, literate culture. Writers could embellish and alter events and words to communicate the story they were telling. This was a completely acceptable way of writing in the culture of that time.

These historical writers were not being devious. Mixing history and storytelling was the accepted practice of that day, and no one questioned whether the account was one hundred percent factual. It was considered a true story because it represented what the author truthfully felt about the heroic figure he was describing. In that day, an author was expected to not only relate factual information about a person, but also to interpret and communicate the meaning of the events.

When we come to the four gospels we find the same feature in operation. Each of the authors felt free to tell the story in his own way, leaving out certain information and adding other details reflecting his understanding of what Jesus actually said and did. They were not intentionally lying or seeking to be deceitful. Yet they weren't giving verbatim, objective journalistic reports either. They were telling the story of a remarkable person, following the common practice of historians/storytellers of that day.

This means that if we want to know who Jesus was, as well as what he said and did, we need to read the gospel accounts carefully and thoroughly, comparing the various accounts of Jesus in the four gospels. When this is done with care and integrity, a clear picture of Jesus's mission in Galilee begins to emerge. What is needed today is clear and courageous Bible study.

TWO VERSIONS OF THE STORY

Once these six basic facts about the New Testament gospels are clear, an important question arises: Did Jesus say and do everything attributed to him in the four gospels?

If the answer to that question is *yes*, it raises an immediate problem: How does one reconcile the version of the Jesus story found in the Synoptic Gospels of Matthew, Mark, and Luke with the version found in the Gospel of John? The first three gospels are called Synoptic Gospels because they present a common picture of the Jesus story. When you read their stories, they look very similar. When you come to the Gospel of John, however, you find a very different picture of Jesus. The stories change, the style and content of Jesus's teaching changes, and you seem to be reading a very different account of the life and teachings of Jesus.

The best way to understand the difference in the two versions of the Jesus story is in the following comparison:

The Synoptic Gospels	**The Gospel of John**
They begin with John the Baptist.	They begin with creation.
Matthew and Luke have birth stories.	There is no birth story.
Matthew and Luke have genealogies.	There is no genealogy.
Twelve disciples are named.	Seven disciples are named.
Jesus speaks in parables.	There are no parables.
Jesus speaks in short, pithy statements.	Jesus speaks in long discourses.
Jesus says little about himself.	Jesus speaks often about himself.
Jesus speaks humbly about himself.	Jesus speaks highly of himself.
Jesus's major theme is the kingdom of God.	His major theme is his own divinity.
Jesus exorcises demons.	No exorcisms are mentioned.
Jesus shows concern for the poor.	No such concern is expressed.
The temple incident is in the last week.	The temple incident is early.
Jesus institutes the last supper.	Foot washing replaces the last supper.

The two portraits painted by John and the Synoptic Gospels are so different they cannot both be accurate. Which Jesus is the Jesus of Nazareth who lived almost two thousand years ago? The Jesus of the Synoptic Gospels who rarely spoke about himself except to say that he was homeless or the Jesus of John's gospel who spoke often about himself? The synoptic Jesus whose major theme is the kingdom of God or the Jesus of John's gospel whose major theme is his own divinity? The Jesus of the Synoptic Gospels who spoke in parables and short, pithy statements or John's Jesus who spoke in long discourses and told no parables? The humble Jesus of Mark 10:18 who responded to a man addressing him as "good teacher" by saying, "Why do you call me good? No one is good but

God alone." Or the Jesus of John's gospel who equated himself with God, saying:

> "I am the bread of life."
> "I am the light of the world."
> "I am the door."
> "I am the good shepherd."
> "I am the resurrection and the life."
> "I am the way, the truth, and the life."
> "I am the true vine."

People sometimes read these statements in the Gospel of John and make the claim Jesus is either who he said he was or he was the biggest liar in history. Those, however, are not the only two alternatives. A third and much more plausible alternative is that Jesus did not make any of those statements about himself. Remember, the Gospel of John was written by someone who had never met Jesus. It was written about seventy years after his death, and was composed outside of the nation of Israel, in the Greek language. These statements actually reflect the view of Jesus held by John and the community for which he wrote, not Jesus's understanding of himself. A Jewish man in first-century Galilee would never equate himself with God. He might consider himself anointed by God for a special purpose. It was only in the Greco-Roman worldview of that day, however (the world in which Paul and the writers of the four gospels lived), that a human being could be considered divine.

Which version (the Gospel of John or the Synoptic Gospels) presents the more accurate picture of Jesus? Biblical scholars have concluded the Synoptic Gospels present a more historically reliable portrayal of Jesus. John's gospel is viewed as a statement of belief by a group of Christians living about seventy years after the death of Jesus rather than a historical account of Jesus's life and teachings. It is basically a meditation on the meaning of Jesus for Christians. For example, the various "I am" statements are really "he is" statements of belief about Jesus, projected backward onto him. The best way to read these affirmations about Jesus is, "We believe he is the light of the world; the bread of life; the way, the truth, and the life," and so forth. There is no harm in believing Jesus is the light of the world for you, or the bread of life for you, or any of the other exalted statements about Jesus. As we said earlier, everyone of that day or our day is entitled to his or her own opinions (or beliefs). The mistake arises when one claims these are factual historical statements Jesus made about himself. This does not mean there is no reliable historical information in John's gospel. It does mean, however, the primary thrust of John is to proclaim strong beliefs about Jesus. Indeed, at the end of his gospel, the writer tells his readers he has written in this manner for the very purpose of helping people to believe in Jesus Christ as the Son of God (John 20:31). He is honest about his motive for writing his gospel in the particular way he did.

This is not to accuse the author of being deliberately misleading when he created the speeches he put into the mouth of Jesus. He is simply following the common practice of the historian/storyteller of that day (see item #6 above).

There is no harm in an author using his imagination to tell the story. The problem arises only when modern interpreters of John's gospel refer to what has been written as factual evidence, without making the effort to distinguish between historical information and material that comes from the writer's imagination. If one wants accurate information about the words and deeds of Jesus as he lived upon this earth, the Gospel of John must be read very carefully with this in mind.

THE SYNOPTIC GOSPELS

This brings us to the three Synoptic Gospels themselves: Mark, Matthew, and Luke. Even within these three gospels, there are significant differences in the accounts of the words and deeds of Jesus. This can be seen most clearly and convincingly by placing the three Synoptic Gospels in parallel columns (See *The New Gospel Parallels* published by Polebridge Press). As mentioned earlier, Mark wrote his gospel first, then Matthew and Luke each individually edited and expanded Mark's gospel into their own version of the Jesus story.

As you look at the three gospels in parallel columns, you can easily see the similarities and differences in their accounts of the same words and deeds of Jesus. You can also note the material Matthew and Luke both included in their gospels, but was not in Mark's gospel. Finally, you can discern the material unique to each of the three writers.

An example of the differences in the three gospels can be seen in a comparison of the accounts of what is regarded as the first Easter morning, reading them in the order in which they were written:

> When the sabbath was over, Mary Magdalene, and Mary the mother of James, and Salome bought spices, so that they might go and anoint him. And very early on the first day of the week, when the sun had risen, they went to the tomb. They had been saying to one another, "Who will roll away the stone for us from the entrance to the tomb?" When they looked up, they saw that the stone, which was very large, had already been rolled back. As they entered the tomb, they saw a young man, dressed in a white robe, sitting on the right side; and they were alarmed. . . . So they went out and fled from the tomb, for terror and amazement had seized them; and they said nothing to anyone, for they were afraid. (Mark 16:1–5, 8)

> After the sabbath, as the first day of the week was dawning, Mary Magdalene and the other Mary went to see the tomb. And suddenly there was a great earthquake; for an angel of the Lord, descending from heaven, came and rolled back the stone and sat on it. His appearance was like lightning, and his clothing white as snow. For fear of him the guards shook and became like dead men. . . . So they left the tomb quickly with fear and great joy, and ran to tell his disciples. Suddenly Jesus met them and said, "Greetings!" And they came to him, took hold of his feet, and worshiped him. Then Jesus said to them, "Do not be afraid; go and tell my brothers to go to Galilee; there they will see me." (Matt 28:1–4, 8–10)

> The women who had come with him from Galilee followed, and they saw the tomb and how his body was laid. Then they returned, and prepared spices and ointments.
>
> On the sabbath they rested according to the commandment. . . .
>
> But on the first day of the week, at early dawn, they came to the tomb, taking the spices that they had prepared. They found the stone rolled away from the tomb, but when they went in, they did not find the body. While they were perplexed about this, suddenly two men in dazzling clothes stood beside them. . . . and returning from the tomb, they told all this to the eleven and to all the rest. Now it was Mary Magdalene, Joanna, Mary the mother of James, and the other women with them who told this to the apostles. (Luke 23:55–56; 24:1–4, 9–10)

One can easily see in the three accounts differences significant enough to warrant the conclusion they cannot all be correct. Looking at the three accounts, ask yourself: Who went to the tomb that morning? What did the women find at the tomb? Did they encounter a young man, an angel, or two angels? What did he/they say? Was there an earthquake or not? Did the women go and tell the disciples or not?

Additionally, the Gospel of John presents a fourth version of the story. In John, it is only Mary Magdalene who comes to the tomb on that morning. She does not encounter an angel or any other figure at the tomb. She finds the stone rolled away, and immediately leaves to tell Simon Peter and the disciples about the empty tomb (John 20:1–2).

Furthermore, Matthew tells a story about the tombs of other deceased people being opened, with many bodies of the saints who were dead coming out of the tombs. After the resurrection of Jesus, these dead bodies went into the holy city of Jerusalem and appeared to many (Matt 27:51–53). Is this an account of a historical event or not? It seems strange none of the other gospel writers mentioned such an unusual and memorable event. The only plausible conclusion is that such an event did not occur. It is a part of the gospel writer's freedom of imagination. Matthew had his own purpose for adding this imaginary story to his gospel, though it is difficult to know what that purpose might have been.

Where does all this confusion about who saw what and when leave us? Clearly, it means the descriptions of the events contradict each other, and they can't all be historically accurate. Thus, even in Christianity's central moment, now considered the first Easter morning, there are significant differences in the vital details reported by the various gospel writers.

It should not be surprising or disturbing to us that these (and many others) gospel accounts do not agree with each other, for the gospel writers were following the storytelling writing style of historians of that period. They had the freedom to use their imaginations in writing their stories about people of history, mixing fact with fiction in a creative storytelling manner accepted by people in antiquity.

It is unfair to the gospel writers for us to demand they measure up to modern standards of writing history, where there is a careful attempt to separate fact from fiction. Today when we read history books or the morning newspaper, we expect the events described to be factually correct. We want the person writing or reporting to be as objective as possible in what is presented. Such was not the case in the writing style of the first century.

The four gospels must be accepted for what they are—the imaginative accounts of the good news about Jesus of Nazareth, a mixture of fact and fiction, providing an important, if imperfect, picture of this remarkable man. Like modern historical fiction, the gospels cannot be considered either pure history or pure fiction. This means they cannot be taken as literally true in every instance. The narrative details of the various gospels simply cannot be reconciled with one another. Therefore, in the manner of a detective, in order to gain an accurate picture of Jesus and what he sought to accomplish in his ministry, the gospel evidence must be examined honestly and carefully.

If not everything attributed to Jesus in the four gospels is historically accurate, how does one determine which of the words and deeds of Jesus are authentic? Sorting through the hundreds of words and deeds of Jesus in the four gospels to determine the ones most likely to be authentic is a daunting task. Most people do not have the scholarly tools to carry out this task.

Fortunately, over the past twenty-five years, the members of the Jesus Seminar and other scholars have devoted a tremendous amount of time to research all of the sayings and deeds of Jesus in the four gospels, in a conscientious effort to determine which words and deeds attributed to him are most likely to have come from Jesus himself. The results of their work provide us with the best evidence of what Jesus most likely said and did, the words and deeds considered to have originated with Jesus.

I don't mean a saying or incident can be proved to originate from the historical Jesus of Nazareth. There are no such proofs; there are only probabilities. Jesus's words and deeds are authentic, then, when good biblical scholarship indicates they probably originated from him and at the same time form a consistent, united pattern.

Thus the four gospels of the New Testament are reliable sources of information about Jesus. They provide excellent information about the historical Jesus. They are not, however, perfect pieces of evidence for understanding Jesus. It is important, therefore, to understand them as historical documents set in the context of their time. Thus they can and must be examined like any other historical document.

Using the image of archeologists at a dig, the New Testament gospels are the top layer of written evidence about the historical Jesus. Digging deeper, however, we find other layers of evidence, documents written prior to the four New Testament gospels. An examination of these prior layers of written evidence will enhance the understanding of Jesus of Nazareth and reveal even more fully his original intention, what he was seeking to accomplish in his mission in Galilee.

4

Examining the Earliest Written Evidence

A GOOD DETECTIVE WILL examine all the evidence, especially the evidence providing the best clues to solving the case. Regarding the case of the missing person Jesus of Nazareth, it is necessary to go beyond the four New Testament gospels, written forty to seventy years after the death of Jesus, to even earlier written evidence. It may come as a surprise to the reader to learn there is written evidence prior to the writing of the four gospels. Such is the case, however, and it is vital to examine that prior written evidence.

Following the death of Jesus in Jerusalem, a group of his original followers remained in Galilee in the northern region of Israel, where Jesus had conducted his mission. These were people who had been with Jesus and knew him personally. I am calling these companions of Jesus who remained in Galilee the Jesus People of Galilee.

Who were these Jesus People of Galilee? They were the poor and destitute of the Galilean villages who were suffering greatly under the oppression of the occupying Roman Empire. As Jesus came to their villages, they responded to Jesus's message and became followers of Jesus. They did not organize churches in our sense of the word. As Jews, they already had synagogues for worship. They formed communities to share a common life together, to continue what Jesus began. They were clearly moved by Jesus's words and deeds.

Why don't we know more about these Galilean companions of Jesus? Through the twists and turns of history, these first-generation followers of Jesus disappeared from the pages of history. It happened around the year 70 CE. A group of Jewish zealots staged an uprising against the Roman rulers in Israel. Rome responded with their traditional scorched-earth policy, destroying the Jewish villages and cities of Israel. In the process, thousands of Jews were killed. At this point in time we lose track of the

Jesus People of Galilee. Some may have escaped to other nearby countries, while others were most certainly killed by the Roman army. In any event, their village communities were destroyed.

These original followers of Jesus did, however, leave two vitally important documents, each containing a collection of sayings of Jesus. They had remembered and compiled Jesus's sayings because his words were important to them in their ongoing life together. All they had to go on as they followed Jesus were his words and deeds, and they preserved these two collections of his teachings.

The two documents have been hidden from us for almost two thousand years. Remarkably, through the careful work of biblical scholars, both documents are now available to us. They provide us with the earliest and most reliable accounts of what Jesus said while he lived upon this earth. In our search for this famous missing person Jesus of Nazareth, our task today is to pay attention to these two early documents from his original followers in Galilee. In seeking to solve a case a good detective will do no less than give special attention to the best available evidence.

THE SAYINGS GOSPEL Q

One document left by the Jesus people of Galilee was not found in an archeological dig. All these years it has actually been embedded in the gospels of Matthew and Luke. It was not until about 150 years ago, however, that scholars in Germany identified this collection of sayings. The discovery of this document is an amazing piece of detective work. Here is how the scholars found this remarkable document.

Mark, as we have seen, wrote his gospel first. Matthew and Luke independently used Mark as the basic source of their gospels, each one editing and changing Mark to suit his own purposes. About 150 years ago, some German scholars noticed that Matthew and Luke have about 250 verses in common not found anywhere in Mark. So the question naturally arose: Since Matthew and Luke wrote independently of each other, how did they come by this shared material not originating in Mark? The scholars concluded that Matthew and Luke used an additional source in the composition of their gospels, some source Mark did not know about, or at least did not use. By examining those verses Matthew and Luke had in common but are not found in Mark, scholars were able to reconstruct this previously unknown document. They gave this lost source the name "Q," from the German word *Quelle*, "source."

Q is an early collection of the sayings of Jesus and thus has been given the name the Sayings Gospel Q. Unlike the four gospels in the Bible, it is not a narrative account of Jesus's ministry. It was compiled by the original followers of Jesus, those who had been with Jesus during his ministry in Galilee, probably first put into written form within ten to twenty years after his death.

The Q document was written in several stages over a period of several years. The first stage of the Q gospel is the original collection of the sayings of Jesus. This stage contains Jesus's understanding of the kingdom of God, viewed as a present reality, not as a future life after death. The later stages add the evolving ideas developing among later followers of Jesus, such as the expectation of a future cataclysmic event signaling the beginning of the end of the world as we know it.

The first edition (or layer) of Q provides a window into a group of Jesus people in Galilee in the 30s and 40s and becomes the primary evidence for what was happening in the life of the original followers of Jesus. Since Jesus did not leave any written words himself, this first stage of Q is a most valuable piece of evidence regarding the mission and message of Jesus.

Q contains no information about the birth of Jesus or his death and resurrection, nor does it ascribe to Jesus any exalted titles such as "Son of God" or "Lord and Savior." In this document there is no call to "believe in Jesus," only a call to follow Jesus. These first followers of Jesus did not worship Jesus as a risen Christ, as did Paul's later congregations. They did not think of themselves as "Christians" or as forming a "Christian church." They were not theologians, nor were they academic. They did not develop theories or beliefs about Jesus.

Since they were struggling with how to get through each day together under the harsh rule of the Roman government, the Jesus People of Galilee focused on what Jesus taught them about how to live in relationship with one another, as well as how to live with others beyond their community. Jesus's radical teachings were kept alive within them and transmitted to one another by word of mouth for a decade or so before they attempted to put his sayings into written form.

Jesus taught them a better way to live than simply enduring the suffering under the Romans, a way open to everyone, no matter what his or her economic status, innate abilities, or ethnic background. Jesus called this new way of living together the "kingdom of God."

Their focus was on following the teachings and example of Jesus, because he put a new spirit and energy into their lives. He taught them how to organize their villages in a profound and startling way, transforming their community life as well as their individual lives. Though he did not claim anything for himself, Jesus became a heroic figure to them. What he taught them was vital to their everyday existence. Therefore, they carefully remembered and preserved his teachings in the original edition of the Sayings Gospel Q. Through the careful research of the biblical scholars, those sayings from the first edition are now available to our generation.

THE GOSPEL OF THOMAS

Another group of Jesus people, who had been with Jesus in his mission in Galilee, also produced a collection of sayings of Jesus. This document was discovered in 1945 by a local peasant near the city of Nag Hammadi in Egypt. It was part of a collection of thirteen Christian writings originally composed in Greek, but the copies found in Egypt are all in a Coptic translation.

No one knows who compiled this list of the sayings of Jesus, but in its opening sentence it describes itself as a revelation to Jesus's disciple Thomas. Thus it has been given the name the *Gospel of Thomas*. It is a collection of more than 114 sayings attributed to Jesus. Like Q, the *Gospel of Thomas* was composed in stages. The original stage was probably written by followers of Jesus in Galilee about the same time as the Sayings Gospel Q—ten to twenty years after the death of Jesus. This stage contains many sayings of Jesus also found in the original layer of Q. This fact gives credence to the conclusion the original layer of the *Gospel of Thomas* also came from Galilee in the early period following the death of Jesus. The original layers of the two sources are very similar, and they demonstrate a common interest in preserving the sayings of Jesus.

Later stages of *Thomas* were added by other followers of Jesus and reflect a Gnostic philosophy of life. Gnosticism was a Greek mystery religion followed by some early Christians. It denied the validity of the physical world, considering it to be evil. The only way of escape was to be initiated into certain mysteries, which necessarily had to be dispensed by a heavenly messenger. For some Christians, Jesus fit this requirement.

Clearly the Gnostic additions to the original layer of *Thomas* did not come from Jesus. As was the case with the Sayings Gospel Q, it is important to distinguish the original layer of the *Gospel of Thomas* from the later additions. It is not good scholarship to dismiss the entire *Gospel of Thomas* because parts of it do not reflect the authentic teachings of Jesus. We must realize the first edition of *Thomas* does indeed contain sayings originating with Jesus and is therefore an important piece of evidence contributing to our understanding of Jesus.

As noted, a goodly number of the same sayings attributed to Jesus occur in the original editions of the Sayings Gospel Q and the *Gospel of Thomas* (see appendix). The value of *Thomas* is not that it adds anything significantly new to our knowledge of the historical Jesus; its importance lies in the way it confirms the existing evidence. *Thomas* provides us with a second, *independent* early source of the sayings of Jesus and gives further evidence these original followers of Jesus in Galilee composed gospels containing only sayings, with no narrative story included—no miracles, no death, no resurrection, and no exalted titles for Jesus.

The Thomas group were also from the villages of Galilee. They, too, suffered under the rule of the Romans and were also poor and destitute. In the original layer of the *Gospel of Thomas*, they preserved the sayings of Jesus important to them.

CONCLUSION: AS CLOSE TO JESUS AS WE CAN GET

We have no record of anything Jesus wrote. The original layer of these two sayings gospels, written before the New Testament gospels and before the letters of Paul, are, therefore, as close to Jesus as we can get. For differing reasons, until recently these two sayings gospels were not known. Now they can be read by anyone interested in Jesus, providing a new avenue for finding the missing person Jesus of Nazareth. It would be foolish (and dishonest) to ignore these two earliest writings from those who were with Jesus in his Galilean ministry.

These two sayings gospels are quite different from the four narrative gospels of the New Testament, and quite different from Paul's understanding of Jesus. These two documents from his original followers provide an alternative viewpoint regarding Jesus and his original intention in his mission in Galilee. They did not seem to know anything about the last supper, the trial and crucifixion of Jesus, or stories of the empty tomb and his resurrection from the dead. Their interest does not appear to be what happened to Jesus in Jerusalem. Their focus is on what he taught them in Galilee about living in the present as real-life members of the kingdom of God here and now.

After the execution of Jesus under Pilate, the Jesus People of Galilee continued to follow the message and program of Jesus in their village life. Even though Jesus was dead, they did not cease being his followers. In their villages they were engaged in a radical lifestyle taught to them by Jesus, explored elsewhere in this book. They produced the original layer of these two sayings gospels and cannot be dismissed as people who somehow failed to understand Jesus and what he was trying to accomplish. The reason they cannot be dismissed is simple—they were with him in his mission in Galilee. The Jesus People of Galilee were numerically and spiritually a vital part of the early Christian movement. These two sayings gospels enable us to know what the first followers of Jesus thought about him before there were any Christian churches of the type founded by Paul.

It should be remembered these first followers of Jesus were all Jews living in Galilee. Jesus's words and deeds lived on in their hearts and minds. They preserved sayings important to them, not just stray teachings of little interest to them. These sayings, mostly pithy one-liners along with a few parables, form the true message of Jesus. Perhaps his followers knew he would most want these teachings remembered and carried on. In any event, this was the message they continued to proclaim and practice in Galilee.

The original stages of these two gospels are two sources going back to those who heard and remembered what Jesus said and did. This oldest layer of the sayings of Jesus can be trusted to provide an accurate picture of what Jesus actually had to say and what his mission was. They are, therefore, the best and most authentic evidence for discovering the missing person Jesus of Nazareth, as well as his vision, program, and original intention for his mission in Galilee.

Amazingly, these two sayings gospels came from the underside of the society of that day, the impoverished, struggling villages of Galilee. It has often been noted that history is written by the victors, the upper classes of a society. In these two documents we have the rare privilege of glimpsing a viewpoint from the lower class of a society, the peasants of Galilee. We should never take for granted the special opportunity we have to examine two documents from the bottom rungs of the ladder in Israel.

Our detective work of examining the written evidence to find the missing person Jesus of Nazareth will involve a serious look at these two early writings, as well as a careful exploration of the four New Testament gospels. Honesty demands we do no less than examine the best evidence available to us.

TIME LINE OF THE WRITTEN EVIDENCE

The dating of the written evidence is important. The closer the material is to the date of Jesus's life, the more accurate and reliable is the information. Without ignoring the importance of the other layers, it is the first layer of written evidence that provides the most reliable evidence regarding the words and deeds of Jesus. With that in mind, using the image of an archeological dig, where the deeper you dig the closer you get to the original source, these are the five layers of the written evidence:

5th Layer	Gospel of John	written circa 95 to 100 CE
4th Layer	Gospel of Luke	written circa 85 to 90 CE
3rd Layer	Gospel of Matthew	written circa 80 to 85 CE
2nd Layer	Gospel of Mark	written circa 70 CE
1st Layer	First editions of	
	Sayings Gospel Q	written circa 40 to 50 CE
	Gospel of Thomas	written circa 40 to 50 CE

5

Examining Jesus's Purpose

THE DETECTIVE'S SEARCH FOR the missing person Jesus of Nazareth begins with the search for his original intention for his mission in Galilee. We begin with the understanding that he had a specific purpose in mind as he began his mission. He did not just wander aimlessly around Galilee. The Gospel of Luke portrays Jesus beginning his mission at around the age of thirty by announcing he saw himself as anointed by God for a special purpose:

> The Spirit of the Lord is upon me,
> because he has anointed me
> to bring good news to the poor.
> He has sent me to proclaim release to the captives
> and recovery of sight to the blind,
> to let the oppressed go free,
> to proclaim the year of the Lord's favor. (Luke 4:18–19)

These words are a quote from Isaiah 61:1–2. Whether or not Jesus actually quoted these words himself we do not know. However, they certainly sum up Jesus's mission in a clear and concise manner. Several important truths emerge from this passage:

A. Jesus had a profound awareness of being anointed by the Spirit of the Lord for a definite purpose. The word "anointed" meant to be called and consecrated to service for God.

B. He believed he was called to bring "good news" to one group in particular—the poor. The evidence will show this is precisely the people to whom Jesus directed his ministry.

C. Jesus saw himself as one sent to proclaim radical social and economic freedom to the "captives," the "blind," and the "oppressed."

D. He believed it was his mission to "proclaim the year of the Lord's favor." Jesus saw the time was right for a new beginning for the peasant villagers in Galilee, and it was his intention to inaugurate that new reality.

Luke reports Jesus then announced to the audience in the synagogue in Nazareth, "Today this scripture has been fulfilled in your hearing" (Luke 4:21). This entire announcement scene as portrayed by Luke confirms the fact Jesus saw himself as a man on a mission from God. This raises the question: Where did Jesus gain his awareness of being called by God for a special mission? The answer is found in the Hebrew Scriptures, what Christians call the Old Testament.

Jesus was a Jew. He was born into a Jewish family and grew up in a Jewish village. We can reasonably assume Jesus went to a synagogue school in Nazareth, where he would have learned the two main parts of the Hebrew Scriptures: The Torah and the Prophets. Based on his brilliant teaching ability as an adult, we can safely assume he was an excellent student, absorbing the content of these two sections of the Hebrew Scriptures.

THE TORAH

The phrase Jesus used in his announcement, "to proclaim the year of the Lord's favor," may seem strange at first glance. Remember, though, Jesus grew up learning the words of the Torah, the first five books of the Hebrew Scriptures. The Torah was especially sacred to the Jews, for it served as the foundational document of the nation of Israel. It contains the Hebrew Law, the set of instructions by which Israel was to live. The underlying theme of the Torah is that God cares for all people equally, so throughout the Torah is a radical egalitarianism. The Torah, therefore, contains some of the most far-reaching economic principles in history, designed to intentionally equalize the economy for the benefit of all the inhabitants of the land. This includes a Sabbath day, a Sabbath year, and every fifty years, the Jubilee Year, the "year of the Lord's favor," as Isaiah and Jesus expressed it. These economic principles are found in three books of the Torah: Exodus, Deuteronomy, and Leviticus. Here is a summary of these principles:

A. The Sabbath Day. The most familiar of these economic principles is the commandment to observe a weekly Sabbath day.

> Six days you shall labor and do all your work. But the seventh is a sabbath to the LORD your God; you shall not do any work—you, or your son or your daughter, or your male or female slave, or your ox or your donkey, or any of your livestock, or the resident alien in your towns, so that your male and female slave may rest as well as you. (Deut 5:13–14)

The weekly cycle of six workdays and a day of rest was established to be a day of rest for each person and each work animal. You will notice the commandment says nothing about a religious observance on the Sabbath day. It was an economic, egalitarian commandment, applied to everyone equally, rich and poor, free and slave, male and female, humans as well as animals. The Sabbath is a day when the inequality of the other six days is set aside and everyone is equally entitled to a day of rest.

B. The Sabbatical Year. After each six-year period a sabbatical year was declared. In this year three steps were to be taken, dramatically altering the social life of the community and reducing inequality among the people:

1. Land Was Given a Rest.

> For six years you shall sow your land and gather in its yield; but the seventh year you shall let it rest and lie fallow, so that the poor of your people may eat; and what they leave the wild animals may eat. You shall do the same with your vineyard, and with your olive orchard. (Exod 23:10–11; see also Lev 25:2–7)

During this sabbatical year crops were not to be planted or harvested. Plants that grew up by themselves were to be left for the poor, and what remained was to be left for the wild animals. Again, this commandment expresses a common concern for all of life, including the poor and the wild animals.

2. Slaves Were Released.

> If a member of your community, whether a Hebrew man or a Hebrew woman, is sold to you and works for you six years, in the seventh year you shall set that person free. And when you send a male slave out from you a free person, you shall not send him out

> empty-handed. Provide liberally out of your flock, your threshing floor, and your wine press, thus giving him some of the bounty with which the Lord your God has blessed you. (Deut 15:12–14; see also Exod 21:1–6)

Most slaves became slaves through indebtedness. After working for six years the slave, male or female, was to be set free. In addition, the owner of a male slave was to give him sufficient provisions to enable him to resume his life as a free person with some degree of dignity and equality. Again, the economic basis of this commandment is evident.

3. *Debts Were Canceled.*

> Every seventh year you shall grant a remission of debts. And this is the manner of the remission: every creditor shall remit the claim that is held against a neighbor, not exacting it of a neighbor who is a member of the community, because the Lord's remission has been proclaimed. (Deut 15:1–2)

The debts were primarily neighborly loans to needy farmers rather than commercial loans. The debt could arise through bad fortune, drought, famine, poor decisions, or death. No matter how the indebtedness occurred, the commandment required the total cancellation of any remaining debts every sabbatical year. This gave each person and each family the opportunity to start over without the inequality of accumulated debt.

In addition to this radical provision, there were two other requirements designed to control inequality among the people of Israel: First, inequality through debt was controlled by the forbidding of interest on loans to Jewish neighbors (Exod 22:25: Lev 25:35–37; Deut 23:19–20). Second, there were strong restrictions on collateral which could be taken on loans (Exod 22:26–27; Deut 24:10–11). These commandments forbidding interest on loans as well as the restrictions on collateral maintained a degree of balance and fairness between the rich and the poor.

C. *The Jubilee Year.* After seven cycles of seven years, in the fiftieth year, a Jubilee Year was declared, in which the most radical economic shake-up was instituted:

> You shall count off seven weeks of years, seven times seven years, so that the period of seven weeks of years gives forty-nine years. . . . And you shall hallow the fiftieth year and you shall proclaim liberty throughout the land to all its inhabitants. It shall be a jubilee

> for you: you shall return, every one of you, to your property and every one of you to your family. That fiftieth year shall be a jubilee for you. . . . In this year of jubilee you shall return, every one of you, to your property. . . . When you buy from your neighbor, you shall pay only for the number of years since the jubilee; the seller shall charge you only for the remaining crop years. (Lev 25:8, 10–11a, 13, 15)

In this fiftieth year, the Jubilee, all land impounded or confiscated for unpaid debts was returned to the original owners of that land. This radical commandment was designed to prevent the rich from profiting at the expense of the poor. People often lost their land through debts they were unable to repay, as poorer farmers borrowed from those who were in a better financial position. The purpose of the Jubilee Year was to prevent the poor from permanently losing their land. When buying a piece of property, the person paid only for the number of years remaining until the next Jubilee Year, and then the property reverted back to the original owner.

The basic principle operating here is that the land ultimately belongs to God. Human ownership was always considered to be provisional and temporary. Accordingly, God commanded, "The land shall not be sold in perpetuity, for the land is mine; with me you are but aliens and tenants. Throughout the land that you hold, you shall provide for the redemption of the land" (Lev 25:23–24).

These Jewish economic regulations in the Torah were radical then, and they still seem radical today. These instructions recognize the fact that some people are better entrepreneurs and financial managers than others and will therefore be in a more advantageous economic position. So every fifty years, the Jubilee addresses these inequities, the gap between the rich and the poor. And it addresses the gap in a dramatic and radical way, canceling all debts and restoring the land to the original owners, thus leveling the playing field in the land once again.

In summing up these commandments regarding the Sabbath, the sabbatical year, and the Jubilee Year, the people of Israel were instructed to always be generous toward the needy members of their communities:

> If there is among you anyone in need, a member of your community in any of your towns in the land that the Lord your God is giving you, do not be hard-hearted or tight-fisted toward your needy neighbor. You should rather open your hand, willingly lending enough to meet the need, whatever it may be. (Deut 15:7–8)

Finally, the promise was given that as Israel lived by these economic principles there would be no one needy in their communities (Deut 15:4). It should also be noted these radical social-economic laws did not eliminate individual creativity and initiative. There was still the opportunity for personal achievement and gain. There was also, however, the need to keep matters in balance, and so a periodic leveling of the playing field was commanded. This was the basis of Hebrew economics in the Torah.

The Jews believed the Torah set forth the instructions by which God wanted them to live. As a Jewish boy growing up studying the Torah, Jesus would have been well aware of these Hebrew economic practices. According to Luke, as he began his mission Jesus announced his original intention to proclaim "the year of the Lord's favor," and it is clear by that phrase he was referring to the Jubilee Year. He believed he had been anointed by God to "bring good news to the poor." There can be little doubt Jesus had these Hebrew economic principles in mind as he declared his intention for his ministry. The evidence will show that he took these Hebrew economic principles and applied them to the situation in the villages of Galilee in his own day.

THE PROPHETS

In addition to knowing the Torah, as a Jew growing up in Israel Jesus would also have known the Prophets, a second main section of the Hebrew Scriptures. The prophets were not primarily predictors of the future but were radical social reformers who spoke out strongly about the social sins of Israel. Any predictions the prophets made related primarily to future outcomes based on whether or not Israel obeyed God's instructions regarding how to live as a nation. Prophecy is not a prediction but a promise or a threat based on Israel's behavior. When Israel strayed from the social-economic teachings of the Torah, the prophets spoke out strongly, condemning the behavior of the nation. Here are the issues that concerned the prophets of Israel, expressed in their own words:

> Wash yourselves; make yourselves clean;
> remove the evil of your doings
> from before my eyes;
> cease to do evil,
> learn to do good;
> seek justice,
> rescue the oppressed,

defend the orphan,
  plead for the widow. (Isa 1:16–17)

Your princes are rebels
  and companions of thieves.
Everyone loves a bribe
  and runs after gifts.
They do not defend the orphan,
  and the widow's cause does not come before them. (Isa 1:23)

The Lord enters into judgment
  with the elders and princes of his people:
It is you who have devoured the vineyard;
  the spoil of the poor is in your houses.
What do you mean by crushing my people,
  by grinding the face of the poor? says the LORD GOD of hosts.
(Isa 3:14–15)

Ah, you who make iniquitous decrees,
  who write oppressive statutes,
to turn aside the needy from justice
  and to rob the poor of my people of their right,
that widows may be your spoil,
  and that you may make the orphans your prey!
What will you do on the day of punishment,
  in the calamity that will come from far away? (Isa 10:1–3)

Is not this the fast that I choose:
  to loose the bonds of injustice,
  to undo the thongs of the yoke,
to let the oppressed go free,
  and to break every yoke?
Is it not to share your bread with the hungry,
  and bring the homeless poor into your house;
when you see the naked, to cover them,
  and not to hide yourself from your own kin? . . .
If you remove the yoke from among you,
  the pointing of the finger, the speaking of evil,
if you offer your food to the hungry
  and satisfy the needs of the afflicted,
then your light shall rise in the darkness,
  and your gloom shall be like the noonday. (Isa 58:6–7, 9b–10)

On your skirts is found
  the lifeblood of the innocent poor,
though you did not catch them breaking in. (Jer 2:34)

For if you truly amend your ways and your doings, if you truly act justly one with another, if you do not oppress the alien, the orphan, and the widow, or shed innocent blood in this place, and if you do not go after other gods to your own hurt, then I will dwell with you in this place, in the land that I gave of old to your ancestors forever and ever. (Jer 7:5–7)

Thus says the Lord: Act with justice and righteousness, and deliver from the hand of the oppressor anyone who has been robbed. And do no wrong or violence to the alien, the orphan, and the widow, or shed innocent blood in this place. (Jer 22:3)

They know no limits in deeds of wickedness;
  they do not judge with justice
the cause of the orphan, to make it prosper,
  and they do not defend the rights of the needy.
Shall I not punish them for these things?
                says the LORD,
and shall I not bring retribution
on a nation such as this? (Jer 5:28b–30)

Woe to him who builds his house by unrighteousness,
  and his upper rooms by injustice;
who makes his neighbors work for nothing,
  and does not give them their wages. (Jer 22:13)

He judged the cause of the poor and the needy;
  then it was well.
Is not this to know me?
  says the LORD.
But your eyes and heart
  are only on your dishonest gain,
for shedding innocent blood,
  and for practicing oppression and violence. (Jer 22:16–17)

Its officials within it [speaking of the nation Israel] are like wolves tearing the prey, shedding blood, destroying lives to get dishonest gain. . . . The people of the land have practiced extortion and committed robbery; they have oppressed the poor and needy, and have extorted from the alien without redress. (Ezek 22:27, 29)

Thus says the Lord:
For three transgressions of Israel,
  and for four, I will not revoke the punishment;
because they sell the righteous for silver,
  and the needy for a pair of sandals—

they who trample the head of the poor into the dust of the earth,
  and push the afflicted out of the way. (Amos 2:6–7)

Therefore because you trample on the poor
  and take from them levies of grain,
you have built houses of hewn stone,
  but you shall not live in them;
you have planted pleasant vineyards,
  but shall not drink their wine.
For I know how many are your transgressions,
  and how great are your sins—
you who afflict the righteous, who take a bribe,
  and push aside the needy in the gate. (Amos 5:11–12)

I hate, I despise your festivals,
  and I take no delight in your solemn assemblies. . . .
Take away from me the noise of your songs;
  I will not listen to the melody of your harps.
But let justice roll down like waters,
  and righteousness like an everflowing stream. (Amos 5:21, 23, 24)

Hear this, you that trample on the needy,
  and bring to ruin the poor of the land,
saying "When will the new moon be over
  so that we may sell grain;
and the sabbath, so that we may offer wheat for sale?
We will make the ephah small and the shekel great,
  and practice deceit with false balances,
buying the poor for silver
  and the needy for a pair of sandals,
  and selling the sweepings of the wheat." (Amos 8:4–6)

Alas for those who device wickedness
  and evil deeds on their beds!
When the morning dawns they perform it,
  because it is in their power.
They covet fields and seize them;
  houses, and take them away;
they oppress householder and house,
  people and their inheritance. (Mic 2:1–2)

He has told you, O mortal, what is good;
  and what does the Lord require of you
but to do justice, and to love kindness,
  and to walk humbly with your God? (Mic 6:8)

As can be seen from these quotations, the prophetic voice of protest against the inequality between the rich and the poor, as well as the mistreatment of the poor by the rich, is constant and consistent. Over and over again the prophets of Israel proclaimed that this inequality runs counter to the will of God. It is a theme found throughout the prophets from beginning to end. The prophets' vision of a new world of peace, compassion, and social justice is neither utopian nor idealistic. It was a practical and pragmatic vision capable of being implemented in this world.

As a Jewish boy growing up in a Jewish family in a Jewish village, Jesus would have regularly heard the reading of the Torah and the Prophets. In a small peasant village like Nazareth there would have been only one copy of the Hebrew Scriptures, which would have been kept in a receptacle known as the Ark. The Jewish people heard the Scriptures read once or twice a week in the synagogue meetings. Since they did not have individual copies of the Hebrew Scriptures, they were very adept at memorizing much of the Torah and the Prophets.

It was the Hebrew Scriptures, the Torah and the Prophets, that nurtured within Jesus an awareness of God's will for his people. Jesus grew up learning (and possibly memorizing) the radical economic principles of the Torah, as well as the prophets' strong protest against inequality among the people of the nation Israel. It was natural, therefore, as he began his mission in Galilee, for Jesus to use a quote from the prophet Isaiah, which also includes the Torah's reference to the Jubilee Year.

Growing up when he did, Jesus saw the huge contrast between God's will for his people and the terrible and worsening economic situation of the poor and destitute in the villages of his home province of Galilee. The Roman taxation system and resulting appropriation of the small land holdings of the village farmers was driving them into deeper and deeper poverty. In addition, the aristocratic Jerusalem priesthood and the wealthy elite of Israel were collaborating with the Romans for their own benefit, ignoring the needs of the poor. Jesus was from one of these peasant villages, Nazareth, and he could readily identify with the situation of the poor and destitute in the villages of Galilee.

Out of the combination of his knowledge of the Hebrew Scriptures and his awareness of the situation of the village poor in Galilee, Jesus formed his sense of being called by God to embark on a mission to "bring good news to the poor."

IT ALL BEGINS WITH JOHN

The Gospels indicate that sometime in his late twenties Jesus left his hometown to join the protest movement led by a prophet called John the Baptist. John's movement was centered in the wilderness area near the Jordan River. Jesus was baptized by John and for a period of time became a member of John the Baptist's protest movement.

John believed God was angry with the Jewish people, especially the priests of the temple in Jerusalem. In John's mind, the brutal Roman occupation was God's punishment of Israel. John proclaimed that any time now God would intervene in this world and clean up the mess that Israel had gotten herself into. He called on people to repent and be baptized in preparation for this visit from God, a visit he believed would occur in the very near future.

It should be noted the word *repent* did not have the same meaning in that day it does in the popular mind today. Repent did not mean to feel sorry for one's sins or to have a feeling of remorse. Rather, the word *repent* meant to turn around, to change one's behavior. It had a very practical application in one's life. According to Luke, John said to the crowds, "Bear fruits worthy of repentance" (3:8).

The Gospel of Luke also reports that when John warned the people the time was near and they should repent, they questioned John about how they should respond:

> And the crowds asked him, "What then should we do?" In reply he said to them, "Whoever has two coats must share with anyone who has none, and whoever has food must do likewise." Even tax collectors came to be baptized, and they asked him, "Teacher, what should we do?" He said to them, "Collect no more than the amount prescribed for you." Soldiers also asked him, "And we, what should we do?" He said to them, "Do not extort money from anyone by threats or false accusation, and be satisfied with your wages." (3:10–14)

John's basic message was that a person could escape the coming vengeful wrath of God by going through the act of baptism and repenting of sin by a change in behavior. His approach was in the tradition of the social prophets of the Hebrew Scriptures. Like these prophets, he told the people God was angry because of the injustices committed by the people of Israel. The evidence of this injustice was the growing large gap between the wealthy elite and the poor.

John was highly popular among the common people, who came out into the wilderness in large numbers to hear him and to be baptized by him. This is attested in both the Gospels and by the Jewish historian Josephus, who describes John's ministry and what happened to him:

> Although John was a good man and exhorted the Jews to lead righteous lives and practice justice toward their colleagues and piety to God, Herod had put him to death. John taught that baptism must not be employed to obtain pardon for sins committed, but as a consecration of the body, implying that the soul was already purified by proper behavior. When others also joined the crowds around John and were greatly aroused by his preaching, Herod grew alarmed that such eloquence could lead to rebellion. Therefore, he decided that it would be better to strike first and get rid of him, rather than wait for an uprising. Although John was brought in chains to Machaerus and put to death in that stronghold, the Jews decided that the destruction of Herod's army was God's vindication of John. (*Ant.* 18.106; Maier trans., p. 267)

The passage speaks for itself. John's fiery preaching attracted huge crowds to the wilderness area. The Roman-appointed ruler of the northern provinces of Israel, Herod Antipas, became nervous about John's popularity and the possibility he may be stirring up the people to revolt. He, therefore, had John arrested and subsequently had him executed.

At the time of John's arrest and execution, Jesus was still a follower of John the Baptist. At this point, Jesus returned from the wilderness to Galilee (see Mark 1:14). Jesus certainly noted that God did not come and intervene dramatically in history on behalf of Israel, as John had predicted. Subsequently, Jesus launched his own mission, with a message quite different from John's message of impending doom.

A MAN ON A MISSION

The word *mission* is the appropriate word to describe Jesus's activity in Galilee, for it refers to activity with a purpose in mind. Jesus had a sense of calling to be on a mission from God. He evidently developed the sense of calling through his knowledge of the Hebrew Scriptures, where God called certain people to be his servants in this world. It is certainly reasonable to assume Jesus had a purpose in mind as he conducted his mission throughout Galilee. He did not wander aimlessly through the countryside. He had something he wanted to accomplish with his mission.

THE ORIGINAL INTENTION OF JESUS'S MISSION

In order to find the missing person Jesus of Nazareth, it is necessary to discover the original purpose for his mission in Galilee. It is not fair to impose on Jesus a preconceived notion about him. It is vital to take an honest look at the evidence. The best evidence is his words and deeds as remembered by his earliest followers. That raises the issue of whether there is enough credible evidence to recover his original intention. If there is not, the quest is hopeless, and should be abandoned.

It is my contention, however, sufficient evidence exists to discover the original intention of Jesus. As in the work of any good detective, the evidence must be sifted through to arrive at a plausible understanding of what Jesus was seeking to accomplish with his Galilean mission.

No one can know, of course, exactly what was in the mind of Jesus. He left no written record of his inner thoughts. There are only his words and deeds remembered by his followers and later put in written form. I have already made the case that not every word and deed attributed to Jesus in the Gospels comes from Jesus himself. Some words and deeds were added by later writers, reflecting their own understanding of Jesus. There are, however, dependable accounts of Jesus's words from the earliest followers of Jesus. These words of Jesus in particular provide the evidence enabling us to discover the original intention of his mission. Jesus must be allowed to speak for himself regarding what he had in mind for his public mission.

What is learned from an examination of the words and deeds of Jesus deemed by the scholars to most likely have originated with Jesus? To what conclusion does the evidence lead regarding Jesus's original intention for his public mission in Galilee? Based on that evidence, here is my conclusion: *The original intention of Jesus's Mission was to transform the villages of Galilee through communal sharing of resources.*

The evidence of the words and deeds of Jesus from the earliest and most reliable gospel sources indicates Jesus did not direct his mission primarily at individuals, but at the small village communities of Galilee. In other words, Jesus was a community organizer first and foremost. He followed the traditional Hebrew viewpoint that individual lives are shaped by the community in which they are raised and in which they live. If you want to produce healthy and wholesome individuals, you start by producing a healthy and wholesome community. The community comes first, individuals second. This means "it takes a village" to produce and maintain a healthy and wholesome individual, whether that individual be a child or an adult. Thus, it could be said that Jesus was a "communitarian," a person who understands the crucial role a healthy and wholesome community plays in developing healthy and wholesome individuals.

Most people are accustomed to thinking of Jesus ministering to individuals, and it may be difficult to realize his own original intention was not simply to reach individuals, but to transform village community life in Galilee. The standard approach to understanding Jesus is to picture him as dealing solely with individual concerns—healing individuals, teaching individuals how to live, and telling them what to do in order to enter heaven upon death.

There are three factors explaining this tendency to think of Jesus as dealing only with individuals. First, part of the problem is that in the original Greek there are two words for "you," a plural "you" and a singular "you," but in Modern English the word "you" can be either plural or singular. Southerners in America long ago recognized this dilemma in the English language and sought to solve it with the combination word "y'all." In the Greek language, the language in which the New Testament was written, the fact is, most of the "yous" in the gospel accounts are plural. Reading an English translation, the only way to determine whether a spoken or implied "you" is plural or singular is by looking at the context of the word. When that is done with Jesus's words, the conclusion is reached that Jesus most often used the plural form of "you" in his teachings.

Second, the traditional teaching of the church through the years has emphasized personal salvation as the purpose of Jesus's ministry. Accordingly, the message has focused on personal decisions to accept Jesus Christ as Lord and Savior. This emphasis on individual decisions is not the only way to understand the purpose of Jesus. The historical and biblical evidence indicates Jesus's mission was aimed primarily at community transformation. In fact, based on the traditional Hebrew viewpoint that transformed communities produce transformed individuals, Jesus envisioned his purpose as developing the suffering Galilean villages into cooperative sharing communities, with the ensuing result being the transformation of individuals.

The third factor influencing the contemporary tendency to interpret Jesus in an individualistic way is the nature of modern American society. We live in a culture emphasizing individual accomplishment and responsibility over community relationships. Americans tend to pride themselves on their "rugged individualism." Sociologists have noted Americans live in the most individualistic society in history.

Considering these three factors, the study of the life of Jesus has a strong tendency to understand his words and deeds as being directed only to individuals. This has led to a one-sided understanding of Jesus. When one keeps in mind, however, the traditional Hebraic understanding of the importance of community, a more complete and balanced picture of Jesus emerges. His vision and program arose from a basic sociological truth found in the Torah and the social prophets of Israel. Individual growth and development arises out of community. It was true then and it is true today. Communities are at their best when there is a spirit of cooperation and sharing. Jesus's teachings are built on that ancient truth. Jesus believed he was called by God to teach the villagers of Galilee the way God wanted people to live in community. He showed them how a community of shared resources could be established in their villages. As one moves beyond the modern individualistic interpretation of Jesus and pays attention to the communal aspect of his teachings, the conclusion that Jesus was a community organizer begins to make sense.

Thinking about Jesus's original intention and purpose for his life, it is sometimes said that Jesus came to die, with the implication that his purpose on earth was to die for our sins. This view of his purpose tends to render his life and his teachings meaningless. An honest examination of the New Testament materials refutes the idea that Jesus thought the purpose of his life was to die. Rather, it is clear from the evidence that what he said and what he did led to his death. He was executed as a threat to the Roman Empire for the things he said and the actions he took.

Examining the New Testament material to determine Jesus's original purpose leads to the conclusion his original intention was to overcome the devastating effects of the Roman rule by calling on the village peasants to change their village life from blaming each other for their dire economic situation to helping one another in a community spirit of sharing of common resources. He led the villagers to return to their traditional Hebrew roots of covenant community. The evidence all points in this direction, beginning with his own statement of his purpose, as stated in the Gospel of Luke.

6

Examining Jesus's Strategic Plan

FURTHER EVIDENCE SUPPORTING THE conclusion that Jesus's original purpose was to transform the villages of the peasants in Galilee is provided by an examination of his mission strategy. As will become clear, Jesus had a carefully developed plan for his mission in Galilee. As any good detective would do, we will examine all the available evidence to determine the contents of his strategic plan. There are five pieces of evidence to be examined.

A. JESUS'S OVERALL PLAN

As noted previously, when Jesus began his mission in Galilee, he publicly announced that God "has anointed me to bring good news to the poor" (Luke 4:18). The evidence shows that Jesus intentionally developed a strategic plan to fulfill that purpose.

When Jesus began his mission in Galilee he first set up a headquarters in the small fishing village of Capernaum, located on the western shore of the Sea of Galilee. In that day, it was the practice of famous teachers and rabbis to set up a headquarters in one location and remain there. Individuals who wished to learn from or be healed by the teacher or rabbi would come to his headquarters for instruction and healing. John the Baptist, for example, followed this practice.

If Jesus had simply wanted to teach and heal individuals he could have followed this pattern and remained in Capernaum and waited for people to come to him. At his headquarters he could have taught and healed individuals. Jesus, however, did not follow the practice of the other teachers and rabbis of Israel. The Gospels portray Jesus traveling continually throughout the province of Galilee. He took his mission of bringing "good news to the poor" to where the people lived. This departure from the traditional pattern of teachers and rabbis of that day leads to the conclusion that Jesus had a specific strategy in mind when he left his headquarters and traveled with his entourage of disciples throughout Galilee.

Where did Jesus go as he traveled throughout Galilee with his disciples? The evidence shows he went to the villages of the region. Remember, the poor lived in the villages, while the rich and those who served them lived in the cities. Interestingly, there is not one single report in the gospel material of Jesus ever going to any of the cities of Galilee. On the other hand, Mark and Luke both describe the mission of Jesus and his disciples as focused on the villages:

> In the morning, while it was still very dark, he got up and went out to a deserted place, and there he prayed. And Simon and his companions hunted for him. When they found him, they said to him, "Everyone is looking for you." He answered, "Let us go on to the neighboring towns, so that I may proclaim the message there also; for that is what I came out to do." And he went throughout Galilee, proclaiming the message in their synagogues and casting out demons. (Mark 1:35–39)

Mark also reports, "he went about among the villages teaching" (6:6b). In addition, Luke notes about Jesus and his disciples, "They departed and went through the villages, bringing the good news and curing diseases everywhere" (9:6).

Why did Jesus focus on the villages? Remember the situation in the villages in Galilee. The population of the villages consisted of farmers who owned small family farms outside the village, as well as a few shopkeepers. The farmers of the villages of Galilee were suffering terribly under the heavy burden of Roman taxes and tribute. Much of their produce was being confiscated by the Roman rulers who lived in the comfort of the cities. Royal taxes, however, were not the only problems faced by the Jewish villagers. They were also required to pay priestly tithes and an annual tax to the temple in Jerusalem. The combination of Roman taxes and temple tithes and taxes put the peasants in a precarious economic situation.

It became impossible for the farmers to produce enough for taxes and tithes, and then to have anything left for their own family. They often had to borrow from the wealthy elite, at very high interest rates, to try to maintain their small family farms. When they were unable to repay these loans, the farmers would lose their farm holdings. They would then become tenant farmers on the land they once had owned, day laborers looking for work on a daily basis, beggars, or worst of all, slaves.

The desperate situation of the peasants under Roman rule was destroying the basic fabric of village community life as the destitute turned against each other in their competition for scarce resources. Village life was breaking down and becoming a bitter struggle to survive as neighbor turned against neighbor. For centuries the traditional Hebrew cooperative spirit had existed in the villages, but due to the harsh conditions under Roman rule, that spirit was disintegrating rapidly during Jesus's time.

This division within the villages worked in the favor of the Roman rulers as they employed the "divide and conquer" principle to maintain absolute control over the villages. As each individual and each family looked after their own interest, the Romans were able to exercise complete power over the populace.

Jesus saw what was happening within the villages, and as a resident of one of those villages he fully understood the plight of the peasant villagers. Jesus felt called to go to the villages where the destitute peasants lived in order to "bring good news to the poor."

What would be "good news" to a peasant who could not even feed his family? Would it be good news for Jesus to say to the poor:

"When you die you can go to a better place called 'heaven.'"

"Your poverty is your own fault because you are lazy and not working hard enough."

"You are all sinners and need to be saved."

Or would the good news be, "I have a plan whereby all of you can have enough to eat and can be free of your indebtedness"?

Clearly, only the last approach of Jesus to the poor would be truly "good news" for the peasants. The evidence shows Jesus taught them a new way of organizing their village life, based on the social-economic principles found in the Torah and confirmed in the words of the Prophets. He reminded them that cooperation rather than competition was God's intention for their villages. By calling the Jewish village peasants back to their Hebrew social-economic principles, Jesus overcame the "divide and conquer" strategy of the Roman government. Jesus brought "good news to the poor" of the villages of Galilee through a plan of communal sharing of their resources.

It should also be noted that Jesus did not travel to the villages alone. He took a community of male and female followers with him. According to the Gospel of John, they shared a common purse, carried by Judas (John 12:6; 13:29). They practiced what Jesus was teaching—a communal sharing of resources. It was an egalitarian community of equals. Thus when Jesus and his entourage entered a village they could rightly say they had been practicing the communal style of life they were encouraging the villagers to adopt.

The fact Jesus and his followers traveled to the villages of Galilee rather than remaining at his headquarters serves as the first piece of evidence demonstrating Jesus's mission was directed to entire villages and not simply to isolated individuals.

B. THREE DIMENSIONS TO JESUS'S STRATEGY

Jesus not only had a strategy of traveling from village to village, he also had a specific strategy within the villages themselves. When the gospel material is examined carefully, the overall strategy Jesus developed as he went into each village comes into focus. Jesus had a very clear intentional plan in mind as he went from village to village. There were three aspects of his strategy, and each dimension was integral to what Jesus was seeking to accomplish in his ministry in Galilee.

1. Teaching

The Gospels often portray Jesus's first strategic action upon arriving in a village as entering the local synagogue (Mark 1:21; 3:1; 6:2). Archeological findings, however, reveal no evidence of any synagogue buildings in the villages of Galilee during Jesus's time. The small villages were evidently too poor to afford a synagogue building. The word *synagogue*, however, does not always refer to a building. It can also be used to describe an assembly of the people of the village. In these once- or twice-a-week gatherings, the villagers prayed, worshiped, and discussed the business of the village. There would not be a formal rabbi to lead the assembly, therefore lay leaders would be in charge of the gatherings. Any adult Jewish male was allowed to speak at the gathering. Jesus's strategy was obviously to be there on the day when the people were assembled together. In that setting he would have the opportunity to share with them his vision and program for redeeming and renewing their village life. If they were receptive to his plan, Jesus and his disciples would remain in the village for a period of time, teaching the specifics of his plan. If they were not receptive, it is likely he would do as he instructed his followers when he sent them out in pairs: he would "wipe the dust" of the village from his feet, and he and his followers would move on to the next village (Mark 6:11; Luke 9:5).

As a teacher, Jesus does not come across as a rabbi interpreting the Scriptures, someone giving lectures on theology, or an instructor imparting knowledge for his listeners to memorize and repeat back to him. Neither was he a philosopher dispensing ideas and timeless truths. He was speaking to a very specific audience, the poor of the Galilean villages, teaching them a radical new way to organize their communities in their very difficult circumstances of living under Roman rule. His teaching, therefore, was highly practical and applicable to their specific situation. For this reason, the villagers heard him gladly and remembered what he had taught them. As Mark reported, those who heard Jesus "were astounded at his teaching, for he taught them as one having authority, and not as the scribes" (1:22).

Jesus apparently saw his words and his works as self-authenticating. He did not appeal to any authority beyond himself, and he refused to perform a miracle on demand as a means of authenticating his work (Mark 8:11–13).

Jesus used two primary methods of communication in his teachings. First, he taught in short, pithy sayings. The wisdom of Jesus is seen in these one-liners. It was, however, not a conventional wisdom. Jesus taught an alternative wisdom, even a subversive wisdom.

Conventional wisdom is the "common sense" of "what everyone knows" to be true. In the time of Jesus, this conventional wisdom was centered on the book of Proverbs, with its practical guidance about rewards for living a good life and punishment for failure to live such a life.

Popular proverbs of today convey this commonsense wisdom: "A stitch in time saves nine"; "A rolling stone gathers no moss"; and "Nothing ventured, nothing gained." Everyone just knows these proverbs are true. It takes no effort to nod one's head in agreement to such conventional wisdom everyone knows.

Jesus's teachings are very different. In his one-liners we see the brilliance of Jesus. He knew wisdom comes not simply by listening to a teacher and nodding one's head in agreement. Wisdom comes through personally wrestling with the issues presented. For example, how would you react to these sayings of Jesus: "Don't let your left hand know what your right hand is doing," or "Be wise as serpents and gentle as doves," or "Love your enemy"? These wisdom sayings leave you scratching your head and struggling to comprehend what the sayings mean and how they apply to your personal life. They also get people's attention, because they go *against* the grain of conventional wisdom.

The other teaching device Jesus used was the parable. A parable is a made-up story, utilizing commonplace activities and events. It is, however, a story with a twist. Jesus's parables were not just simple little inspiring stories. They were stories that caught people by surprise, with unexpected plots and uncommon endings. Jesus's parables begin with the everyday world of the first-century Galilean peasants, but end with a surprising new way of looking at reality. Like Jesus's one-liners, his parables stand in contrast to conventional wisdom. Again, the listener has to think twice about the parable.

His parables were open-ended. They have no set ending to which the listener can simply nod his or her head in agreement. Jesus's parables were more like discussion starters. They were told to a group of peasants who were struggling to survive under the Roman domination system. The end of the parable would invite the peasants to discuss and ponder the application of the parable for their situation. Unfortunately, we have no records of the conversations the parables generated. What we do have is a record of the parables written down forty or more years after they were told, sometimes placed in a framework different from the one in which they were first spoken. In order to understand Jesus's parables, the best we can do is attempt to hear them in the context of first-century peasants suffering tragic economic deprivation through the rule of the Romans and the Jewish elite.

In summary, to comprehend Jesus's one-liners and parables, the specific audience he was addressing, the poor of Galilee, must be kept in mind. When his words are taken out of that context, many of his teachings make little or no sense. If his teachings are treated as timeless truths, they lose their impact. Today, people simply ignore the teachings they find inconvenient, difficult to follow, or incomprehensible to modern ears. Jesus's teachings can be applied to today's circumstances only if they are first heard in the context in which they were spoken.

Jesus must have been a brilliant communicator, for he took on the task of teaching the villagers of Galilee a radical new way of organizing their village life, and people don't change their whole lives easily. Even more importantly, Jesus must have communicated unconditional acceptance and love, for people will not listen to a person unless they feel they are accepted as they are. If they feel they are being judged or condemned, the ideas will seem outlandish and wrong to them. If they sense they are being cared for, they will be more open to hearing what is being communicated. Jesus uniquely combined the qualities of brilliant communication and unconditional acceptance in such a way that the people heard him gladly.

Jesus addressed the village people in a manner that enabled them to understand the message he was communicating. He used images from the culture of their rural life, enabling them to comprehend what he was saying about the kingdom of God. Many of these images, however, are foreign to our modern world and need to be examined carefully in order to understand what Jesus taught. In this regard, the biblical scholars who have thoroughly studied Jesus's teachings can be immensely helpful in bringing these teachings into focus for our day. A later chapter will explore the specific instructions Jesus taught the villagers. These instructions provide the details of his new social-economic plan for the villages of Galilee.

It is also important to note that Jesus was not simply a dispenser of heavenly or spiritual truths for individuals. If that had been the case, he could have lived to a ripe old age. Jesus's teachings were subversive to the Roman rulers, and they perceived him to be a threat to their way of life. The only way to understand the arrest and public execution of Jesus by the Roman rulers is to know they viewed his teachings with suspicion. They were right to be suspicious of Jesus, for as we shall see in the next chapter, his teachings and program were indeed subversive to the Romans economic and political domination of the peasants in Galilee.

2. Healing

Disease and sickness were rampant in Israel of that day, especially in the small villages where the poor lived. Unlike the cities, the villages had very little in the way of sanitary conditions. The result was that villagers often suffered from illnesses, especially eye problems and skin diseases. Healing from illness was a major need in every village.

There were physicians in the society of that day. Medical care, however, was primitive and was mainly confined to the cities where the elite lived. The poor in the villages had no access to medical care, and in any case, they could not have afforded it. Any illness could easily turn fatal. Every illness, therefore, was very frightening to the individual, and since many illnesses were highly contagious, every illness was also a danger to the village community.

In that day, it was assumed a person with an illness was being punished by God for some sin. Thus the sick or diseased person would often be shunned and isolated from the village. Being ill placed a double burden upon an individual, for the ill person had the combined suffering of both the physical illness and social isolation from the village.

The sick person, of course, had a strong desire to be well again. The villagers, therefore, would welcome anyone who might be able to provide them with relief from their distress. Mark reports, for example, that news about Jesus's healing power "spread everywhere throughout the surrounding region of Galilee" (1:28). His reputation as a healer would provide Jesus an entree into a village.

Another feature of illness in that day was the common belief that sickness and disease were caused by demons. The sick person was often thought to be "possessed" by demons. Thus an important aspect of healing was the act of "driving out" the demons from the ill person. This act was called "exorcism" and was expected to be a part of every healer's ministry. The Gospels include many accounts of Jesus offering healing and exorcisms as he traveled from village to village. Many of Jesus's healing and exorcisms occurred in the setting of the village synagogue, the public assembly of the people of the village. When Jesus came to this public assembly he carried out two major aspects of his mission strategy: healing and teaching.

There were other religious healers and exorcists in Galilee and other parts of Israel. In that day, spontaneous healing was not considered impossible or even unusual. However, healers and exorcists expected people to pay for their services, and they used their healing power to enrich themselves and to become famous. On the other hand, the healing Jesus offered was free to everyone. No one had to pay him for the healing he provided. This was an expression of his oneness with the poor of the community. Health care was delivered to all—lepers, children, women, and others who were generally considered "lesser persons" or outcasts in that society.

The free healing mission of Jesus was a sign of the arrival of the kingdom of God in the village. Jesus's healing mission gave the village people confidence in what Jesus was teaching them: how to set up the kingdom of God as a communal arrangement in their village. Jesus would move beyond the personal healing of individuals and teach the villagers how they could live in a new social-economic arrangement that would relieve their suffering under Roman rule and make life more manageable for everyone.

There is never a report of Jesus claiming for himself the power to heal or seeking to draw attention to himself with the healing aspect of his mission. There is no record of Jesus ever saying to an individual, "my power has healed you." His healing of individuals was never used as a proof of divinity or of his being the long-awaited messiah.

Over and over we read accounts of Jesus saying to the person who has been healed, "your faith has made you well." Jesus always gave credit to the individual for the healing that occurred. It was the faith of the individual person, not the power of Jesus himself, providing the healing. The Gospels make it clear that Jesus's only motive for healing was compassion for the sick. The free healing ministry of Jesus was an expression of the way God wanted the villagers to live in a new social-economic communal arrangement, an arrangement he called "the kingdom of God."

3. Communal Meals

The third feature of Jesus's mission in the villages was the communal meal. In reading the Gospels we get the distinct impressions that Jesus spent a large amount of time at meals. Jesus himself says that he came "eating and drinking" (Luke 7:34). He taught the villagers to share together in a common meal whatever food they had available. Food and drink were offered equally to everyone as an expression of the egalitarian kingdom of God in their midst. It was a practical and specific method demonstrating the value of communal sharing. These festive communal meals must have had a great impact upon the poor and destitute of the villages.

In the world of that day meals set boundaries of who was included and who was excluded. The sharing of a meal was a form of social inclusion. Refusing to share a meal with someone was an expression of social exclusion. The upper class ate only with the upper class. As is usually the case today, the lower class was not invited to the homes of the elite for a meal.

Meals expressed friendship, closeness, and social acceptance. Jesus's meals were open to everyone, rich or poor, sick or healthy, male or female, Jew or Gentile, child or adult. This made Jesus unique among his contemporaries. It was a radical departure from the custom and etiquette of that day. For this reason Jesus drew heavy criticism from the religious leaders of Israel for eating with the wrong people, those who were not considered pure and clean:

> When the scribes of the Pharisees saw that he was eating with sinners and tax collectors, they said to his disciples, "Why does he eat with tax collectors and sinners?" (Mark 2:16)

> All who saw [Jesus eating with Zacchaeus] began to grumble and said, "He has gone to be the guest of one who is a sinner." (Luke 19:7)

> And the Pharisees and the scribes were grumbling and saying, "This fellow welcomes sinners and eats with them." (Luke 15:2)

> [Jesus said,] "the Son of Man came eating and drinking, and you say, 'Look, a glutton and a drunkard, a friend of tax collectors and sinners!'" (Luke 7:34)

The terms "tax collectors" and "sinners" refers to those who were not socially acceptable in the eyes of the religious leaders of Judaism. "Tax collectors" were Jews and others who worked for the Roman government, collecting the Roman taxes and tribute. "Sinners" were those Jews who did not pay their tithes and temple taxes or follow the many rules regarding ritual cleanliness. The village poor could not always afford to pay the temple tax and the annual tithes, nor could they keep all the rules related to ritual purity. Thus they were considered "sinners" by the religious elite.

For Jesus and his entourage of followers, to eat with these kinds of people was to eat with those who were considered outcasts in society. It was to treat them as equals, and this the religious leaders of that day could not accept. Jesus's practice of table fellowship demonstrated the acceptance of all in a kingdom of equals, even those who were rejected by the elite and the religious authorities. In God's egalitarian kingdom, everyone was treated equally and invited to share in the meal on an equal basis. This would enable the poor and destitute to see themselves as clean and acceptable, in a society that saw them as unclean and unacceptable.

The open meals with the villagers where everyone was invited provided an excellent setting for teaching. While eating, real conversation and dialogue could take place. It is easy to imagine many issues being discussed as Jesus taught the villagers during the communal meals.

Jesus's meals expressed the principle that cooperation, not competition, is the basis for community life in the kingdom of God. In a time when the village people were having a difficult time finding enough food for their families and in desperation were turning against each other, the shared meals were a concrete example of what cooperation could accomplish. When the villagers shared their food together in a common meal, they found there was enough for everyone. Jesus's encouraging words in the beatitudes, "You will be filled" and "You will laugh" (Luke 6:21), came true in the practice of joyous cooperative sharing of meals.

Like a three-legged stool, each aspect of Jesus's strategy in the villages undergirded his plan of developing communities of shared resources. All three parts of his intentional strategy were integral to his purpose. Each one reinforced the other. His free teaching ministry, his free healing ministry, and the mutuality of his communal meals all reveal his concept of the community of shared power and shared resources as a concrete expression in the villages of the major theme of his ministry: the kingdom of God. These three dimensions of his village strategy serve as important pieces of evidence leading to the conclusion that Jesus's original intention was to develop share-communities in the villages of Galilee from the bottom up, in contrast to the Roman rulers' and Jewish elites' concept of greed-communities established from the top down.

C. JESUS'S ORGANIZATIONAL STRATEGY

Jesus also had a clear organizational strategy for his mission. Jesus realized his ambitious goal of taking his message of the kingdom of God to the many small villages of Galilee could not be accomplished by himself alone. Therefore, he developed a plan to send the followers he had recruited and trained to the villages he himself would not be able to visit. There are four gospel accounts of Jesus sending his followers out to the villages (Matt 10:5–14; Mark 6:7–13; Luke 9:1–6; 10:1–11).

Jesus's strategy becomes clear in the specific instructions he gave them regarding their behavior as they traveled to each village:

> He ordered them to take nothing for their journey except a staff; no bread, no bag, no money in their belts; but to wear sandals and not to put on two tunics. He said to them, "Whenever you enter a house, stay there until you leave the place." (Mark 6:8–10)

> He sent them out to proclaim the kingdom of God and to heal. He said to them, "Take nothing for your journey, no staff, nor bag, nor bread, nor money—not even an extra tunic. Whatever house you enter, stay there, and leave from there." (Luke 9:2–4)

> Carry no purse, no bag, no sandals; and greet no one on the road. Whatever house you enter, first say, "Peace to this house!" And if anyone is there who shares in peace, your peace will rest on that person; but if not, it will return to you. Remain in the same house, eating and drinking whatever they provide, for the laborer deserves to be paid. Do not move about from house to house. Whenever you enter a town and its people welcome you, eat what is set before you. (Luke 10:4–8)

Since they were going to villages where the residents were poor and destitute, they were to travel without any "extras" that would put them in a better position than the villagers. Hence, they were instructed to carry no bread, no money in their belts, no sandals, and only one piece of clothing. The instruction not to wear sandals must have been particularly difficult, considering the rocky terrain and the poor condition of the unpaved roads. They were also instructed not to take a beggar's bag with them, for they would not come to the village as beggars. They were to be neither superior nor inferior to the villagers. It was a "kingdom of equals" they were introducing to the villages, and the instructions of Jesus reflect that reality.

When they arrived at a village, they were to find a receptive house in which to stay, and then remain at that house, eating and drinking whatever the hosts provide. In other words, don't go looking for a better place to stay. It is again clear that Jesus had a specific plan in mind for them as they went to the villages. They were not on a mission of converting or changing individual lives, but of cultivating a new social-economic life in the villages of Galilee, by which each individual's life would be changed for the better.

These instructions must also reflect Jesus's own lifestyle and strategy, for certainly he would be one who practiced what he preached. If he had not lived in the manner he instructed them to live, they surely would not have been so devoted to him. Jesus's strategy for himself was to go from village to village with no sandals, no money, no staff for protection, and no extra clothes. In this way he and his disciples could identify with the poor of the villages, coming to them as equals.

The communal program of Jesus is also seen in the fact he did not tell his disciples to go out and bring people to him. He told them to go out and do what he had been doing—heal the sick and proclaim the presence of the kingdom of God within the villages. Jesus did not see himself as the unique conveyor of his message. Jesus never said, "I am the kingdom of God," or "I have the kingdom of God." Jesus never claimed special powers for himself, nor did he seek to make himself the center of his kingdom movement. He did not tell them to heal in his name. His followers were expected to be able to do what he was doing. His was indeed a communal endeavor.

This was in contrast to the practice of John the Baptist, who was the only one in his movement who could perform baptisms. When John was arrested and executed, therefore, the movement died. On the other hand, when Jesus was arrested and executed, his movement continued on, for it did not depend solely upon him for its success. His followers were expected to be able to do what he did: create sharing communities in the villages of Galilee.

D. JESUS'S INSTRUCTIONS TO HIS FOLLOWERS REGARDING REJECTION

Perhaps the best evidence in the Gospels confirming Jesus's mission as focused on villages, not simply on individuals, is found in the mission instructions given to his followers regarding their appropriate response if a village rejected them. Again, both Luke and Mark report this instruction from Jesus:

> Whenever you enter a town and they do not welcome you, go out into its streets and say, "Even the dust of your town that clings to our feet, we wipe off in protest against you. Yet know this: the kingdom of God has come near." (Luke 10:10–11)
>
> If any place will not welcome you and they refuse to hear you, as you leave, shake off the dust that is on your feet as a testimony against them. (Mark 6:11)

If Jesus had wanted them to only change individual lives, he could have told his disciples to focus on receptive individuals and ignore the others. From these instructions, however, it is clear the reception or rejection by the entire village determines the disciples' reaction. If the village is not open to hearing the "good news" about Jesus's new social-economic plan (the kingdom of God) for their village, then they should leave that village, wiping the dust of the town off their feet in protest against that village.

Luke also reports that Jesus instructed his followers as they leave to tell the villagers what they have missed. They are to say to the villagers, "the kingdom of God has come near you." The villagers are being told they have missed the opportunity to experience the kingdom of God, life as God intends it to be lived in community. The kingdom of God had indeed come near to them, if the villagers had only had the wisdom to accept this new communal arrangement of organizing their village. The kingdom of God is not a heavenly existence in the afterlife, or simply an individual spiritual state in this life. It is a radical social-economic plan, God's will for how people should live together in community. Some villages accepted this new plan and others rejected it.

Jesus's emphasis on the entire village community is also seen in the final words of his instructions, as reported by Luke, "I tell you, on that day it will be more tolerable for Sodom than for that town" (10:12). The reference here is to the account in the Hebrew Scriptures regarding the destruction of the town of Sodom for their unethical behavior. Why would Jesus pronounce judgment on the whole village when they rejected the disciples? Were there not individuals who might have listened and responded? Could not some of them have been receptive as individual villagers? If Jesus's mission had been focused on individuals he would not have told his disciples to pronounce a word of warning against the whole town for its rejection of the "good news."

Jesus's instructions to his disciples on how to leave a village when it is unreceptive to them, as well as his condemnation of the entire village, make it clear his mission was directed at the entire village community rather than simply to individuals.

E. JESUS'S STRATEGY IN A VILLAGE

As we have seen, Jesus's strategy was to go from village to village in Galilee, teaching the peasants how to organize their lives in a cooperative manner. A typical village would have one hundred to two hundred residents, mostly peasant farmers operating small family farms, and a few shopkeepers.

Now imagine Jesus and his entourage arriving at the outskirts of a small Galilean village. Jesus and his companions would enter the village, first seeking hospitality in homes of the villagers. It was a strong tradition in the Mediterranean area of the Middle East to show hospitality to strangers and travelers, even welcoming them into one's home. Not every homeowner in a village, however, would be open to welcoming strangers. So the first step upon arriving in a village was to ask someone where the hospitable homes were, then seek out those homes and knock on the door with the expectation the door would be opened to them. If not, Jesus and his companions would go to other homes in the village until they found a place where they would be welcomed.

In exchange for hospitality, Jesus would provide healing for the ill and the diseased, as well as teaching the villagers a new way to organize their life together. This practice of healing and teaching reinforced the principle of equality in the kingdom of God. Jesus was not looking for handouts, nor was he seeking to be paid for what he was doing. He came as an equal with the villagers, neither above nor below them.

On the day of the village synagogue meeting, the assembly of the village, Jesus would attend the gathering. Now imagine Jesus standing up in the synagogue assembly of the peasant village to speak. According to the Sayings Gospel Q he began his teaching with these now familiar words from the so-called Sermon on the Mount (Matthew) or Sermon on the Plain (Luke):

> Blessed are you who are poor,
> for yours is the kingdom of God.
> Blessed are you who are hungry now,
> for you will be filled.
> Blessed are you who weep now,
> for you will laugh. (Luke 6:20–21)

Other translations replace the word *blessed* with the word *fortunate* or *congratulations*. It is clear Jesus was addressing the specific audience of the struggling village peasants: "Blessed are *you* who are poor . . . *you* who are hungry now . . . *you* who weep now." In these opening words to the villagers, he was already fulfilling the original purpose of his mission to bring "good news to the poor."

It should be noted Matthew's more popular version of Jesus's opening statement makes small, yet significant, changes in the wording. His version has Jesus saying:

> Blessed are the poor in spirit, for theirs is the kingdom of heaven.
> Blessed are those who mourn, for they will be comforted.
> Blessed are the meek, for they will inherit the earth.
> Blessed are those who hunger and thirst for righteousness, for they will be filled. (Matt 5:3–6)

Neither Matthew nor Luke was present when Jesus spoke these opening words to the villagers. They were both quoting from the written document the Sayings Gospel Q. One of them has changed the wording. Which one? Due to the context, New Testament scholars conclude it is Matthew who changed the words to fit his own purposes. He has altered the wording into more generalized statements that do not address the needs of the poor. What in the world does "poor in spirit" mean? If it means humility, the peasants certainly do not need to be reminded to be humble. They have already been humbled by the Romans and the Jewish elite. That statement would have meant little or nothing to the villagers. Further, in Matthew's version the "you" words are replaced with the impersonal word "the," as in "the poor" instead of "you poor." Can you imagine Jesus speaking to a village assembly of peasants and addressing them as "the poor"? Matthew's version of these opening words of Jesus robs the words of their original power and impact, and does not fit the situation of Jesus addressing peasants in a Galilean village.

In Luke's version Jesus speaks directly to his audience, the village peasants. They would certainly have wondered what Jesus could possibly mean by referring to them as "blessed" and saying the kingdom of God is theirs. No one had ever called the poor "blessed" or indicated the kingdom of God belongs to them. Those words would have immediately grabbed their attention.

When Jesus said the kingdom of God would belong to the poor, he was stating that as a literal fact. The kingdom of God, the share-communities he was establishing among the poor in the villages of Galilee, was a literal expression of the kingdom of God. It would be a unique way of humans living together in the midst of a world dominated by greed, divisiveness, competition, and selfishness. The kingdom of God, the way God wanted people to live, would belong to the poor.

As Jesus continued these opening statements, he addressed two major concerns of the poor: hunger and sorrow. First, the peasants were struggling to find enough food to feed their families, and he made the astounding promise they would have enough food to eat. Second, the peasants lived with daily grief over their desperate situation—living on the edge of starvation, their children dying of hunger and disease, and a gnawing sense of hopelessness. Jesus made the amazing promise they will be able to laugh again.

Imagine the reaction of the villagers to these words of Jesus. The words would certainly have struck them as too good to be true. They would have begun to question Jesus about these rather grandiose promises he has made to them. They would ask: How can this be true for peasants like us? What do you mean, we are "blessed," and how in the world will the kingdom of God be ours? How can we who are hungry expect to be fed? How will we have enough food to feed our families? In our desperate circumstances, how will we be able to laugh again? Jesus better have a plan for making his statements a reality, or he will quickly be run out of town.

The very first statement Jesus made when he spoke to the villagers included the promise that the "kingdom of God" would be theirs. What could Jesus possibly have in mind when he used this phrase with those Galilean peasants? It was not a term much in use in Jesus's day. Yet Jesus made it the fundamental theme of his teaching. In order to understand and follow Jesus, it is vital to have a clear picture of what Jesus meant by this central theme in his teaching, "the kingdom of God."

Jesus was not promising the poor they will attain "heaven" when they die. He did not teach them how to behave or what to believe in order to get into heaven in a life to come. Nor did he teach them they could enter some "spiritual" kingdom now. Jesus did not tell them to read the Bible, attend worship services, or practice other acts of piety. He did not teach them theological or philosophical concepts. None of this would have been helpful to the poor in their current circumstances. Nor would it have been "good news to the poor."

Jesus had something very practical and revolutionary in mind for the villagers when he used the term "the kingdom of God." He taught the village people what life could be like when lived under the reign or rule of God—life lived as God intended it to be lived. When they organized their villages according to God's will as seen in the Torah and the Prophets of the Hebrew Scriptures, Jesus promised that their village would be a place where there would be enough food to eat and they would be able to laugh again. Their village would be a local expression of the kingdom of God (the way God wanted life to be lived) in a practical, down-to-earth way.

Their social-economic life would be organized and lived according to the will of God, and the results would be wonderful for everyone. This was indeed "good news to the poor."

SUMMARY OF THE EVIDENCE

The five pieces of evidence regarding Jesus's strategic plan for his mission in Galilee makes a compelling case for the conclusion that Jesus's mission was aimed at entire village communities, not simply at individuals. His original intention was to transform the peasant villages of Galilee into a new social-economic pattern of communal sharing of resources that would enable them to withstand the oppressive and debilitating rule of the Roman government and the elite Jewish aristocracy who collaborated with the Romans. Jesus went to the villages of Galilee to bring this good news to the poor. These new village share-communities were concrete expressions of the kingdom of God. All the evidence points in the direction of Jesus as a community organizer in the villages of Galilee.

7

Let Jesus Speak for Himself

IF WE ARE GOING to find the missing historical person Jesus of Nazareth, we must let him speak for himself. We owe him that. Fortunately, we have a goodly number of his one-liners and parables preserved for us by his original followers in Galilee. We also have the help of biblical scholars to enable us to separate out teachings originating with Jesus of Nazareth from other teachings attributed to him, but not originating with him. Our final piece of detective work will involve listening to what Jesus of Nazareth had to say.

As we have seen, Jesus's strategy was to go from village to village in Galilee, teaching the peasants how to organize their lives in a cooperative, sharing manner. The fact Jesus traveled from village to village meant he probably used his one-liners and parables numerous times. Those who traveled with him to the various villages probably heard these teachings many times. This enabled them to remember the teachings that meant the most to them. For the original followers of Jesus in Galilee, his words were everything. In fact, based on the writings they left, it was the teachings of Jesus more than anything else about him they remembered. This gives us confidence the teachings of Jesus compiled by his original followers are indeed from Jesus himself. The first editions of the two earliest writings available to us, the Sayings Gospel Q and the *Gospel of Thomas*, are highly reliable sources for the authentic teachings of Jesus.

In addition, the Synoptic Gospels of Matthew, Mark, and Luke each contain some original teachings of Jesus. As we have seen in the examination of the written evidence related to Jesus, however, not every word attributed to Jesus in these gospels goes back to Jesus. It was common practice for writers of that day to place their own words in the mouth of the person about whom they were writing. This practice was not considered devious in any way. It does, however, significantly alter the original message of Jesus. Fortunately, biblical scholars have been able to carefully examine all the words in the Gospels attributed to Jesus, and from that research determine those teachings most likely to have originated from Jesus himself. In order to recover the original message of Jesus it is vital to utilize the results of these biblical scholars.

The instructions Jesus gave to the village peasants regarding their village life will be the final and most decisive major piece of evidence in the search for the missing person Jesus of Nazareth and his purpose in his mission in Galilee.

Jesus went to the villages in Galilee to establish a new kind of village life, one he called "the kingdom of God." I am using the more contemporary term "the Beloved Community," to describe what Jesus had in mind by the phrase "the kingdom of God." It was Dr. Martin Luther King Jr. who coined the term during the civil rights movement of the 1960s. Both words of the term are important. The word *beloved* means the community is to be a place where each person is valued and treated as a person of worth and dignity. The word *community* refers to the understanding that it is not just a collection of individuals but a group of people living in trust and unity with one another, with a sense of belonging to one another.

In order to comprehend Jesus's message and purpose, it will be important to keep in mind the audience to whom he was speaking. Jesus did not proclaim his message in a vacuum. He was addressing a specific audience: the peasants in the villages of Galilee who were suffering severe economic hardship under the rule of the Roman government and the Jewish elites who collaborated with the Romans. When that audience is kept in mind, his teachings and instructions to them come alive for us in a refreshing and enlightening way.

Where more than one version of a saying or parable exists, I will use the version considered by the scholars to be more likely to have originated with Jesus of Nazareth. We start with the prayer he taught them to share in their community life together.

THE PEASANTS' PRAYER

Jesus taught the peasants a simple prayer, one they probably used as the communal blessing at their daily evening meal together. What is traditionally called "The Lord's Prayer" (though that title does not appear in the Scriptures), is found in the first layer of the Sayings Gospel Q. There are two different versions of the prayer, found in Matthew 6:9–12 and Luke 11:2–4. Matthew and Luke each altered the original version of the prayer to suit their own purposes, so it is necessary to piece together the prayer using both versions. According to New Testament scholars, this is the prayer as Jesus most probably expressed it to the Galilean peasants:

> Father, hallowed be your name. (Luke 11:2)
> Your kingdom come,
> your will be done. (Matt 6:10a-b)
> Give us this day our daily bread. (Matt 6:11)
> And forgive us our debts,
> as we also have forgiven our debtors. (Matt 6:11)
> And do not bring us to the time of trial. (Luke 11:4b)

Though the church later began to label it "The Lord's Prayer," it is actually a prayer for the peasants. By naming it "The Lord's Prayer" the meaning and purpose of the prayer has been radically changed. That move by the historical church took all the power out of the prayer by relegating it to the spiritual realm, whereas Jesus was so clearly grounded in the daily life of real people's material livelihood. It removed the prayer from the context of the peasant village life of Galilee and turned it into a generalized prayer, resulting in the loss of its original impact. When the prayer is labeled what it is, namely "The Peasants' Prayer," it takes on new meaning for us.

The Peasants' Prayer contains three petitions or prayer sentences about concrete economic matters affecting the everyday life of the poor in the villages: food, debt, and the difficult situations they were facing. Jesus knew the issues faced by the peasants and taught them a way to pray addressing those issues. When looking at this prayer in the context of Galilean village life, it becomes obvious Jesus was not teaching them a timeless prayer about heaven or life after death, but about the here-and-now life of the peasants. It was a prayer quite specific to the situation of the peasants in the villages of Galilee. This made the prayer memorable to them, and eventually the first followers of Jesus put it into written form in the Sayings Gospel Q.

There are five distinct segments of the Peasants' Prayer.

A. Father, hallowed be your name.

Witty man, that Jesus. Do you get Jesus's joke? If not, here is the explanation, though it loses something in the translation. Everybody in that day knew the name of God was *Yahweh*. It was an inscrutable name, reflecting the idea of a distant God in the sky. God was considered all-powerful (omnipotent) and all-knowing (omniscient), a god who could keep his eye on you and be aware of what you were doing at all times (omnipresent). God was the ultimate judge who meted out punishment to those who disobeyed his laws. The name of God, *Yahweh*, was always to be revered (hallowed), not even to be used in normal conversation. God was an impersonal deity who could only be approached through the temple and the priests. This concept of God was, of course, advantageous to the temple priests, who eagerly taught the peasants to understand God in this way, thus enabling them to preserve their own powerful standing in Israel.

Jesus, however, gave God a new name: Abba/Father. *Abba* is an Aramaic word (the language of Jesus) young children used to address their father. It is much like the English word *daddy*. The word reflects both Jesus's sense of closeness to God and the warm, personal relationship with God, available to everyone. This word for God, so familiar today, would have come as a surprise and shock to the peasants of Galilee. It was incongruous to link the intimate word *abba* (daddy) with the God of the universe, but that is exactly what Jesus did. By combining the new name for God, *Abba/Daddy*, with the traditional Jewish phrase, "hallowed be your name," Jesus gave a humorous new twist to the image of God. From now on, a Galilean peasant could pray to God with a twinkle in his eye and a smile upon his face. God was no longer a powerful deity in the sky, but a loving and generous *abba/daddy* who was also the God of the universe, available to them on a daily basis. Like any good father, Abba now provided for their material needs through the kingdom of God on earth, the peasant share-communities. Jesus also retained the traditional Jewish phrase "hallowed (or revered) be your name." Putting these two opposite concepts of God together was Jesus's joke about God.

Writing fifty years after the time of Jesus, Matthew didn't get the joke. He inserted the grandiose statement, "who dwells in heaven," after the opening word *abba/daddy*, which negates the humor of the startling contrast Jesus intended. Matthew didn't understand Jesus's humorous new image of

God. By the time he wrote, the shock value of Jesus's joke had worn off and *abba* had become a more common term for addressing God.

What was Jesus's image of God? Obviously Jesus called God *Abba/Daddy*. What kind of daddy/father, however, is God, according to Jesus?

The Bible presents two contrasting images of God. One image of God is a powerful, finger-pointing, judgmental father who makes and enforces rules. This is the patriarchal view of God as the strong, domineering, strict, law-enforcing father. God becomes a punishing, even vengeful, judge, meting out terrible punishments to people who violate God's laws. In this view, God is seen as ruthless and demanding. This image of God has been called the "strict father" image and is very popular in some religious circles today.

The other image of God running throughout the Bible is a nurturing, caring, compassionate father. This image of God is more intimate and personal, a God who is more approachable. With his use of the intimate word *abba*, Jesus indicates his image of God is the "nurturing parent" who cares for all humans upon this earth. God is seen not as a harsh judge, but as a loving and generous parent. The God revealed through Jesus is not a violent, punishing God. Jesus's image of God is one of compassion, love, care, and forgiveness, images traditionally associated with feminine, motherly characteristics. The specific teachings of Jesus reinforce this image of God as a nurturing, compassionate parent, rather than an all-powerful, punishing judge.

Our image of God matters. It determines the kind of life we lead and the kind of society we want. Do we understand God as an all-powerful, all-knowing, punishing, judgmental God? Or do we see God as a compassionate, nurturing, caring God? It is clear that Jesus's image of God is that of a nurturing parent. If we want to follow Jesus, we must pay attention to his understanding of God as *abba/daddy*.

B. Your kingdom come, your will be done.

As we have seen, Jesus taught the kingdom of God as a reality here on earth, not a place to go after death. The plea here is for this new way of life to happen upon this earth. The second phrase, "your will be done," explains the first phrase. A kingdom is a specific area of land where people live under the rule and will of a king. The kingdom of God is the place on earth where a community lives in accordance with God's will for humankind, founded on social justice and based on the principle of mutual care for one another. Each community has the potential to be an expression of the kingdom of God.

In his teachings, Jesus makes it clear that God's will is for people to live in a spirit of cooperation, not competition, with each other. This cooperation is radical—it involves a communal sharing of resources. The prayer is for this way of life (the kingdom of God where God's will is done) to come to the peasant villages of Galilee, and beyond, to the rest of Israel and the whole world. This is Jesus's vision, and he devoted his life to enabling that vision to begin to be realized in the villages of Galilee. He stayed true to that vision, even unto death.

C. Give us this day our daily bread.

This simple sentence prayer would certainly be the prayer of a peasant who did not know where his next meal was coming from and who wondered how he would be able to feed his family. This petition makes no sense as a general prayer for those who are middle class or wealthy. They know where their next meal is coming from; they have ample food to eat for this day and beyond. The peasant, on the other hand, lives from hand to mouth, so to speak, and would only ask for enough food to eat for that one day.

Jesus had a specific plan for all the peasants in the village to have enough food to eat each day. The plan is both simple and profound: rather than competing with one another for scarce resources, through the communal sharing of resources in the village, there would be food enough for everyone. The prayer for daily bread was answered through intentional sharing. Each peasant was thus freed from the daily anxiety about having enough food to feed his family. In Jesus's planned communities there was a regular communal meal, probably the evening meal each day, where there would be enough food for everyone.

D. Forgive us our debts, as we have also forgiven our debtors.

Jesus is dealing with peasants for whom debt is a huge problem, so the word *debts* rather than *sins* or *trespasses* is the appropriate word. *Debts* is the word used in Matthew's version of the prayer. Luke, writing fifty-five years after the time of Jesus, and also writing in another country, did not realize the importance of the issue of debt in the lives of the village peasants, so he changed the wording to "forgive us our sins, for we ourselves forgive everyone indebted to us" (11:4). This takes the prayer out of the specific context of peasant village life and turns it into a generalized, timeless prayer.

With the recent dramatic increase in taxes and tithes, the village peasants of Jesus's day were always on the verge of falling into serious debt. First, they had to borrow from each other in order to survive, and this indebtedness to one another created many tensions in the village life. It wasn't like today, where you owe your mortgage to a faceless corporation. Imagine running into your creditors in town every day! In addition, many farmers were falling into serious debt to the wealthy elite, often losing their farms as they were unable to repay their debts. Indebtedness was a very real and serious problem for the peasants in the villages of Galilee.

Jesus was very aware of the reality of debt and the problems it was causing the peasant villagers. He told this story to make the peasants aware of the importance of debt forgiveness:

> The kingdom of heaven may be compared to a king who wished to settle accounts with his slaves. When he began the reckoning, one who owed him ten thousand talents was brought to him; and, as he could not pay, his lord ordered him to be sold, together with his wife and children and all his possessions, and payment to be made. So the slave fell on his knees before him, saying, "Have patience with me, and I will pay you everything." And out of pity for him, the lord of that slave released him and forgave him the debt. But that same slave, as he went out, came upon one of his fellow slaves who owed him a hundred denarii; and seizing him by the throat, he said, "Pay what you owe." Then his fellow slave fell down and pleaded with him, "Have patience with me, and I will pay you." But he refused; then he went out and threw him into prison until he would pay the debt. When his fellow slaves saw what had happened, they were greatly distressed, and they went and reported to their lord all that had taken place. Then his lord summoned him and said to him, "You wicked slave! I forgave you all that debt because you pleaded with me. Should you not have had mercy on your fellow slave, as I had mercy on you?" And in anger his lord handed him over to be tortured until he would pay his entire debt. (Matt 18:23–34)

Jesus knew the first step in establishing a communal sharing of resources was to deal with the issue of indebtedness. In this story, the slave who would not cancel a small debt after he had just been forgiven a huge debt is the villain. The behavior is so outlandish the story would catch the attention of the listeners. The peasants who heard the story naturally would be horrified at his callous behavior. In this parable, Jesus challenged the villagers to think about the whole issue of their indebtedness to one another. Quite likely, following the telling of this parable, a lively conversation ensued among the villagers as they began to realize the new community they wanted must begin by forgiving their debts to one another. A sharing of resources on an equal basis cannot start with squabbling about who is in debt to whom and demanding repayment of neighborly loans. The villagers must start with a clean slate, canceling their indebtedness to one another.

Interestingly, this sentence prayer also asks God to forgive the peasants their debts to God. What debt did the peasants owe to God? The answer is the temple tax and the annual tithe to the temple. It was an obvious answer to the Jewish peasants, but time and cultural distance have made the answer obscure to us. Each adult male in Israel was obligated to pay a portion of his annual income to the temple. The priests sent out tax collectors to the various villages to collect the peasants' obligation or "debt to God." The peasants of Galilee were poor and destitute, so they often found themselves in a difficult situation, having to choose between paying their tithe and tax to the temple or feeding their family. Faced with such a choice, they naturally opted to feed their family rather than pay their obligation to the temple, as anyone would. This clearly angered the religious authorities. In an effort to extract the temple tax and tithe from the peasants, the tax collectors used the social stigma of shame against the peasants. The peasants were declared to be "sinners" in violation of God's laws, and thus unable to worship in the temple in Jerusalem. Due to their inability to pay tithes and temple taxes, they were tainted as ritually impure—unholy and unclean. The temple authorities who claimed to speak for God used threats of a vengeful God to intimidate the peasants into paying their tax and tithe. Thus the peasants, in addition to the guilt over their inability to pay their "debt to God," also now faced social ostracism within the village community. They were in a double bind.

Jesus came to the village with the dramatic teaching that God would forgive the peasants their obligation to the temple if they would forgive their debts to one another. It was a win-win situation for the peasants. According to Jesus, they did not need to feel guilt or shame about their inability to pay the temple tax and tithe. It did not make them unworthy of God's love and blessings, nor were they ritually unclean. Jesus was totally discrediting the power of the temple and the purity laws that had given the wealthy priests leverage over the peasants. His powerful teaching gave the peasants freedom from guilt and shame, as well as a new lease on life. On the other hand, this teaching of Jesus obviously upset the temple religious establishment and their money collectors, creating strong animosity among them toward Jesus. The powerful wealthy elite had good reason to hate Jesus. He leveled the playing field and pulled the rug out from under the whole unjust system that kept the poor "in their place."

With this prayer sentence, Jesus is essentially saying to the peasants, "We are returning to the Jewish traditional roots and Jubilee system. All debts to one another are cancelled, and your debt to the temple is also cancelled. God is your abba/father who understands your financial plight. Don't worry about the temple tax and tithe. Feed your family first." Coming from an authority figure like Jesus, this was welcome news.

In this prayer petition, Jesus demonstrated his awareness of the difficult circumstances of the peasants in the villages. Rather than a timeless teaching about sins, Jesus was addressing the specific situation of the poor in Galilee. He brought them good news on the issue of debt, offering them a practical plan for dealing with their guilt over their "debt to God" as well as their indebtedness to one another. This prayer petition about debts made great sense to the village peasants of Galilee and was indeed "good news to the poor."

E. Please do not bring us to the time of trial.

There is debate among the scholars whether this petition was taught by Jesus or was added later by the early followers of Jesus. It is simply a request that God not subject people to test after test of their faith and trust. It is a prayer anyone, peasant or otherwise, could pray, so it is difficult to know whether Jesus would have included it in his teaching to the peasants of Galilee. In any event, it does not alter the main thrust of the prayer in any significant regard.

In the Peasants' Prayer, it should be noted, all the petitions are in the plural. Jesus taught the peasants to move from "me" to "we" in their thinking, from the individual to the community. It is another indication Jesus's mission was directed, not just to individuals, but to the entire community. It was a communal not simply an individual prayer, probably meant to be prayed at the evening communal meal.

When we see the Peasants' Prayer in its original context, it becomes a very meaningful prayer for that day, and therefore, for our day.

JESUS'S INSTRUCTIONS TO THE BELOVED COMMUNITY

Much of Jesus's authentic teaching is devoted to providing the villagers the principles and guidelines for their relationships within the Beloved Community, the kingdom of God. Since Jesus was teaching the villagers a radical new social arrangement, they needed very practical and specific guidance. Also, the majority of the villagers did not know how to read or write. Jesus needed to teach the villagers in a way they could remember what he said. This he did through his memorable parables and one-liners.

Fortunately, those who traveled with Jesus, as well as the villagers themselves, remembered many of Jesus's teachings about their village life and preserved them in written form. We now examine the majority of the teachings of Jesus, letting him speak for himself. For convenience in examining these teachings, I have divided them into twelve categories:

1. Signs of the Kingdom of God

In Jesus's day, the Jews in Israel were suffering terribly under the harsh rule of the Roman government. There was a great hope that God would one day in the near future intervene in human history and violently establish his powerful kingdom upon the earth. Many Jews were looking for signs God was about to make a dramatic entrance, bringing his kingdom to the earth, as seen in these reports:

> Once Jesus was asked by the Pharisees when the kingdom of God was coming, and he answered, "The kingdom of God is not coming with things that can be observed; nor will they say, 'Look, here it is!' or 'There it is!' For, in fact, the kingdom of God is among you." (Q in Luke 17:20–21)

> Another time his disciples said to him, "When will the (Father's) imperial rule come?" Jesus said, "It will not come by watching for it. It will not be said, 'Look, here!' or 'Look, there!' Rather, the Father's imperial rule is spread out upon the earth, and people don't see it" (*Thom.* 113:1–2).

Jesus did not endorse the understanding of the kingdom of God as a dramatic divine intervention. He responded to the questions of the Pharisees and his disciples by noting the kingdom cannot be observed with outward signs indicating it is about to arrive. In fact, he said God's kingdom was already among them. They just did not recognize its existence. The communal sharing of resources in the villages was the kingdom of God here on earth. It was life structured according to God's will. Those who were waiting on a dramatic arrival of the kingdom of God were blinded to the fact that God's kingdom was already among them on earth.

When Jesus added the comment, "The kingdom of God is among you" (Luke 17:21), he was referring to the Beloved Community in the villages of Galilee. The kingdom is not something "within" an individual. Rather, the individual is within the kingdom, the Beloved Community. All the images and parables Jesus used in his teaching about the kingdom of God involve a reality into which one enters. He never refers to the kingdom as an internal event. It is always a communal concept.

It is clear Jesus did not expect or announce an imminent end of the world or a divine intervention in history. His words and deeds were aimed at improving the conditions of the peasants living in the villages of Galilee. His efforts in this regard would have made no sense if the end of the world was imminent, or if things were so bad only a divine intervention could make them right. Jesus's focus was practical and down-to-earth in the here-and-now, not speculating about what might possibly happen in the future. Some of his later followers did begin to speculate about a second coming or the end of the world, and even put words in his mouth to this effect (see Mark 13), but this was not the focus of Jesus's ministry. In fact, Mark reports Jesus speaking extensively about the end times, and then saying, "Truly I tell you, this generation will not pass away until all these things have taken place" (13:30). Clearly "these things" did not take place, and still have not taken place. So either Jesus was wrong about the timing of God's dramatic intervention in history, or Mark was wrong. From all the other evidence of Jesus's words and deeds, it would seem it was Mark who was speculating about the end times, and it was Mark who was wrong, not Jesus.

Jesus also told this parable about the presence of the kingdom of God:

> The kingdom of God is as if someone would scatter seed on the ground, and would sleep and rise night and day, and the seed would sprout and grow, he does not know how. The earth produces of itself, first the stalk, then the head, then the full grain in

> the head. But when the grain is ripe, at once he goes in with his sickle, because the harvest has come. (Mark 4:26–29)

According to Jesus, the kingdom of God arrives quietly, without a person even being aware of it. "Someone" scatters seed on the ground, and the kingdom (the share-community) grows quietly in each village. When the kingdom is fully established in the village, the result (harvest) is obvious to everyone. In this agricultural parable about the kingdom of God, Jesus makes it clear the kingdom does not come with dramatic signs everyone can see. The kingdom comes quietly like a seed planted and growing into a healthy grain. When the kingdom, the Beloved Community, is fully established in a village, the results can be easily seen because everyone is benefiting equally from the new social-economic sharing of resources, built on principles of social justice, equality, nondiscrimination, and tolerance.

One of the accusations Jesus's opponents used against him was that he performed healing and exorcisms by the power of Satan. This was a sign, they said, he was not doing the work of God, but of Satan. Jesus responded to his accusers by asking them in whose name do their own people cast out demons. They acknowledge it is done in God's name. Jesus concludes with this strong statement, "if it is by the finger of God that I cast out the demons, then the kingdom of God has come to you" (Q in Luke 11:20). He is saying he, too, drives out demons with God's power, and furthermore, his exorcisms are a sign of the presence of God's kingdom. According to Jesus, his healing of the ill and infirm came from God, not Satan, and was a demonstration of the presence of the kingdom of God among them.

Jesus also made this observation, "I watched Satan fall from heaven like a flash of lightning" (Luke 10:18). The establishment of the kingdom of God, the Beloved Community, means Satan (evil) no longer has power. The divisiveness and greed existing among the peasants was a sign of evil's rule over them. However, evil has no chance against God's love and justice based on equality. The old way of competition and scrambling for scarce resources has no power or strength against the kingdom of cooperation and compassion. As Jesus expressed it, "if a house is divided against itself, the house will not be able to stand" (Mark 3:25).

The new spirit of unity and cooperation among the peasants provides them with a strength they previously lacked. Jesus used the image of a strong man being overcome to describe their new strength through communal sharing:

> No one can enter a strong man's house and plunder his property without first tying up the strong man; then indeed the house can be plundered. (Mark 3:27)

> When a strong man, fully armed, guards his castle, his property is safe. But when one stronger than he attacks him and overpowers him, he takes away his armor in which he trusted and divides his plunder. (Q in Luke 11:21–22)

Jesus came to the villages of Galilee on a mission from God. He had something to offer stronger than divisiveness, individual self-interest, and greed: a powerful message of love, unity, and sharing that overcomes the ways of evil and cancels the oppressions turning people against each other in a competitive struggle. The establishment of the Beloved Community in the villages is the sign of the presence of the kingdom of God.

Jesus is often reported to have said, "Let anyone with ears listen." He is saying that his message about the kingdom of God is clear and obvious to those who pay attention to its truths. All one has to do is listen and observe. The kingdom of God is not a theological concept, nor is it something mysterious and secret. It is obvious and in plain sight, easy to see. His kingdom message is not private or hidden. The kingdom of God is ordinary and practical, not grandiose and powerful. It is the communal sharing of resources in the peasant villages of Galilee, and anywhere else God's will is done on earth, as it is in heaven.

2. The Beloved Community Is Built on Trust in God

When Jesus came to a village, he first assured the villagers of God's care for them, and then he called them to overcome the social and economic conflicts causing their village life to deteriorate rapidly. He taught them about a beloved community built first on the solid foundation of trust in God:

> I tell you, do not worry about your life, what you will eat, or about your body, what you will wear. For life is more than food, and the body more than clothing. Consider the ravens: they neither sow nor reap, they have neither storehouse nor barn, and yet God feeds them. Of how much more value are you than the birds! And can any of you by worrying add a single hour to your span of life? . . . Consider the lilies, how they grow: they neither toil nor spin; yet I tell you, even Solomon in all his glory was not clothed like one of these. But if God so clothes the grass of the field, which is alive

> today and tomorrow is thrown into the oven, how much more will he clothe you—you of little faith! (Q in Luke 12:22–25, 27–28)
>
> Don't fret, from morning to evening and from evening to morning, about what you are going to wear. You're much better than the lilies, which neither card nor spin. (*Thom.* 36:1–2)
>
> Are not five sparrows sold for two pennies? Yet not one of them is forgotten in God's sight. But even the hairs on your head are all counted. Do not be afraid; you are of more value than many sparrows. (Q in Luke 12:6–7)
>
> Is there anyone among you who, if your child asks for bread, will give a stone? Or if the child asks for a fish, will give a snake? If you then, who are evil, know how to give good gifts to your children, how much more will your Father in heaven give good things to those who ask him! (Q in Matt 7:9–11)

The community of shared resources with one another is built upon trust in God's care for humankind. Jesus saw God as a loving being whose essential nature is caring, compassionate, forgiving, generous, and peace loving. As noted previously, Jesus's image of God is that of a nurturing, caring parent.

Jesus's words, "do not worry about your life . . . ," are difficult to follow in a capitalistic society where everyone is on their own. The way American society is organized works against the teachings of Jesus. Over and over again Jesus said, "Fear not," but Americans struggle to follow that guidance because of fear there won't be enough in the future. Thus each one anxiously stores up and saves as much as possible for the unknown and risky future. In fact, if you were advising your children on financial planning would you teach them, "take no thought for tomorrow"? Or would you advise them to carefully plan for the future, for the future is uncertain and one needs to have as much stored up as possible? Obviously, a parent would advise the child to ignore what Jesus taught and store up and plan carefully for the unknown future lying ahead. In a capitalist society, it would be irresponsible to do otherwise.

The only way Jesus's teachings about trusting in God for the needs of life make sense is in the context of a community of shared resources. Jesus taught we are all in this together, and thus we can relax because through the community there is enough for everyone on into the future. Jesus perceived God as a parent who gives good gifts to his children, who are then expected to trust enough to share what they have with everyone. Each person in the community can live a more relaxed and carefree life because of God's care. But the question naturally arises: *How* does God provide for the needs of his children upon this earth? Jesus's answer is straightforward and practical: "Ask, and it will be given you; search, and you will find; knock, and the door will be opened for you. For everyone who asks receives, and everyone who searches finds, and for everyone who knocks, the door will be opened (Q in Matt 7:7–8)

Jesus's answer to the question about God's care for humanity is this: God provides for humankind, not by sending food, clothes, and other necessities floating down from heaven, but through a community of shared resources. For example, anyone who sat down at the community table would be fed, no questions asked. Trust in God meant trust in the share-community arrangement Jesus taught them. As everyone shares their resources and no one seeks his or her own personal wealth, there is enough for everyone. When you ask for what you need, it will be given you; when you search for help, you will find it; and when you knock on someone's door, it will be opened to you. This spirit of generous sharing with one another enables everyone's needs to be met. The villagers could trust in God to provide because the community sharing of resources will meet their needs.

3. The Beloved Community Is Built on Trust in One Another

The Beloved Community is also built on the foundation of mutual trust. This meant, for example, that in the community there are no secrets about the way the business of the community is conducted. Everything is open and above board. Jesus expressed it these various ways:

> For there is nothing hidden, except to be disclosed; nor is anything secret, except to come to light. (Mark 4:22)
>
> For nothing is covered up that will not be uncovered, and nothing secret that will not become known. (Q in Matt 10:26b)
>
> For nothing is hidden that will not be disclosed, nor is anything secret that will not become known and come to light. (Q in Luke 8:17)
>
> For there is nothing hidden that will not be revealed. (*Thom.* 5:2)

Secrets are deadly to community life. In the Beloved Community, everyone is knowledgeable about the affairs of the community. To have secrets, secret pacts and groups, secret societies and schemes, leads to the destruction of the community. Information is power, and secret information gives one person power over another. In the community there is to be no secret information. There is no power bloc and no hierarchy. Everyone has access to all the information. Jesus let the villagers know that everything will be open and above board in the operation of the communal sharing of resources: no stashing the best food for yourself. What is said and done must be open for all to hear and see. Secrets destroy relationships; therefore, no secrets.

Another way this mutual trust expressed itself was in the minimal number of rules within the village community. A community of trust is built on a few commonly accepted principles, but does not require a large number of rules for the members to follow. Jesus taught this truth in regard to two matters of importance to the villagers: the keeping of the Sabbath and the food regulations.

The fourth of the Ten Commandments is "Remember the sabbath day, and keep it holy" (Exod 20:8). In Jesus's day the religious authorities had added numerous rules about what could and could not be done on the Sabbath, much like the former Blue laws in the southern United States prescribed what behaviors were allowed on Sundays. These ancient regulations were complicated and difficult for the peasant villagers to follow. They were always in danger of violating one of the many Sabbath rules.

Jesus took the pressure off the villagers by stating this basic principle, "The sabbath was made for humankind, and not humankind for the sabbath" (Mark 2:27). With this simple statement, Jesus overcame hundreds of Sabbath regulations that had been imposed on the villagers. The spirit of trust meant they did not have to monitor each other's behavior. They did not have to judge one another, nor did they need to always be fretting about violating some Sabbath rule, and thus being declared "sinners" by the religious authorities.

In Jesus's day the religious leaders had also established numerous rules about what foods could and could not be eaten. The regulations were again complicated and difficult for the average person to follow. The villagers lived in fear of violating one of the laws regarding food intake, which would make them ritually unclean, requiring offerings (food or money) they didn't have in order to be declared pure, holy, and supposedly in God's good graces again. Another way Jesus expressed the fact that a community built on trust did not need numerous food rules was in this statement of principle, “Listen to me, all of you, and understand: there is nothing outside a person that by going in can defile, but the things that come out are what defile” (Mark 7:14–15).

In these two statements about Sabbath observance and food intake, Jesus makes it clear a community of trust is built on a few principles, not on numerous rules and regulations. Jesus was basically removing the oppressive layers of dogmatic legalistic teachings that had accumulated within Judaism through the centuries. The lack of specific rules in Jesus's teaching was another expression of mutual trust within the village community.

Jesus summed up these twin foundations of community life—trust in God and trust in one another—by quoting these two commandments from the Jewish Scriptures:

> The first is, “Hear, O Israel: the Lord our God, the Lord is one; you shall love the Lord your God with all your heart, and with all your soul, and with all your mind, and with all your strength.” The second is this: “You shall love your neighbor as yourself.” There is no other commandment greater than these. (Mark 12:29–31)

In these two commandments Jesus addressed two great needs of humanity: a connection with God and a connection with other people. Love was certainly at the heart of Jesus's teaching: love your neighbor, love your enemy, be compassionate as God is compassionate, give to everyone who begs from you. For Jesus, love is not simply a warm, fuzzy emotion. Love is something you do. It is an action word. In fact, love changes everything. It changes communities and therefore it changes individuals.

4. The Inclusive Kingdom

In a series of one-liners, Jesus teaches the peasants that the kingdom of God is inclusive rather than exclusive, open to everyone in the village, whoever they may be. First, he said, “Let the little children come to me; do not stop them; for it is to such as these that the kingdom of God belongs” (Mark 10:14). This saying about children may seem sweet and innocuous to us. In the Roman world, however, children were regarded as nobodies. Children could be disposed of at the whim of the parents. They had no rights and no status. Furthermore, children had no money or means of support. They had nothing to commend them. For Jesus to make the statement the kingdom of God is made up of such is to declare it an inclusive kingdom where everybody is a nobody and thus everybody is a somebody.

There is no hierarchy of status or power. Everyone is equal in the Beloved Community. It is an egalitarian kingdom Jesus is building, a kingdom for ordinary humble people in contrast to those of wealth and power.

Jesus also indicates the inclusiveness of the kingdom by stating, "Whoever is not against us is for us" (Mark 9:40). In contrast to communities whose primary concern is establishing social boundaries, separating those on the inside from those on the outside, Jesus is establishing an open, welcoming community in the villages of Galilee.

Jesus also said, "Why do you wash the outside of the cup? Don't you understand that the one who made the inside is also the one who made the outside?" (*Thom.* 89). This saying in *Thomas* is an attack on those who would separate insiders from outsiders. When one is washing a cup, both the inside and the outside of the cup are washed. There is no distinction. Further, Jesus said, the one who made the cup made both the inside and the outside of the cup. God has made everyone, and there is no distinction between inside and outside in the kingdom of God.

In addition to these one-liners, Jesus told a parable about a man who was hosting a dinner party:

> Someone gave a great dinner and invited many. At the time for the dinner he sent his slave to say to those who had been invited, "Come; for everything is ready now." But they all alike began to make excuses. The first said to him, "I have bought a piece of land, and I must go out and see it; please accept my regrets." Another said, "I have just bought five yoke of oxen, and I'm on my way to try them out. Please excuse me." Another said, "I have just been married, and therefore I cannot come." So the slave returned and reported this to his master. Then the owner of the house became angry and said to his slave, "Go out at once into the streets and lanes of the town and bring in the poor, the crippled, the blind, and the lame." And the slave said, "Sir, what you ordered has been done, and there is still room." Then the master said to the slave, "Go out into the roads and lanes, and compel people to come in, so that my house may be filled." (Q in Luke 14:16–23)

This parable may well have been about the communal meals of the villages. These were the village "banquets." Normally only the elite get invited to banquets. The village banquets, however, were for everyone, including the poor, the lame, and even the untouchables. All one has to do is accept the invitation to participate. The village peasants have nothing to commend them except their willingness to attend. This parable again reveals the inclusive nature of the communal sharing in the kingdom of God, where the poor and the infirm are welcome, even though they may have very few resources to share. This must have indeed come as "good news to the poor."

The inclusiveness of the kingdom is also revealed in Jesus's relationship with women, a relationship radically different from the customs of the culture and religion of his day. According to Luke, "many" women traveled with Jesus and his male companions on their mission throughout Galilee:

> The twelve were with him, as well as some women who had been cured of evil spirits and infirmities: Mary, called Magdalene, from whom seven demons had gone out, and Joanna, the wife of Herod's steward Chuza, and Susanna, and many others, who provided for them out of their resources. (Luke 8:1–3)

Mark, writing about the crucifixion of Jesus, mentions three specific women who had traveled with Jesus, along with "many other women" who were with Jesus in his travels:

> There were also women looking on from a distance; among them were Mary Magdalene, and Mary the mother of James the younger and of Joses, and Salome. These used to follow him and provided for him when he was in Galilee; and there were many other women who had come up with him to Jerusalem. (15:40–41)

Both men and women traveled with Jesus, probably about twenty to twenty-five in number. Feeding that many people daily would be quite an undertaking, and Jesus's mission continued for over a year. From these two Scripture references, it is clear that a group of women underwrote the cost of the mission of Jesus and traveled with him.

It was a major violation of the social codes of that day for women to travel publicly with men. This breach of conduct by Jesus was highly scandalous. The fact Jesus was willing to transcend the normal social etiquette and include women in his traveling party is a strong indication of the inclusive nature of his community. Women were considered inferior to men in that culture, but Jesus treated women as equals. In fact, there is no indication in any of the gospel materials that Jesus considered women to be inferior to men. In his inclusive egalitarian kingdom, everyone was seen as an equal. In a tradition dominated by adult males, Jesus included women and children within the new community, a remarkable achievement indeed.

Jesus himself may have experienced what it is like to be treated as an unwelcome outsider in his own hometown, and even by his own family. In several different sources he is reported to have made comments about this:

> Prophets are not without honor, except in their hometown, and among their own kin, and in their own house. (Mark 6:4)

> Truly I tell you, no prophet is accepted in the prophet's hometown. (Luke 4:24)

> No prophet is welcome on his home turf; doctors don't cure those who know them. (*Thom.* 31:1–2)

Jesus himself evidently did not even have a home or a hometown, for he is reported to have said, "Foxes have holes, and birds of the air have nests; but the Son of Man has nowhere to lay his head" (Q in Luke 9:58). The phrase "Son of Man" was a common way of referring to oneself, so it is clear Jesus is speaking about himself as being homeless. Jesus was an itinerant, traveling from village to village throughout Galilee. In a very real sense he was always a stranger in town, an outsider.

Jesus also had strong comments to make about family ties:

> Whoever comes to me and does not hate father and mother, wife and children, brothers and sisters, yes, and even life itself, cannot be my disciple. (Q in Luke 14:26)

> The disciples said to him, "Your brothers and your mother are standing outside." He said to them, "Those here who do what my Father wants are my brothers and my mother." (*Thom.* 99:1–2; see also Mark 3:31–33)

These statements need to be read in the context of the world of that day. The family was a rigid multigenerational social unit. People remained with their family unit their entire lives. The family was also patriarchal, with total power and authority being exercised by men. The family unit was the basis of economic production, making it the primary source of one's material security and personal identity. The family structure, therefore, held powerful control over an individual's life.

Jesus, however, had left his family to go out on his own with his mission to the villages of Galilee. He had made the break from family control, and perhaps the result was rejection by his family for a period of time. In any event, Jesus placed priority of loyalty to the community of shared resources over loyalty to family. It is doubtful Jesus meant a complete rejection of family, given his other teachings about love of neighbor and even love of enemies. He did, however, dramatically teach the importance of commitment to the values and ideals of the new community as the source of security and identity. The new family, in which one finds his true mother, brothers, sisters, is the Beloved Community, dedicated to finding and doing the will of God.

Evidently, Jesus knew what it was like to be treated as an outsider, even an outcast. He was determined that the Beloved Community would not treat anyone in that manner. He was known to have associated with pagans, tax collectors, lepers, women, children, and other outcasts of society. Jesus broke down the barriers separating people into the categories of insiders and outsiders. He did not distinguish between those who were in and those who were out. In the share-community, everyone was welcome. His kingdom of God communities included everyone, even those considered to be outsiders and outcasts.

5. The Rich and Communal Sharing

Jesus made some strong and rather controversial statements about wealth and the community of shared resources. In one instance he said, "How hard it will be for those who have wealth to enter the kingdom of God! . . . It is easier for a camel to go through the eye of a needle than for someone who is rich to enter the kingdom of God" (Mark 10:23, 25).

In this statement, Jesus acknowledges that the wealthy will find it very difficult to enter into the kingdom of God. The reason is obvious. The kingdom of God involves a mutual sharing of all resources, so the wealthy have the most to lose. A wealthy person would naturally be reluctant to enter into such an arrangement. It is so difficult, Jesus says, for a rich person to want to enter the kingdom of God, the share-communities, it is like a camel going through the eye of a needle, a humorous picture indeed. This is not a judgmental observation, but a statement of fact. A wealthy person will not likely choose to be a part of the kingdom of God, the community of shared resources. In one sense, the wealthy don't have to enter into such an arrangement, as they can provide for themselves. In another respect, how sad and lonely a choice that is, especially considering how much wealthier the community would be if the wealthy joined, thus making the wealthy rich in ways other than money.

Jesus also stated, "No slave can serve two masters; for a slave will either hate the one and love the other, or be devoted to the one and despise the other. You cannot serve God and wealth" (Q in Luke 16:13). A person has a choice to make: one can be devoted to God or wealth, but not to both. God's kingdom means a sharing of resources, not selfishly holding on to what one has.

Further, Jesus said those who refuse to join the Beloved Community and try to hold on to things for themselves will lose what they have, while those who are willing to lose what they have as members of the community will keep the fullness of life.

Jesus also said, "Strive to enter through the narrow door; for many, I tell you, will try to enter and will not be able" (Q in Luke 13:24). Jesus declared that the door to the kingdom of God is narrow, and many will try to enter and not be able to do so. Why is that the case? The reason is that the door leads to a new social-economic arrangement involving the communal sharing of resources. People of means can see the benefits of the arrangement and will want to enter, but will not be able to do so, because they are unwilling in the end to place their resources in the community share program. Would you want to enter into a community of shared resources, sharing your resources with other community members? It would not be an easy choice to make for someone who has ample resources.

Finally, Jesus told two parables about a person wanting to hoard his resources for himself. One is a farmer, the other an investor:

> The land of a rich man produced abundantly. And he thought to himself, "What should I do, for I have no place to store my crops?" Then he said, "I will do this: I will pull down my barns and build larger ones, and there I will store all my grain and my goods. And I will say to my soul, "Soul, you have ample goods laid up for many years; relax, eat, drink, be merry." But God said to him, "You fool! This very night your life is being demanded of you. And the things you have prepared, whose will they be?" (Q in Luke 12:16–20)

> There was a rich person who had a great deal of money. He said, "I shall invest my money so that I may sow, reap, plant, and fill my storehouses with produce, that I may lack nothing." These were the things he was thinking in his heart, but that very night he died. (*Thom.* 63:1–3)

Each of these men had the "silo mentality": wanting to accumulate as much as he could for his own future security. Neither even thought to use his good financial fortune for the sake of others. Jesus highlights the futility of such an approach to life by closing each parable with the sudden death of the person hoarding resources for himself.

All of these teachings of Jesus on wealth and the kingdom of God make sense only in the context of a communal sharing of resources. If they are taken out of context and made into timeless truths for individuals to follow, most people in a capitalist society where everyone is on their own will find them impractical or impossible to follow. The result is they will simply ignore them. If the context of communal sharing of resources in the peasant villages of Galilee is kept in mind, these teachings on wealth and success are completely understandable. If you "give up" your wealth by placing it in the community pot, you ensure that you, your descendants, and the whole village will have ample for years to come. Your wealth lives on in the community instead of going to no use, dying with you.

6. Generous Compassion in the Beloved Community

At the heart of Jesus's instruction to the community was the spirit of generous compassion toward one another. This spirit of compassion is rooted in the generosity of God toward humanity. Surprisingly, Jesus does not have much to say about God. Jesus's focus is on the kingdom of God, how God wants people to live in relationship to one another upon this earth. What Jesus does have to say about God, however, is quite revealing, God "makes his sun rise on the evil and on the good, and sends rain on the righteous and on the unrighteous" (Q in Matt 5:45). Here Jesus made the obvious observation that God distributes rain and sunshine on both the righteous and the unrighteous without discrimination. God doesn't judge whether a person deserves sunshine or rain, and then punish the wicked by withholding either sunshine or rain from them. Jesus did not view God primarily as a judge eager to inflict punishment for wayward human behavior, but as a compassionate father providing for the needs of all human beings, regardless of their behavior.

Accordingly, Jesus stated that our compassion is based on God's compassion, "Be as compassionate as your Father is" (Q in Luke 6:36, Scholar's Version). In this statement, Jesus called on the members of the community to imitate God by being compassionate. In his rendering of this statement from the Sayings Gospel Q, Matthew replaced the word *compassionate* with *perfect*. That is unfortunate, for trying to imitate God by being "perfect" would be an impossible task. In fact, it creates a perfectionist streak in people. Think of all the harm done by someone trying to be a perfect child, a perfect student, a perfect friend, a perfect athlete, a perfect male or female body type, a perfect spouse, a perfect parent, a perfect worker, or a perfect Christian. Compassion, as opposed to perfection, is a quality within reach of each person as well as the community as a whole.

Jesus's words about compassion also include this instruction, "Give to everyone who begs from you" (Q in Luke 6:30). Beggars were a common sight in the villages of Galilee. The oppressive Roman rule had made life precarious for peasants. Some lost their farms entirely, being forced to become day laborers, working on those days when work was available. Others were unable to work due to poor health or age. And others simply could find no work at all, becoming beggars. Jesus instructed the community to give to everyone who begs. The village community would have a storehouse of shared resources of food and clothing. Those resources were to be shared not only with each other, but also with every needy person who came along. There is no instruction from Jesus for the community to judge whether the person "deserves" the help. Just as God does not judge whether a person "deserves" sunshine or rain, the community is not to set itself up as a judge of a person's merits. If there is a need, they are instructed to meet that need. Period.

Again, it should be noted this instruction makes sense only within a community context. If the individual peasant gave to "everyone" who begged from him, it would not be long before he would be completely out of funds. Even today, you as an individual probably do not feel comfortable giving to "everyone" who begs from you. Though everyone is expected to be compassionate, this saying of Jesus fits the context of the new village community, rather than being an instruction for individuals.

Jesus also emphasized generous compassion in this statement, "If you have money, don't lend it at interest. Rather, give it to someone from whom you won't get it back" (*Thom.* 95). This instruction is again part of the communal spirit of sharing of resources. Those who have more than others will be giving to those who have less. It is all part of the compassionate spirit within the community, the kingdom of God.

The compassionate spirit within the Beloved Community is also expressed in the instruction on forgiveness of one another, "Forgive and you will be forgiven" (Q in Luke 6:37c). Members of the community were to be forgiving of one another in their daily lives. Forgiveness, however, is a two-way street. In order to receive forgiveness from others, a person must have a forgiving spirit.

Finally, this spirit of compassion is to be expressed in a nonjudgmental attitude toward one another:

> Why do you see the speck in your neighbor's eye, but do not notice the log in your own eye? Or how can you say to your neighbor, "Friend, let me take out the speck in your eye," when you yourself do not see the log in your own eye? You hypocrite, first take the log out of your own eye, and then you will see clearly to take the speck out of your neighbor's eye. (Q in Luke 6:41–42)

It is easy to see small flaws in the lives of other people while ignoring our own faults and shortcomings. Jesus warns against the tendency to play judge about other people's behavior. A judgmental spirit is destructive of the spirit of compassion within the community.

Jesus also told two parables with surprising twists to express the importance of generous compassion in the village community:

> A man was going down from Jerusalem to Jericho, and fell into the hands of robbers, who stripped him, beat him, and went away, leaving him half dead. Now by chance a priest was going down that road; and when he saw him, he passed by on the other side. So likewise a Levite, when he came to the place and saw him, passed by on the other side. But a Samaritan while traveling came near him; and when he saw him, he was moved with pity. He went to him and bandaged his wounds, having poured oil and wine on them. Then he put him on his own animal, brought him to an inn, and took care of him. The next day he took out two denarii, gave them to the innkeeper, and said, "Take care of him; and when I come back, I will repay you whatever more you spend." (Luke 10:30–35)

As the peasants heard this story they would nod with understanding when they heard of the temple priest and Levite passing by on the other side. They would look at each other knowingly and say, "Yes, that is what you would expect from those aristocrats in the temple." Now the audience would anticipate the story will continue with a peasant coming by and helping the stranger. The Jewish peasant would be the hero of the story. Jesus, however, catches them by surprise by making a Samaritan the compassionate hero. The Jews and the Samaritans were long-time bitter enemies, and for a Samaritan to be the heroic character in the story was a shock to the Jewish peasants. Today, it would be like saying to an American audience (post 9/11) the hero who took pity on the victimized American was a terrorist. In this story, Jesus forced the villagers to struggle with what it meant to show generous compassion to others. If a hated Samaritan can show compassion, then their understanding of generous compassion must expand to include even those they considered outsiders and outcasts. This meant they were being challenged to receive compassion from those they don't care for and give compassion to those they don't like.

The second parable about generous compassion involves laborers in a vineyard:

> The kingdom of heaven is like a landowner who went out early in the morning to hire laborers for his vineyard. After agreeing with the laborers for the usual daily wage, he sent them into his vineyard. When he went out about nine o'clock, he saw others standing idle in the marketplace; and he said to them, "You also go into the vineyard, and I will pay you whatever is right." So they went. When he went out again about noon and about three o'clock, he did the same. And about five o'clock he went out and found others standing around; and he said to them, "Why are you standing here idle all day?" They said to him, "Because no one has hired us." He said to them, "You also go into the vineyard." When evening came, the owner of the vineyard said to his manager, "Call the laborers and give them their pay, beginning with the last and then going to the first." When those hired about five o'clock came, each of them received the usual daily wage. Now when the first came, they thought they would receive more; but each of them also received the usual daily wage. And when they received it, they grumbled against the landowner, saying, "These last worked only one hour, and you made them equal to us who have borne the burden of the day and the scorching heat." But he replied to one of them, "Friend, I am doing you no wrong; did you not agree with me for the usual daily wage? Take what belongs to you and go; I choose to give to the last the same as I give to you. Am I not allowed to do what I choose with what belongs to me? Or are you envious because I am generous?" (Matt 20:1–15)

This is a parable not about God, but about the kingdom of God. It is not about the character of God, but the character of the Beloved Community. As with the previous parable in which the Samaritan was the hero, so the hero of this parable is someone the peasants would not normally admire. As they heard the story from their cultural perspective, the peasants would know the landlord was a member of the despised elite of Israel, probably seen as a greedy opportunist. Jesus gives us clues to his wealthy status. He owns a vineyard, and vineyards were most likely owned by the rich elite. He has a "manager" to supervise workers in the vineyard, so it must be a large vineyard. Then his crop is so abundant he cannot estimate the number of workers he will need, so he has to keep going back to the marketplace to hire more day laborers. The villagers would see him as a despised figure in the parable, a member of the elite who continually took advantage of the peasants. They would identify with the day laborers who were looking for work, not the hated landlord. It is the landlord, however, who hires unemployed peasants at the last hour of the workday, then pays them a full daily wage. The ones who had worked the whole day naturally complain about the landlord's behavior. He responds by saying he has been fair to all of them, and asks why any of them should begrudge his generosity.

The peasants who heard this story would have to ponder the meaning of a seemingly generous landlord, which wouldn't make sense to them. Should they side with the workers who got paid the same no matter how long they had worked? Or should they side with the peasants who had worked all day? Or should they be on the side of the landlord? As they struggled with this issue, they would also have to deal with the whole issue of unconditional generous compassion. Imagine today a story of a corporate construction company treating its employees in this same manner. Whose side would you take?

In these two shocking and challenging parables, Jesus taught the peasants that generous compassion (exemplified by a hated Samaritan and a despised landlord) is at the heart of what God wants in their behavior toward one another.

Jesus told one additional parable to remind the peasants of the importance of compassion:

> Suppose one of you has a friend, and you go to him at midnight and say to him, "Friend, lend me three loaves of bread; for a friend of mine has arrived, and I have nothing to set before him." And he answers from within, "Do not bother me; the door has already been locked, and my children are with me in bed; I cannot get up and give you anything." I tell you, even though he will not get up and give him anything because he is his friend, at least because of his persistence he will get up and give him whatever he needs. (Luke 11:5–8)

When he introduced this parable with the phrase, "suppose one of you had a friend," Jesus placed each person in his audience at the center of the story. Hospitality and sharing was a tradition in the Jewish villages, and in the parable a villager wants to honor that tradition by providing a meal for someone who has arrived at midnight to his home. However, he does not have food in the house to provide a proper meal for his newly arrived guest. By tradition, the sojourner who has arrived at the man's home is considered a guest of the entire village, not just the individual villager. Therefore, the host can go to the homes of others in the village and ask for help in providing a hospitable meal for his guest. As he does so, he asks the first villager for three loaves of bread. However, because the man is already in bed, he refuses to give him anything. Jesus concludes the parable by noting he will not get up and give the host anything out of friendship, but because of the persistence of the friend he will give him whatever he needs.

The village peasants who heard this parable would have to wrestle with how this applied to their village life. Had they lost their sense of caring for one another? Were they competing with each other for scarce resources and finding excuses for not helping one another? As they struggled with the meaning of the parable and how it applied to them, perhaps they would be reminded of the importance of generous compassion toward one another and toward guests who came to their village.

In summary, Jesus instructed the peasants to imitate God by being compassionate. Jesus, however, didn't simply tell them to be compassionate. He demonstrated compassion with the way he lived his life. Throughout the Gospels Jesus is portrayed as showing compassion toward those who are poor and infirm, the outcasts and outsiders of society. As seen in the life and teachings of Jesus, unconditional generous compassion is the hallmark of the kingdom of God.

7. Celebration in the Community

Jesus taught the peasants, who were living in very hard and difficult times, the importance of celebration:

> To what then will I compare the people of this generation, and what are they like? They are like children sitting in the marketplace and calling to one another,
> "We played the flute for you,
> and you did not dance;
> we wailed, and you did not weep."
> For John the Baptist has come eating no bread and drinking no wine, and you say, "He has a demon"; the Son of Man has come eating and drinking, and you say, "Look, a glutton and a drunkard, a friend of tax collectors and sinners!" (Q in Luke 7:31–34)

In this saying, Jesus contrasts his behavior with that of John the Baptist. John was known for his austere lifestyle, surviving on locusts and honey. The religious leaders criticized John for his unusual behavior. Jesus, on the other hand, came eating and drinking and celebrating with all kinds of people, and they criticized him for that behavior. Some people you just cannot please. If you play the flute in joy, they will not join in by dancing, and if you are sorrowful, they will not feel the sorrow. Jesus obviously encouraged a lifestyle of joyful celebration, and the communal meals he instituted in the villages were certainly celebrations of food and drink for the peasants. They were peasant versions of the banquets the elite held for themselves.

One time when it was pointed out to Jesus that both the disciples of John the Baptist and the Pharisees fasted, Jesus responded, "The wedding guests cannot fast while the bridegroom is with them, can they? As long as they have the bridegroom with them, they cannot fast" (Mark 2:19). Weddings and fasting simply do not go together. Guests do not fast while the celebration is going on, as long as the bridegroom is around. Life in the village community is meant to be a joyous celebration of sharing communal resources together. It is a life of celebration, not one of fasting.

Jesus also told two parables having in common the theme of celebration, one featuring a male and one a female:

> Which of you, having a hundred sheep and losing one of them, does not leave the ninety-nine in the wilderness and go after the one that is lost until he finds it? When he has found it, he lays it on his shoulders and rejoices. And when he comes home, he calls together his friends and neighbors, saying to them, "Rejoice with me, for I have found my sheep that was lost." . . .
>
> Or what woman having ten silver coins, if she loses one of them, does not light a lamp, sweep the house, and search carefully until she finds it? When she has found it, she calls together her friends and neighbors, saying, "Rejoice with me, for I have found the coin that I had lost." (Luke 15: 4–6, 8–9)

The twin stories of the lost sheep and the lost coin each have a note of humor in them. In the first, a shepherd has one hundred sheep and one of them becomes lost. The shepherd leaves the ninety-nine and goes looking for his lost sheep. The peasants hearing the parable would immediately recognize this to be an irresponsible act on the part of the shepherd. He abandoned the ninety-nine sheep, thereby exposing them to the dangers of the wilderness. More of the sheep may wander off, or wild animals may attack the flock.

Furthermore, when he finds the lost sheep, the shepherd (surprisingly) does not even return to the ninety-nine he left in the wilderness. He takes the sheep home with him and calls for his friends and neighbors to come celebrate with him. In that culture, the host would normally be required to provide the meat for the celebration, meaning he would need to slaughter the lamb he has found. Therein lies the humor of the story.

In the second story, a woman who is evidently a widow has ten coins, representing her life's savings. She loses one of the coins, searches and finds it, then calls her friends and neighbors to come and celebrate with her. She spends her newly found coin to celebrate with her friends and neighbors the finding of her lost coin. From a practical point of view, neither her behavior nor the behavior of the shepherd makes sense. But then celebrations don't have to make much sense, especially in the Beloved Community. Any excuse will do to hold a joyful celebration.

The communal meals with Jesus were a time of joy, food, drink, and conversation. They were celebrations in and of themselves. Everyone was invited to the communal meals. Each meal was a joyful expression of the kingdom of God, a happy event with enough food and drink for everyone.

Jesus also told a major story highlighting the theme of celebration. Known as the Parable of the Prodigal Son, found in Luke 15:11–32, it is the story of a father who pampers his younger son and ignores his older son. Basically, it is the story of a dysfunctional family. A man has two sons, and the younger son asks for his share of the inheritance to be given to him right away. The father indulges this son and gives him the money. Through extravagant living the young man squanders his entire inheritance in a foreign land. Famine strikes the land, and his situation worsens. He looks for a job, and the only work he can find is feeding pigs. The Torah declares pigs to be unclean. He has reached the bottom in humiliation for a Jewish man: feeding pigs. In his poverty and shame, he returns home, asking his father to receive him back as one of the servants. The father, however, welcomes him back royally, and throws a huge party to celebrate the son's return. The older son, who has remained faithful at home, is unhappy about this turn of events and complains to the father. The father assures him that he, too, is loved, but says it is necessary to celebrate the return of the long lost son. Is the father being overly indulgent by throwing a party for this wayward younger son? Is he being unfair to the older son? The listener is left to ponder these questions.

This story is not an allegory in which the father represents God and the prodigal son represents a wayward sinner who repents and comes back to his heavenly father. It is a story about a human father and his two sons. As Jesus told it, the parable is a straightforward story about a father's attempts to deal with his two sons and his celebration over the homecoming of a lost son. The villagers could enter into a vigorous discussion about the father's actions and the behavior of each of the sons. At the end, they might realize anew the vital role celebration plays in human relationships.

Jesus taught the peasants to celebrate. In a compassionate community of shared resources each peasant can celebrate life because there is enough for everyone. Everything given up to the community multiplies the happiness of everyone exponentially.

8. How to Deal with Your Enemy

A major issue for the village peasants was what to do about their hated enemy, the Roman rulers and the Jewish elite who collaborated with them. In what is perhaps his most radical statement, Jesus said, "Love your enemies. . . . If you love those who love you, what credit is that to you? For even sinners love those who love them" (Q in Luke 6:27, 32).

The peasants certainly knew who was the enemy. First and foremost, the enemy was the Roman rulers in the cities and their ever-present military forces. Secondarily, it was the wealthy Jewish elite and the aristocratic temple priests, both of whom collaborated with the Roman rulers for their own welfare. All these "enemies" made life miserable for the peasants.

It was easy to hate these enemies. In fact, it is not uncommon to build a community life on the hatred of "the Other." Leaders of nations have thrived on instilling hatred and fear of enemies as a way of maintaining control and power over the populace. Jesus made it clear the kingdom of God was not going to be built on hatred of the enemy.

Jesus taught a new way of relating to the enemy. Jesus said, "Love your enemies." Love here is an action word, not simply a feeling. Jesus is not asking the peasants to feel loving toward their enemies, but to act loving toward them. This injunction to "love your enemies" can apply to both an individual and to the entire community. It can be read as both singular and plural.

The teaching had to be both challenging and troubling to the peasants in the villages. They were suffering terribly because of their enemies. When they heard Jesus tell them, "love your enemies," the peasants must have asked, "*How* exactly are we supposed to love our enemies, the ones who are making life so miserable for us?" Jesus responded with three savvy strategies for dealing with the enemy, each one applicable to situations in which the peasants found themselves as they dealt with those who were their masters and rulers.

First, Jesus somewhat surprisingly said, "if anyone strikes you on the right cheek, turn the other also" (Q in Matt 5:39). Jesus is telling the peasants if a superior person (such as a Roman official, a military person, a master, or a boss) strikes you on the *right* cheek you are to turn the other cheek to that person also. The peasants were accustomed to receiving such blows from those who were considered their superiors. To strike someone on the right cheek a right-handed person would necessarily use the back of the right hand. This was a way of humiliating the peasant and demonstrating that one holds a superior position over the peasant. Jesus surprisingly instructs the peasant, when struck on the *right* cheek, to turn the other cheek so the "superior person" can strike him again. Since the left hand was not used to hit someone, the one doing the hitting would have to strike the peasant with the open palm of his right hand. This puts the "superior" in a quandary, for now he does not know what to do. To hit the "inferior" with his right fist or open palm would be to sink to the level of a common fistfight with the peasant, and the superior person would lose his "superior" status in relation to the peasant. By turning the other cheek, the peasant has retained his dignity as an equal in a potentially humiliating situation. He is saying to the superior, "I am a person of equal worth to you."

Second, Jesus said, "If anyone wants to sue you and take your coat, give your cloak as well" (Q in Matt 5:40). Jesus is saying that if a superior person sues a peasant and insists on taking his coat as collateral for the debt, the peasant is to give his cloak also. The peasants of that day wore only two pieces of clothing, an outer coat and an inner cloak. Indebtedness was a major problem for the peasants, who often had to borrow money from a wealthy person in order to have funds to plant crops and feed their families. The wealthy charged the peasants exorbitant interest, from 25 percent to over 100 percent. In many instances the peasant was unable to repay the loan on time. The wealthy person could take the peasant to court and claim his coat (the outer garment) until the loan was repaid. The peasant had no chance of winning a case in the courts. The legal system was stacked against him. So Jesus surprisingly suggested when the wealthy person demanded the peasant's coat he should right then and there give his cloak also (the inner garment). Since they did not have underwear, this would leave the peasant standing in court completely naked. The wealthy person would be embarrassed for having caused this spectacle. By taking this action, the peasant had undermined the sense of superiority of the wealthy person. The peasant also had made fun of the legal system and the way it favored the rich over the poor by allowing the confiscation of one-half of the peasant's clothing. It was a dramatic way for the peasant to retain some dignity in an extremely unfair system.

The third example Jesus employed involved the Roman military. Jesus told the peasants, "if anyone forces you to go one mile, go also the second mile" (Q in Matt 5:41). Under Roman law a Roman soldier could conscript a Jewish male to carry the soldier's heavy armor and equipment for the distance of one mile, but no more. It did not matter what activity the Jew might be engaged in, he had to stop what he was doing and carry the soldier's pack the distance of one mile. It was an onerous and humiliating burden imposed on the peasants by the enemy soldiers, rubbing the Jewish peasants' noses in their own powerlessness. Jesus, again surprisingly, suggested at the end of the one mile, the peasant insist on carrying the pack a second mile. This put the Roman soldier in a real quandary. If he allowed the Jewish peasant to carry his pack a second mile, the soldier would be in trouble for violating the law. If he refused the offer, he looked silly. The peasant had again gained the upper hand in the situation and retained his dignity in the presence of a supposed superior.

In all three situations, Jesus taught the peasants a brilliant strategy for responding to the violent behavior of "superiors" in a nonviolent, yet active manner. These were nothing short of radical acts of social justice and nonviolent resistance. It is much easier to "love your enemies" if you can do so in a way that also undermines the entire power structure of your unjust society, puts your oppressors in a quandary, and retains your own sense of dignity. This was guidance the peasants desperately needed as they questioned Jesus about his radical instruction to "love your enemies."

With these strategies, Jesus taught the peasants they could love their enemies in an active way that carried a social message, without being doormats. Jesus was not teaching them to passively absorb the abuses of the elite and powerful. Nor was he counseling the peasants to love their enemies in the hope of changing the enemies into friends. The resulting outcome of their behavior was not the issue. He was teaching them there is a way to act in a loving manner and still retain one's dignity.

Jesus knew that this behavior would not be easy for the peasants. For them to live in nonviolent dignity in their situation, Jesus counseled, "be as sly as snakes, and as simple as doves" (*Thom.* 39:3). He called on the peasants to combine two seemingly contradictory qualities: be sly as snakes and as simple as doves. It is not easy to love one's enemies, and it takes a combination of great wisdom and gentle innocence to respond to violence with nonviolence, without simply being a victim.

Jesus also told the peasants what to do when someone of the wealthy elite, "the enemy," to whom they owe money, takes them to court for repayment of a loan:

> When you go with your accuser before a magistrate, on the way make an effort to settle the case, or you may be dragged before the judge, and the judge hand you over to the officer, and the officer throw you in prison. I tell you, you will never get out until you have paid the very last penny. (Q in Luke 12:58–59)

Jesus knew the legal system was stacked against the peasants. For a peasant to go before a judge was to be at a great disadvantage. So Jesus advised the peasants to seek to arrange a settlement of the debt prior to appearing before the judge. Within the Beloved Community, the peasants could cancel their debts to one another, which was all well and good, but they would have to repay the wealthy person to whom they owed money. Jesus's advice to try to settle with the wealthy lender before going to court was both practical and sensible in their situation.

Further, Jesus taught them what to do regarding taxes owed to another enemy, the Roman rulers. The peasants were burdened by the heavy taxes imposed on them by the Romans, and they wondered if they should continue to pay their hard-earned money to the brutal Roman government. According to the *Gospel of Thomas*, they showed Jesus a gold coin and said to him, "The Roman emperor's people demand taxes from us." Jesus knew if the peasants refused to pay their Roman taxes, they would be thrown in prison and perhaps executed, so he taught them, "Give the emperor what belongs to the emperor, give God what belongs to God" (*Thom.* 100:2). The point of Jesus's response is that the members of the new community must sort out their own obligations and then fulfill them. They must give the emperor what is due him, and they must also give to God whatever is their responsibility. This was wise advice from Jesus in that situation.

Jesus had one more thing to say about the Romans. The Jews, especially the peasants, chafed under the oppressive rule of the occupying Roman military power. There was a strong desire to rise up and overthrow the Roman rulers. Insurrection was in the air. Jewish zealots all around Galilee were seeking to stir up a spirit of violent rebellion against the Romans. The peasants in the villages certainly asked Jesus about the wisdom of trying to violently overthrow the Romans who were occupying and enslaving the nation of Israel. Jesus answered them with this straightforward advice, "Do not resist an evildoer" (Q in Matt 5:39). Jesus knew violent rebellion against the evil Roman government was futile and suicidal. Jesus did not agree with the Zealots in their attempt to stir up rebellious actions to the Roman rule, and he advised against reacting violently to "the one who is evil."

To help the peasants sort through their feelings on this matter, Jesus told this parable:

> A person owned a vineyard and rented it to some farmers, so they could work it and he could collect its crop from them. He sent his slave so the farmers would give him the vineyard's crop. They grabbed him, beat him, and almost killed him, and the slave returned and told his master. His master said, "Perhaps he didn't know them." He sent another slave, and the farmers beat that one as well. Then the master sent his son and said, "Perhaps they'll show my son some respect." Because the farmers knew that he was the heir to the vineyard, they grabbed him and killed him. (*Thom.* 65:1–7)

Mark also has a version of this parable (12:1–12), but the version in *Thomas* is more likely to have originated with Jesus. On first reading, the parable seems strange to us. It appears to promote the idea of violence. Yet it was a parable the peasants could understand. They knew about wealthy landowners and tenant farmers. The farmers did all the work and the landowner (who had probably confiscated the farm from a peasant in the first place) took the lion's share of the crop. The farmers were left with very little for themselves and their families. They would naturally be angry at the wealthy landowner. The action of beating the landowner's slaves and killing his son, though, would be seen as self-defeating. The peasants hearing this parable would be able to finish the story. They knew this tactic would never work. The farmers in the story were foolish to think that by killing the landowner's son they would somehow get the land back. If you did something to harm the landowner's servants or his family, he would simply call in the military police. The farmers would be arrested and thrown in jail, and probably executed. Their violent behavior would have gained them nothing but trouble and even death.

Jesus knew violence only begets more violence, and it would be futile to stage a violent rebellion against the Roman rulers. It cannot be known whether or not Jesus was a pacifist in principle. The case can be made either way. What can be known is that in this specific situation in first-century Galilee, Jesus advised the peasants not to rebel via war or terrorism against the Roman rulers. This was wise and practical advice for the circumstances of that moment in time. It would be unfair to Jesus to use his words on this occasion to argue for or against pacifism as an operating principle for all time, but it is clear he favored its application as the only moral tool for change in their particular circumstances.

Jesus had wise words for the peasants about how to deal with enemies. These words, however, need to be understood in the context of first-century peasant village life. Too often these teachings of Jesus have been interpreted as telling victims of violence to "turn the other cheek" and submit to further violence. They have been used, for example, to tell battered women to submit to those who are abusing them, which is an absurd and horrendous idea. It is always important to keep in mind the audience to whom Jesus was speaking and the specific situation the village peasants were facing. Keeping an oppressed population down (such as battered women or other victims of violence) seems exactly opposite of Jesus's message, given its radical anti-oppression foundations.

The major issue of improving the daily quality of life for the peasants involved how to deal with the hated Roman rulers and military. They asked Jesus: What can we do about our enemies? What options do we have beyond rebellion or resigning ourselves to our miserable fate? What can we do to survive the difficult situation in which we find ourselves? Jesus gave them practical help with this issue in a way that made sense to the village peasants. The ultimate answer was the Beloved Community, where they shared their resources with one another and found strength in their new way of living together, but he also provided concrete examples of social justice activism to help them reclaim their humanity, their sense of dignity, and their personhood when they inevitably had to deal with "the enemy" in the outside world.

Finally, it should be noted that Jesus and his early followers did not try to reform Roman society. That would have been impossible for them.

The Roman Empire allowed no right of public protest. Any attempt by Jesus to change the Roman society would have been met with prompt arrest and death. It is thus quite understandable that Jesus had a different strategy in mind in dealing with the Romans. That strategy was the establishment of the communes in the village, enabling the peasants to survive, and perhaps even thrive, in the midst of Roman oppression.

9. *The Kingdom Community as an Irritant*

Jesus taught the peasants their community would be an irritant to the Romans and the Jewish elite who collaborated with them. The Romans exercised their control of Israel through the familiar tactic of "divide and conquer, divide and rule," a universal strategy of all oppressors. It was to the Romans' advantage that the village peasants were turning against one another in a desperate attempt to survive and feed their families. Poverty was pitting the peasants against one another, isolating them in their competition for scarce resources. The more divided the peasants were against one another, the easier it was for the Romans to control them.

Jesus came with a new way of organizing the social-economic life of the villages, a way that would bring them together rather than divide them. This new way of living together, life as God wanted it to be lived, would be an irritant to the Romans and to their elite Jewish collaborators. The Beloved Community Jesus was establishing in the villages was not open military rebellion against the Romans, but it was certainly seen as an irritating threat.

Jesus told the peasants, "I have cast fire upon the world, and look, I am guarding it until it blazes" (*Thom.* 10). He taught the peasant villagers to live together in a way that threatened the Roman rulers. They didn't know what to make of it, this kingdom of God. Jesus said he was guarding the Beloved Community until it was well established, until the fire was blazing. At that point, the peasant villagers would be strong enough in their newfound life together to stand on their own in the face of Roman opposition.

As was often his custom, in dealing with this subject, Jesus told one parable from the male viewpoint and one from the female point of view: the Parable of the Mustard Seed and the Parable of the Leaven. Unless the culture of that day, as well as the situation the peasants faced, is kept in mind, these two parables can easily be misinterpreted. In the first parable, Jesus said:

> What is the kingdom of God like? And to what shall I compare it? It is like a mustard seed that someone took and sowed in the garden; it grew and became a tree, and the birds of the air made nests in its branches. (Q in Luke 13:18–19)

Here Jesus compares the kingdom of God to a mustard seed someone sowed in a garden. Right away the peasants would know something was up. The mustard plant is a nuisance plant, a weed. No one in his right mind would purposely sow a mustard seed in a garden, unless he had an ulterior motive. Mustard is an aggressive plant, difficult to control. It thrives where it is not supposed to be. It is certainly not to be planted in a garden. Next, the mustard seed grows to become a tree, attracting birds to the garden. This is the last thing a farmer would want. Birds are unwelcome in a garden. They will eat the seeds of the garden plants and ruin his garden. Yet Jesus compares the establishing of the kingdom of God in the villages to the planting of the mustard plant, a nuisance weed, in a garden.

Jesus is saying he is purposely planting something in the midst of the Roman occupation of Israel that will be an irritant to the Roman rulers. Jesus knows they will not like the fact he is organizing the villagers in a way that unites them together and gives them strength in the face of the oppressive rule of the Romans. It counteracts the Romans' "divide and rule" philosophy. Jesus said their kingdom community, the mustard plant, would thrive and grow, but it would be a nuisance in the midst of the Roman "garden." The peasants would like the fact their Beloved Community of resource sharing would be an irritant to the Roman rulers and the Jewish elite. This parable would have appealed to them.

The second parable is about a woman who is baking bread:

> To what shall I compare the kingdom of God? It is like yeast that a woman took and mixed in with three measures of flour until all of it was leavened. (Q in Luke 13:20–21)

This parable describes a typical activity of a rural peasant woman. Yet Jesus's hearers would immediately know something was up when he tells them she mixes yeast (leaven) in with the dough, enough so that the whole batch is leavened. In the Jewish culture of that day, leaven was considered to be a pollutant. It was an extremely negative image, associated with corruption and even death. Leavened bread was considered swollen, empty bread, like a swollen corpse. The Jews ate only unleavened bread. No Jewish woman baking bread would put leaven in the dough.

The leaven would ruin the bread. Yet Jesus compared the kingdom of God to a woman putting a substantial amount of polluting leaven in a batch of dough, until "all" of the dough was leavened.

Jesus was making the same point with the leaven as with the mustard seed. He was saying the kingdom of God, the new social-economic arrangement of the villages, would be an irritant to the Roman rulers. Within their oppressive dominating rule of Israel, the kingdom of God in the local villages would be a pollutant to their military kingdom, causing Romans and Jewish elites to be disgusted at the highly effective actions of the Beloved Community. It threatened their control of the peasants and was tremendously irritating to them.

Finally, the mustard weed in the garden and the leaven in the dough, once started, are difficult to stop. Once established, the Beloved Community, Jesus said, would be difficult to overcome.

The kingdom of God villages of Galilee were a source of united strength for the peasant villagers but a thorn in the side of the Roman rulers and those who collaborated with them. Through the kingdom of God, both via the communal sharing of resources and the acts of passive resistance, the peasants now had strength in numbers. This is good news for the peasants, bad news for the Romans. Jesus's Beloved Community program was a threat to the Roman way of life and to the comfortable lives of any Jews wealthy or powerful enough to benefit from collaborating with the Romans. This put Jesus and his mission in jeopardy and caused the Romans to watch him carefully.

10. The Uncertain Future in the Beloved Community

Jesus taught the peasants in the Beloved Community there were no guarantees about the future. It is open-ended and uncertain. He made this point in two very brief parables. First, he said, "The kingdom of heaven is like treasure hidden in a field, which someone found and hid; then in his joy he goes and sells all that he has and buys that field (Matt 13:44).

For a peasant, finding unexpected treasure in a field is like winning the lottery. It is beyond the expectations of everyday life. It is almost like getting something for nothing, a dream come true. Buried treasure was not uncommon in ancient Israel. With no banks available, it was the only way to keep one's money from being stolen. So the dream of finding buried treasure was strong within the mind of a peasant, a sudden bonanza quickly lifting the peasant out of his poverty. Very much like our lotteries today, the chances were slim, but the hope of this cultural myth or pipe dream was powerful.

In this parable, though, there is one problem. The field where the buried treasure is found belongs to someone else. Nevertheless, the finder of the treasure is filled with "joy" over his good fortune. He keeps the information to himself, sells all that he has, then goes and buys the field from the unsuspecting owner. The story ends there, and should be seen as a conversation starter. We have the parable Jesus told, but we don't have any record of the conversation of the villagers. Is the finder of the treasure wise or foolish in his behavior? He has sold "everything he has" in order to buy the field. He now has no assets on which to live. Plus, in the culture of the small villages of Jesus and his audience there was very little privacy. Everyone would be aware of what the treasure-finder had done in tricking the owner of the field. If he began to spend the treasure he had found, people would be suspicious. Thus, the man who found the treasure now had something useless to him. He cannot spend it without his wrongdoing being discovered by his fellow villagers. So, is his situation better or worse now that he has spent everything to buy the field?

Imagine the lively discussion that occurred among the hearers of the parable. They would have to ask themselves: What does this parable mean for us? The most probable answer was the new social-economic arrangement in the village was the treasure in the field, and each of the peasants is expected to put all they have into it. They would have to give up their individual produce for the common good, which would truly be quite hard, seemingly a risk, even though they didn't own much. Still, it was all they had. Would it be worth it? Are there any guarantees about the future? How will it all turn out? The peasants would have to wrestle with these questions among themselves and find their own answers.

Jesus made the same point in the telling of the short story of the treasured pearl, "the kingdom of heaven is like a merchant in search of fine pearls; on finding one pearl of great value, he went and sold all that he had and bought it" (Matt 13:45).

The peasants who heard this story would know about pearls, but none of them would have owned one. A valuable pearl was a dream of the peasants, but only the wealthy actually owned pearls. The peasants could identify with a merchant who suddenly finds an unexpected treasure, a pearl of immense value. The merchant in the story realizes his good fortune, sells all that he has, and buys that hugely valuable pearl. As with the parable of the treasure, this story has no ending. We don't know what happened to the merchant when he sold everything he had to buy a single valuable pearl. What will he do to provide for himself and his family? What will he do with the pearl? Was he wise or foolish to sell everything to buy a pearl, even an extremely valuable pearl?

Again, a lively discussion would ensue among the hearers of the story, helping make the story both interesting and memorable. But finally the hearers would ask: What does this parable mean for us? The answer is that the community sharing of resources is the pearl of great value; but is it worth the risk of each of us pooling our resources for the greater good of everyone in the community? Will we gain more than we lose? What will the future look like? Again, as with the Parable of the Treasure in the Field, the peasants would have to wrestle with these questions. Jesus offered no guarantees about the future, but he did offer them a new way of organizing their village economic life filled with new possibilities. This new way of living together is one in which each peasant could gain more than he would lose, even though at first that might not appear to be the case.

11. Leadership in the Beloved Community

Every organization, group, or community must have leaders. The only issue is what kind of leadership will the leaders exhibit. Here is what Jesus taught the villagers about leadership:

> Whoever wants to be first must be last of all and servant of all. (Mark 9:35b)

> You know that among the Gentiles those whom they recognize as their rulers lord it over them, and their great ones are tyrants over them. But it is not so among you; but whoever wishes to become great among you must be your servant, and whoever wishes to be first among you must be slave of all. (Mark 10:42b–44)

Leadership in the Beloved Community was meant to be different than leadership in other relationships in life. In government, business, and the military, there is a definite hierarchy of leadership, with those higher up the organizational ladder having (often unquestioned) authority and power over those below them. When Jesus noted that the Gentile leaders lord power over their subjects and are tyrants over them, he probably had in mind the Roman rulers who controlled Galilee. They ruled with an iron fist and made life very difficult for the peasants. It would be different, he said, in the kingdom-of-God communities. In the village of communal sharing, there are to be no rulers, and those who are leaders are servants of all. They do not lord it over others in the Beloved Community.

Jesus also had strong negative words to say about both the Pharisees and the scribes who loved to have special privileges and honors in the community:

> Woe to you Pharisees! For you love to have the seat of honor in the synagogue and to be greeted with respect in the marketplaces. (Q in Luke 11:43)

> Beware of the scribes, who like to walk around in long robes, and love to be greeted with respect in the marketplaces, and to have the best seats in the synagogues and places of honor at banquets. (Q in Luke 20:46)

In this same vein, Jesus told a parable about two men who went to the temple to pray, one a Pharisee and the other a collector of the temple taxes:

> Two men went up to the temple to pray, one a Pharisee and the other a tax collector. The Pharisee, standing by himself, was praying thus, "God, I thank you that I am not like other people; thieves, rogues, adulterers, or even like this tax collector. I fast twice a week, I give a tenth of all my income." But the tax collector, standing far off, would not even look up to heaven, but was beating his breast and saying, "God, be merciful to me, a sinner!" I tell you, this man went down to his home justified rather than the other. (Luke 18:10–14a)

In the parable, the Pharisee is obviously full of pride about his own behavior, while at the same time seeking to shame the tax collector. The tax collector refuses to let that condemnation stifle him, and he prays directly to God for mercy. Jesus was roundly condemned by the religious leaders for being a friend of tax collectors and sinners, so it is not difficult to understand why the humble tax collector is the good person in this parable. Jesus had a special place in his heart, it seems, for those who were humble in their life and in their relationships with one another. He had another view of those who were haughty and prideful.

It is not known how leaders were chosen within the communities that established Jesus's prescribed social-economic arrangement. A typical pattern for making choices in that culture was the casting of lots, mentioned numerous times in the Hebrew Scriptures (the Old Testament). The casting of lots involved putting stones, perhaps of various colors, into a vessel to be shaken until one fell out. This was meant to remove the human element, so God could make the choice. There was no concept of democratic voting or elections. When Judas had to be replaced as one of the twelve, for example, the decision on his replacement was made by casting lots (Acts 1:24–26). Ancient records indicate that a later Christian group, the Gnostics, chose their leaders by casting lots. The casting of lots meant there was no campaigning for leadership, no popularity contests, no power grabbing, and no entrenched leadership. Whatever way the lots fell was considered to represent the will of God for that moment in time.

Not only did the Christian Gnostics cast lots for their leaders, they also rotated leadership on a regular basis. A person in the community might be the leader for a period of time, and then take a lesser position within the group, while a person who had been in a lesser role might become the leader of the community for another stretch of time. Perhaps this is what Jesus had in mind when he said, "the last will be first, and the first will be last" (Q in Matt 20:16).

A rotation system of leadership ensured there was no permanent hierarchy in the community. You could be the president at one time and a dishwasher the next. No one person could usurp power unchecked. This approach represented egalitarian leadership, and evidence suggests it may well have been instituted by Jesus in the villages. Jesus had established a community of equals, where all distinctions of class, race, and gender were eliminated, including in the leadership roles.

12. The Beloved Community as an Example

Jesus certainly understood the ancient concept of the nation of Israel being established by God to be a "light unto the Gentiles." He wanted the village share-communities to be an example to others of the way God wants humans to live in relation to one another. The Beloved Community was a pilot project, a demonstration community for others to see. We humans learn how to do something, not by reading a book, but by observing others doing the activity and trying to imitate them. Jesus gave specific instructions about how to live as a village commune. If they lived in this manner with one another, others could learn from this living example and see the good arising from it. Here is how Jesus described the share-communities as examples for others:

> A city built on a hill cannot be hid. (Matt 5:14)
>
> No one after lighting a lamp puts it under the bushel basket, but on the lampstand, and it gives light to all in the house. (Q in Matt 5:15)
>
> Is a lamp brought in to be put under the bushel basket, or under the bed, and not on the lampstand? For there is nothing hidden, except to be disclosed; nor is anything secret, except to come to light. (Mark 4:21–22)
>
> No one after lighting a lamp hides it under a jar, or puts it under a bed, but puts it on a lampstand, so that those who enter may see the light. (Q in Luke 8:16)
>
> No one after lighting a lamp puts it in a cellar, but on the lampstand so that those who enter may see the light. (Q in Luke 11:33)

The Beloved Community was not a secret to be hidden. It is like a city on a hilltop that can be seen by everyone. Or it is like a lighted lamp, which no one would put under a bushel basket, or beneath the bed, or in a cellar, but on a lampstand so it can give light to everyone in the house. In each of these images, Jesus is saying the Beloved Community is a sample of the product. If one wants to see evidence of the kingdom of God, all one has to do is look at these villages in operation, as living examples of communal sharing of resources with one another in a spirit of love, compassion, and cooperation.

Jesus knew there would be difficulties and challenges for the villagers as they learned this new way of living, so he told them this parable:

> A sower went out to sow. And as he sowed, some seed fell on the path, and the birds came and ate it up. Other seed fell on rocky ground, where it did not have much soil, and it sprang up quickly, since it had no depth of soil. And when the sun rose, it was scorched, and since it had no root, it withered away. Other seed fell among thorns, and the thorns grew up and choked it, and it yielded no grain. Other seed fell into good soil and brought forth grain, growing up and increasing and yielding thirty and sixty and a hundredfold. (Mark 4:3–8)

When the peasants heard this parable their first reaction would have centered around the sower, and how careless and wasteful he was in the way he sowed the seed, throwing it where it had little chance to grow. They would have then pondered about the three negative places where the seed had fallen and what that might mean in their village as they tried to build the Beloved Community. Who were the birds? What about those who have initial enthusiasm and then quickly become discouraged? Where are the thorns in our village? And what is this about a thirty, sixty, and hundredfold yield from the seed falling into good soil? Does Jesus mean if we adopt his sharing community plan we will all benefit many times over? The villagers would have had quite a lively conversation among themselves about this parable as it applied to their village life.

Jesus realized the challenges of establishing the Beloved Community in a village would cause some peasants to want to quickly abandon the whole idea. He, therefore, counseled patience by telling them this parable:

> A man had a fig tree planted in his vineyard; he came looking for fruit on it and found none. So he said to the gardener, "See here! For three years I have come looking for fruit on this fig tree, and still I find none. Cut it down! Why should it be wasting the soil?" He replied, "Sir, let it alone for one more year, until I dig around it and put manure on it. If it bears fruit next year, well and good; but if not, you can cut it down." (Luke 13:6–9)

It was not unusual for a fig tree to be growing in a vineyard. This particular tree, however, has evidently been neglected, and it is not producing fruit. The owner is ready to give up on the tree and have it cut down. The vintner, however, who has perhaps been neglecting the tree, now argues for giving him another year to tend to the tree, with the hope it might bear fruit in that time. The peasant farmers who heard this parable might wonder about the farming abilities of each of these two characters with their fig tree.

Perhaps Jesus meant the "three years" literally as applied to the village share-communities. If for the past few years the villagers had been neglecting to care for their village life, the result would be the deterioration of their life together. If they were now to tend to their village life through their share-communities, they could have good results for their village within the next year. It is worth a try to get their new social-economic arrangement functioning in a fruitful way.

Finally, Jesus said the results of this new way of life would speak for themselves:

> You will know them by their fruits. Are grapes gathered from thorns, or figs from thistles? In the same way, every good tree bears good fruit, but the bad tree bears bad fruit. (Q in Matt 7:16–17)

Elsewhere, Jesus expressed it this way, "Figs are not gathered from thorns, nor are grapes picked from a bramble bush" (Q in Luke 6:44b). The Beloved Community, living in love and compassion with one another, is the good fruit capable of being seen and evaluated by everyone. It is the obvious demonstration on earth of the kingdom of God, life lived as God wants it to be lived, with spirituality, equality, and social justice going hand in hand.

SUMMARY

These, then, are the majority of the teachings attributed to Jesus considered by a consensus of New Testament scholars to have originated with Jesus. They serve as the major piece of evidence in making the case that Jesus's original intention in his mission was to transform the villages of Galilee into communities of shared resources.

It is also important to note what Jesus did not say in his teachings. First, he did not provide conventional wisdom to his audience. He did not exhort them to avoid being idle, to work hard and earn one's own living. He did not give advice on family life, or friends, or raising children, or other topics of common wisdom. He had a single-minded focus on establishing the Beloved Community in the peasant villages. He clearly saw himself as a person called by God to be on a mission "to bring good news to the poor" (Luke 4:18).

Second, Jesus did not have much to say about himself, and when he did he spoke of himself as homeless, having "nowhere to lay his head" (Luke 9:58). He is also reported to have responded to an inquirer who addressed him as "good master" with the words, "Why do you call me good? No one is good but God alone" (Luke 18:19). He did not call himself the divine Son of God, and certainly did not speak of himself as the second person of the Trinity.

Third, Jesus did not speak about individual salvation. The Jewish people did not worry about whether or not they were "saved." Most of them believed there would be a life after death, and they looked forward to this life. They did not, however, need to be saved or believe in a certain person in order to enter the life to come. As Jews, they were already God's people, and God had given them both the land and the Law. If they failed to live up to the Law, God forgave them on the Day of Atonement. Jesus, therefore, did not make it his mission to "save" individual Jews, or to get their "souls" into heaven. Jesus did not focus on life after death, but on building the new community in the villages of Galilee in this world. He did not concern himself with the world to come after death.

The followers of Jesus who collected his teachings focused on his words and deeds in the villages of Galilee. For them, this is what made Jesus special. He taught the villagers a joyful, egalitarian new way of life together, firmly rooted in traditional Jewish economic principles, giving the peasants a newfound sense of economic and social dignity. He transformed the villages from despair to hope, and for this they remembered him as their hero and carefully remembered and eventually wrote down the truths he had taught them. Therefore, in our examination of the evidence, it is vital to let Jesus speak for himself.

8

Corroborating Evidence: James the Brother of Jesus

CONTINUING WITH THE THEME of detective work, a good detective will, after assembling the major evidence in a case, gather corroborating evidence in support of the case. This corroborating evidence puts the finishing touches on the case and sometimes clinches it.

In the previous chapters, we have made the case that Jesus's original intention in his mission was to transform the deteriorating village life of Galilee into communal sharing villages. The primary evidence for this case has been presented in the previous chapters. It is now time to turn to the secondary evidence, beginning with James the brother of Jesus.

A FORGOTTEN HERO

Jesus had brothers and sisters. The brothers are named and the sisters referred to in Mark's gospel. At the beginning of his mission, when Jesus returned to his hometown and began to teach in the synagogue, the townspeople wondered where he got his wisdom and power, and they asked, "Is not this the carpenter, the son of Mary and brother of James and Joses and Judas and Simon, and are not his sisters here with us?" (Mark 6:3). There are a total of seven references in the New Testament to Jesus having natural siblings.

James was apparently the eldest of the brothers of Jesus, since he was named first among the brothers listed in Mark. Being the eldest also accounts for the fact he became the leading figure from Jesus's family.

Yet in many ways James is a forgotten hero. He actually played a more prominent role in the early Jesus movement in Israel than is portrayed in the New Testament. Many people, therefore, do not understand his contribution to helping us understand what Jesus was trying to accomplish in the villages of Galilee. James, however, is quite important in helping us perceive Jesus's original intention in his Galilean mission, thereby finding the missing person Jesus of Nazareth.

There is great debate about the relationship of Jesus with his family. The evidence is mixed. There is evidence of hostility between Jesus and his family members, but there is also evidence his family was supportive of his ministry. Most scholars conclude that James, and perhaps some other brothers of Jesus, traveled with Jesus during at least part of his ministry. They may not have belonged to the group listed as the twelve disciples, but the evidence is strong they were frequently in the company of the followers of Jesus. Also, since Acts reports the brothers as present among the believers in Jerusalem immediately after the death of Jesus (1:14), it is reasonable to assume they must have been active in Jesus's mission in Galilee.

James is mentioned several other times in the book of Acts where, following the death of Jesus, he is obviously the leader of the church in Jerusalem (12:17; 15:13–21; 21:17–26). The account in Acts 15 is particularly significant. Paul had come to Jerusalem asking the Jerusalem church to make a decision regarding requirements for Gentile converts. It is important to note it is James who is in charge of the proceedings and who renders the decision on behalf of the Jerusalem church, indicating again his position of leadership in the church.

The earliest evidence regarding James's leadership of the Jerusalem church, however, comes from the letters of the apostle Paul. This is a firsthand account of the situation in Jerusalem, providing the best evidence available.

In his letter to the Galatians, Paul reports that three years after his conversion experience he went to Jerusalem, where he stayed with Peter for fifteen days. This event took place five to eight years after the death of Jesus. About this event Paul wrote, "but I did not see any other apostles except James the Lord's brother" (Gal 1:19). Here Paul names James as an apostle and makes it clear he is the brother of Jesus. This suggests that within a few years of Jesus's death James was already a leader of the Jerusalem followers of Jesus.

Paul also indicates that fourteen years after his conversion he returned to Jerusalem, where he met with the three "pillars" of the church, namely, James, Peter, and John (Gal 2:1–12, esp. v. 9). James is named first, indicating his established position as leader of the church. In his account of the meeting, Paul expresses concern he might be working in vain unless the pillars approve his mission and methods, signifying the importance and authority James had not only in Paul's mind, but in the church at large as well (Gal 2:2). James was the leader of the Jerusalem church, the church considered to be the "mother church" of the Christian movement. Thus, the church led by James had primacy over all other churches.

References to James are also numerous beyond the New Testament. What is remarkable about these sources is they all agree that Jesus himself passed his leadership role to his brother James, who is widely known in these early writings.

A primary source of information about James and his prominent role in the early Christian movement is found in the writing of the highly regarded first-century Jewish historian Josephus. His works *The Jewish War* and *The Antiquities of the Jews* were written toward the end of the first century. In these important histories, Josephus refers several times to James and his leadership in the Jerusalem church. Here is his account of a plot to kill James and the reaction of some of the leading citizens of Jerusalem:

> Upon Festus' death, [the Roman governor of Judea] Caesar sent Albinus to Judea as procreator. But before he arrived, King Agrippa had appointed Ananus to the priesthood, who was the son of the elder Ananus. . . . The younger Ananus, however, was rash and followed the Sadducees, who are heartless when they sit in judgment. . . . Convening the judges of the Sanhedrin, he brought before them a man named James, the brother of Jesus who was called the Christ, and certain others. He accused them of having transgressed the law, and condemned them to be stoned to death.
>
> The people of Jerusalem who were considered the most fair-minded and strict in observing the law were offended by this. Some of them even went to meet Albinus, who was on his way from Alexandria, and informed him that Ananus had no authority to convene the Sanhedrin without his permission. Albinus angrily wrote to Ananus, threatening vengeance. King Agrippa, because of this action, deposed Ananus from the high priesthood, which he had held for three months. (*Ant.* 20.197; Maier trans., 275–76)

The *Gospel of Thomas* includes a collection of 114 sayings attributed to Jesus. In Saying 12, the disciples acknowledge they are aware Jesus will be leaving them. They ask, "Who will be our leader?" The response attributed to Jesus is, "No matter where you are, you are to go to James the Just, for whose sake heaven and earth came into being." The second part of the sentence reflects the Jewish idea that the world exists and is sustained because of the virtues of a small number of righteous or "just" individuals. James was known for his great virtue and thus came to be known as "James the Just."

A major source of information about James comes from two early documents written in the second century, both now lost. The first was composed by Hegesippus (90–180), a Jewish Christian historian from Palestine, while the second came from Clement of Alexandria (150–215) who was a Christian teacher in Egypt. Both are quoted extensively by the later Christian historians Eusebius of Caesarea (260–340) and Epiphanius of Salamis (367–340).

Hegesippus is quoted by Eusebius:

> But James, the brother of the Lord, who, as there were many of this name, was surnamed the Just by all from the days of our Lord until now, received the government of the Church from the Apostles. (*Ecclesiastical History* 2.23.3-4; quoted in Eisenman, *James*, 198)

Eusebius also quotes Hegesippus regarding the high esteem in which James was held by the Jewish leaders in Jerusalem:

> They assembled and said to James, "We beseech you to restrain the people, who are going astray after Jesus as if he were the Christ. We beseech you to persuade all who are coming to the feast of the Passover rightly concerning Jesus; for all obey you. For we and all the people testify you are Righteous and do not respect persons. Therefore, persuade the people not to be led astray after Jesus, for all the people and ourselves have confidence in you. Therefore, stand on the Pinnacle of the Temple that you may be clearly visible from above and your words readily heard by all the people. (*Ecclesiastical History* 2.23.11; quoted in Eisenman, *James*, 210)

In addition, Eusebius quotes Josephus, indicating the cause of the fall of Jerusalem was the killing of James by some of the Jewish leaders:

> So admirable a man, indeed, was James, and so celebrated among all for his Righteousness, that even the wiser part of the Jews were of the opinion that this was the cause of the immediate siege of Jerusalem, which happened to them for no other reason than the crimes against him. Josephus, also, has not hesitated to superadd this testimony to his works: 'These things happened to the Jews to avenge James the Just, who was the brother of him that is called Christ, and whom the Jews had slain, notwithstanding his preeminent Righteousness.' (*Ecclesiastical History* 2.23.20; quoted in Eisenman, *James*, 399)

Eusebius joined the chorus of those who indicated the leadership role James held in the Jerusalem church:

> James, the brother of the Lord, was allotted the episcopate in Jerusalem by the Apostles. James, who as the Sacred Scriptures show, was generally called the brother of Christ, was the first to receive the episcopate of Jerusalem from our Savior himself. (*Ecclesiastical History* 2.7.19; quoted in Eisenman, *James*, 196–97)

Many other ancient sources refer to the righteousness and virtue of James the brother of Jesus as well as his unique leadership role in the Jerusalem church. There can be no doubt James was the undisputed leader of the Jerusalem church for over thirty years until his death in 62 CE. He and his brothers, as well as his mother, Mary, had gone with Jesus on his final journey to Jerusalem. After the death of Jesus some of his followers, including members of his family, remained in Jerusalem. They formed a community there, headed by James.

James regarded his brother as the human Jewish Messiah, from the line of David. He was conceived in the normal way by his parents, Joseph and Mary. What was remarkable about Jesus was his vision and program for transforming village life in Galilee and beyond. James and the other followers of Jesus in Jerusalem saw themselves as faithful Jews who followed the Jewish Messiah. They remained in Jerusalem and formed a community there, most probably because they believed this is where the completion of the mission of the Messiah would occur. Their conception of a Messiah was that of a human being "anointed" or "called" by God for a special mission and purpose. They did not regard Jesus as divine or as a god himself. They were observant Jews who felt their belief in Jesus as the Jewish Messiah in no way conflicted with their faithfulness to Jewish religious practice. They continued to observe the purity laws, the holy days and seasons, circumcision, and regular participation in worship at the temple.

They also did think of themselves as founding a new religion. Like Jesus, James and the earliest followers of Jesus were practicing a certain form of Judaism, similar to a denomination in today's world. There were many different sects of Judaism in the first century, and the Jerusalem community was one of those branches. So when I refer to the Jerusalem community led by James, I do not mean to indicate a new or separate religion distinguished from Judaism.

Who better to corroborate the evidence about Jesus's original intention than his brother who literally grew up in the same household with him and traveled with him during at least part of his mission in Galilee? James is an important direct link to Jesus. By examining James and the Jerusalem community he led, a clearer picture of Jesus and his mission emerges.

THE JERUSALEM COMMUNITY

The author of Acts offers these striking descriptions of the Jerusalem community, led by James the brother of Jesus:

> All who believed were together and had all things in common; they would sell their possessions and goods and distribute the proceeds to all, as any had need. (2:44–45)

> Now the whole group of those who believed were of one heart and soul, and no one claimed private ownership of any possessions, but everything they owned was held in common. (4:32)

> There was not a needy person among them, for as many as owned lands or houses sold them and brought the proceeds of what was sold. They laid it at the apostles' feet, and it was distributed to each as any had need. (4:34–35)

The reader might well ask: Where did James get the idea to form a socialistic community in the city of Jerusalem? It was a community where "no one claimed private ownership of any possessions, but everything they owned was held in common." The answer is clear: James and the Jerusalem community of believers patterned their social-economic practices after the distinctive communal arrangement Jesus had established in the villages of Galilee. They simply continued the life they had lived with Jesus. They were away from their homes and occupations in Galilee, sharing their life together as followers of Jesus. Evidently they each had their own means of earning an income in Jerusalem, and then pooled their income into a common purse.

The distribution of the income from the common purse was an important aspect of their life together. First, the apostles distributed the funds "to each as any had need." As a result, Acts tells us "there was not a needy person among them." Second, they distributed aid to needy persons in the city of Jerusalem. Acts reports one of the first organizational steps of the Jerusalem church was to appoint seven men to administer the aid to the needy (6:1–6). The distribution of mutual helpfulness to those within the community as well as beyond the community was an important feature of their life together. Evidently, the single use of the common purse was for mutual aid and assistance.

For these followers of Jesus the kingdom of God was a reality in the present time, not an event in the future. What was important to them was the fact they were living a kingdom life now. Again the author of Acts describes their life together, "day by day, as they spent much time together in the temple, they broke bread at home and ate their food with glad and generous hearts, praising God and having the goodwill of all the people" (2:46–47).

From this statement it is obvious the Jerusalem community of Jesus followers met in the Jewish temple for worship and in their homes for their meals. The author of Acts reports they ate their food with "glad and generous hearts." Through their joyful spirits and their generous hearts, they were winning the goodwill of the people of Jerusalem.

As was the pattern in the share-communities Jesus established in the villages of Galilee, they ate together in the evening, the chief meal of the day. The common meals were an essential part of their life together. It was a full meal and would be especially important to the poor. The meal would function as a social occasion where everyone is the equal of all. The meal would bring the community close to one another, as it had done in their time with Jesus.

The common meals are an indication that the church was organized for more than just worship, or for teaching and preaching. The church was organized for the administration of their common life together. The church in Jerusalem was a communal life together with a religious foundation. Their common purse and common meals expressed this reality.

The Jerusalem church was a socialistic community, patterned after what James and the other followers of Jesus had learned from him in Galilee. Thus, the Jerusalem group led by James the brother of Jesus serves as strong collaborating evidence that the mission of Jesus was to establish communal sharing groups in the villages of Galilee. They continued in Jerusalem what they had experienced in Galilee.

THE LETTER OF JAMES

The Letter of James is an important and unique book of the New Testament, reinforcing and corroborating Jesus's authentic teachings. This letter provides a window into James's understanding of the teachings of Jesus and what Jesus sought to accomplish.

It is not known whether James the brother of Jesus actually wrote the Letter of James. Most scholars, however, conclude that either James wrote the letter or, at a minimum, it contains the thoughts and ideas of James, though a later editor may have put it into its final form. The Letter of James is considered to be a trustworthy expression of the thinking of James. We can be confident the letter that bears his name reflects the thinking of James the brother of Jesus.

In the letter, James does not comment on every subject related to following Jesus. He focuses primarily on a community ethic and how members of the community should relate to each other. James describes the commune as a community of equals. He does not use words of hierarchy, but addresses his audience as brothers and sisters. He does not want the members of the community to act in the manner of secular leaders, exerting power and control over others. His desire is for the community to live by the principles of love and compassion.

In all of this, he reflects the teachings and values of his brother Jesus. The ethical content of James's letter parallels the authentic teachings of Jesus. What is remarkable about the Letter of James is that, in spite of its brevity, it contains more than thirty direct and indirect references to the teachings of Jesus himself. The Letter of James thus serves as a direct link to the teachings of Jesus during his mission in Galilee. James was with him for at least part of that mission, and in his letter he passes on what he learned from his brother. This letter is a reflection of the original message of Jesus as he traveled throughout Galilee.

A look at the evidence in the Letter of James corroborates the essential message of Jesus. Here, then, are the core teachings of James from the New Testament letter attributed to him:

> If any of you is lacking in wisdom, ask God, who gives to all generously and ungrudgingly, and it will be given you. (1:5)

> For the sun rises with its scorching heat and withers the field; its flower falls, and its beauty perishes. It is the same way with the rich; in the midst of a busy life, they will wither away. (1:11)

Be doers of the word, and not merely hearers who deceive themselves. (1:22)

Religion that is pure and undefiled before God, the Father, is this: to care for orphans and widows in their distress, and to keep oneself unstained by the world. (1:27)

If a person with gold rings and in fine clothes comes into your assembly, and if a poor person in dirty clothes also comes in, and if you take notice of the one wearing the fine clothes and say, "Have a seat here, please," while to the one who is poor you say, "Stand there," or "Sit at my feet," have you not made distinctions among yourselves and become judges with evil thoughts? Listen, my beloved brothers and sisters. Has not God chosen the poor in the world to be rich in faith and to be heirs of the kingdom that he has promised to those who love him? (2:2–5)

What good is it, my brothers and sisters, if you say you have faith but do not have works? Can faith save you? If a brother or sister is naked and lacks daily food, and one of you says to them, "Go in peace, keep warm and eat your fill," and yet you do not supply their bodily needs, what is the good of that? So faith by itself, if it has no works, is dead. (2:14–17)

Who is wise and understanding among you? Show by your good life that your works are done with gentleness born of wisdom. But if you have bitter envy and selfish ambition in your hearts, do not be boastful and false to the truth. . . . For where there is envy and selfish ambition, there will also be disorder and wickedness of every kind. But the wisdom from above is first pure, then peaceable, gentle, willing to yield, full of mercy and good fruits, without a trace of partiality or hypocrisy. (3:13–14, 16–17)

Those conflicts and disputes among you, where do they come from? Do they not come from your cravings that are at war within you? You want something and do not have it; so you commit murder. And you covet something and cannot obtain it; so you engage in disputes and conflicts. You do not have, because you do not ask. You ask and do not receive, because you ask wrongly, in order to spend what you get on your pleasures. (4:1–3)

Do not speak evil against one another, brothers and sisters. Whoever speaks evil against another or judges another, speaks evil against the law and judges the law; but if you judge the law, you are not a doer of the law but a judge. There is one lawgiver and judge

> who is able to save and to destroy. So who, then, are you to judge your neighbor? (4:11–12)

> Beloved, do not grumble against one another, so that you may not be judged. (5:9)

> We call blessed those who showed endurance. You have heard of the endurance of Job, and you have seen the purpose of the Lord, how the Lord is compassionate and merciful. (5:11)

> Above all, my beloved, do not swear, either by heaven or by earth or by any other oath, but let your "Yes" be yes and your "No" be no, so that you may not fall under condemnation. (5:12)

These teachings in the Letter of James all have parallels in the teachings of Jesus. The writings of James focused not on Jesus the person but upon what Jesus taught. He saw Jesus as a teacher, an example to follow. There is no evidence James worshiped Jesus or considered him divine.

The Letter of James also stands in sharp contrast to Paul's teaching of salvation by faith alone. This contrast becomes clear in the second chapter of James's letter, "What good is it, my brothers and sisters, if you say you have faith but do not have works? Can faith save you? . . . So faith by itself, if it has no works, is dead. . . . You see that a person is justified by works and not by faith alone. . . . For just as the body without the spirit is dead, so faith without works is also dead" (14, 17, 24, 26).

James, Jesus's own flesh and blood, had a different view of the Christian faith than did Paul, who never met Jesus and never studied under any of the original followers of Jesus. This whole section of the letter develops the concept of righteousness based on works as opposed to righteousness based on faith alone. In 2:24–25 James uses Abraham as the example of works-based righteousness, indicating his viewpoint is clearly in opposition to Paul's teaching, for in the fourth chapter of Romans, Paul had already used Abraham as an example of righteousness by faith.

In his letter, James emphasizes the behavior of the followers of Jesus in their community life together. He stresses the importance of works over faith, the doing of good deeds over simply having a sympathetic concern for others. The teachings of James, as reflected in this letter, confirm and corroborate the teachings of Jesus.

A SAD TWIST OF HISTORY

James and the Jerusalem community serve as strong secondary evidence for Jesus's original intention to transform the suffering villages of Galilee into communal sharing villages that he called "the kingdom of God" and we call the Beloved Community.

Eventually, the Jerusalem community was lost to the Christian movement, and Paul's version of Christianity became the accepted version throughout the Roman Empire. The versions of Christianity taught by the followers of Jesus in Galilee and Jerusalem, who knew Jesus and had been with him in his mission in Galilee, were systematically eliminated by the followers of Paul. The story of how that occurred is one of the strange twists of history. It all revolves around the pivotal year of 70 CE.

The Jews of Israel had long chafed under the cruel domination of the Roman Empire. A spirit of rebellion was in the air. Around the year 66 CE, Jewish zealots led a revolt against the Roman occupation, seeking to drive the Romans out of Israel and establish Israel once again as an independent nation. The Romans reacted swiftly and harshly, sending a mighty military force into Israel to crush the rebellion. The Jewish resisters held out as long as they could, with the walled city of Jerusalem as their last refuge. In the year 70 CE the Romans finally entered the city and killed most of the remaining Jewish refugees in the city. The Romans completely destroyed the Jewish temple, the longtime center of Jewish worship. By the time they had finished crushing the rebellion, the Romans had killed hundreds of thousands of Jews throughout Israel.

In the rebellion, the original Jewish followers of Jesus in Jerusalem and Galilee were either killed or scattered. This resulted in their communities being destroyed and their understandings of Jesus becoming lost to history. Through the circumstances of history, therefore, the Jesus story as taught and lived by those who knew Jesus was hidden from view for almost two thousand years. From that time forward the leadership of the Christian movement shifted from Israel to the churches in the Greco-Roman world founded by the Apostle Paul. The Christian movement lost its foundational roots in Israel, becoming a movement centered in the Gentile world outside of Israel.

The churches founded by Paul throughout other parts of the Roman Empire were not affected by the Jewish rebellion in Israel. Shortly after the year 70 CE, the various books of the New Testament, including the

Gospels, began to be written. They were all written from the point of view of Paul's understanding of Christianity. The writings of Paul and his followers dominate the New Testament material, so one gets the impression that his ideas and point of view were those generally prevailing in the early Christian movement. As we have seen, such was not the case. The fact is the social vision of the Jerusalem church and the Jesus People of Galilee is not adequately presented in the New Testament. The Christian reader of the New Testament thus gets an impression of the Christian faith that is bound to be one sided. And even more to the point, the missing person Jesus of Nazareth became lost to history, hidden within the New Testament.

CONCLUSION

James was Jesus's own beloved brother and was witness to what Jesus was teaching and doing in his mission in Galilee. Who better to corroborate the evidence regarding Jesus's original intention and help us find the missing person Jesus of Nazareth than his own brother, James? The evidence for James serving as a direct link to Jesus is threefold:

A. His role as the leader of the Jerusalem church following the death of Jesus
B. The Letter of James in the New Testament confirming the authentic teachings of Jesus
C. The socialistic community James founded in Jerusalem as an urban counterpart to the village sharing communities Jesus established in Galilee

When we read in the early chapters of Acts about the communal sharing arrangement of the church in Jerusalem, led by James, we ask: Where did James get the idea for such a community? The answer is clear: from his brother Jesus. Thus, James provides an important glimpse into the mission and message of Jesus in Galilee, and greatly assists us in our detective work of finding the missing person Jesus of Nazareth.

9

A Case of Mistaken Identity?

One of the perils in the search for a missing person occurs when it becomes a case of mistaken identity. This happens when one believes the missing person has been found, but it turns out to be another person. This eventuality can be disheartening, to say the least, but it also means the search for the missing person must be continued. In the search for the missing person Jesus of Nazareth, we now examine a possible case of mistaken identity.

THE APOSTLE PAUL

Saul of Tarsus, known to most people by his Roman name, Paul, was a young man, probably in his thirties, when Jesus died. There is no evidence Paul ever met or knew Jesus.

Paul was a Jew raised in Tarsus, in the area of what is now Turkey. He was not from Israel. He was well educated, a learned man who was knowledgeable of both the Jewish traditions and the Greek culture all around him. Both factors seem to have influenced his understanding of Jesus.

We first come to know Paul as he joined with Annas, the high priest of the temple in Jerusalem, in attempts to suppress and arrest the followers of Jesus. This was soon after the crucifixion of Jesus. Three or four years later, Paul had a conversion experience in which he claims to have "met" the risen Christ. In his letters Paul does not indicate where the event occurred. The author of Acts, writing about fifty years later, says the event occurred as Paul was on his way to Damascus (in modern-day Syria). In any event, Paul believed he received a revelation from Jesus in which he was called to preach the good news of salvation through faith in Jesus Christ to the Gentile world.

Paul writes about his experiences in his letter to the Galatians. Following his call to preach, he writes, "I did not confer with any human being, nor did I go up to Jerusalem to those who were already apostles before me" (Gal 1:16–17). He indicates he went away at once to Arabia, and then returned to the city of Damascus. After three years, Paul went to Israel to the city of Jerusalem, where he stayed with Peter for fifteen days. He also visited with James the brother of Jesus on that visit. Paul then describes another visit to the Jerusalem followers of Jesus fourteen years later. Paul does not provide any information about his activities during those fourteen years.

During this visit, Paul met with the "pillars" of the Jerusalem church, namely James, Peter, and John. Though Paul insisted he did not need anyone's permission to pursue his mission to the Gentiles, while he was in Jerusalem the three leaders did endorse the plan for Paul to take his gospel message to the Gentiles. Paul makes it clear in his letter to the Galatians that he had received his authority to preach his gospel directly through revelations by the risen Christ, not from any human commission or authorities. He also indicates that his contact with James, Peter, and John had been minimal. He writes, what these leaders were "made no difference to me" and they "contributed nothing to me" (Gal 2:6). Paul seemed to take pride in the claim that his authority came directly from Christ and he needed no earthly approval (Gal 1:1, 11–12).

Around the year 50 CE Paul began his mission to the Gentiles of the Roman world. He went to various cities within the Roman Empire, where he founded churches comprised primarily of Gentile converts. Shortly after his first missionary journey Paul began to write letters to the churches he had founded, and it is primarily through these letters we get to know Paul. The letters were written over a period of about ten years, including his imprisonment in Rome. Paul died in Rome in the early sixties, about ten years prior to the writing of the first New Testament gospel by Mark.

Since Paul had never met Jesus, he could not claim the human Jesus had taught him what he was preaching. Paul, therefore, developed his particular interpretation of the Christian gospel based on his own mystical experiences. There is no way, of course, to evaluate whether or not a person has actually experienced such a mystical revelation. One can only know what the person claims to have experienced. For example, in 1827 in upstate New York, Joseph Smith claimed to have received from the angel Moroni golden tablets from which, with the help of special stones set in silver bows, he translated the *Book of Mormon.* If one is a Mormon then one accepts the *Book of Mormon* as valid scripture and affirms Joseph Smith's claim. If one is not a Mormon, then Joseph Smith's claim to a direct revelation from an angel is not viewed as credible. There is, therefore, no method to judge the authenticity of Paul's claim of direct revelation from Jesus. The most that can be done is to accept the fact Paul claims such revelations came to him, and then evaluate the content of the message Paul indicates he received from Christ.

Paul believed strongly in his own gospel message, while being hostile toward any other version of the gospel. He referred to his message about Jesus Christ as "my gospel" and called his gospel "the revelation of the mystery that was kept secret for long ages, but is now disclosed" (Rom 16:25). He also pronounced a curse upon anyone who preached any other gospel than the one he preached (Gal 1:9).

PAUL'S VERSION OF CHRISTIANITY

Paul taught that Jesus was a preexistent heavenly being who existed in the "form of God" and was "equal with God" (Phil 2:6). According to Paul, Jesus Christ voluntarily "emptied himself" and took on human form. His purpose for becoming human was to die on the cross as an atonement for the sins of the world. God then raised him from the dead and thus proclaimed him as the long-awaited Messiah ("Christ" in the Greek language).

In agreement with James the brother of Jesus and the Jerusalem church, Paul may have originally seen Jesus as the human Jewish Messiah. This may have been the reason the leaders of the Jerusalem church were able to endorse Paul's mission to the Gentiles. Paul, however, transformed this Jewish Messiah into a divine universal Messiah who died for the sins of the world. This was a radical departure from the understanding of Jesus held by James and the Jerusalem followers of Jesus.

In Paul's view, through the death of Jesus Christ, God was able to reconcile a sinful world unto himself. Those who accepted the atoning sacrifice of Christ's blood were forgiven of their sins and given the gift of eternal life. People were made right with God by faith in Jesus Christ and the efficacy of his death upon the cross, not by good deeds, such as caring for the poor or other acts of kindness. In fact, Paul insisted his Gentile converts were not required to live by the teachings of the Torah, the Jewish law. Paul also expected Jesus to return in his own lifetime, and assured his followers that when Christ appeared both the living and the dead would rise in the air to meet Christ in the clouds of heaven (1 Thess 4:13–18). Paul believed the return of Christ would bring an end to history and render judgment on everyone. He felt called to prepare the members of his congregations for a "second coming" of Jesus as Messiah. Obviously, Paul was wrong in his expectation Christ would return during his own lifetime.

In all honesty, it must be noted that Paul's theology differs from Jesus's teaching of everyday justice and the earthly presence of the kingdom of God. Jesus's primary message is the kingdom of God, the beloved community in which one can live in the here and now. Paul's primary message was the risen Christ, the salvation based upon his death upon the cross, his resurrection and exaltation as the Lord and Savior of the world, and personal faith in Jesus Christ. Paul shows little interest in what Jesus actually said or did. He is not concerned with following the path the human Jesus set forth. Paul's primary interest appears to be in the heavenly world and life after death, in stark contrast to Jesus's message about how to live in this present world. Thus, in the writings of Paul the message *of* Jesus has been transformed into a message *about* Jesus.

THE VERSION THAT PREVAILED

Even though Paul never met Jesus, the message he taught about Jesus became the accepted version of Christianity throughout the Roman world. The versions of Christianity taught by the followers of Jesus in Galilee and Jerusalem, who knew Jesus and had been with Jesus in his mission in Galilee, were systematically eliminated by the followers of Paul. In the previous chapter on James the brother of Jesus I recounted the story of how that occurred. You will recall there was a rebellion by some Jews against the Roman occupation of Israel. In the year 70 CE Rome crushed the rebellion, killing hundreds of thousands of Jews in the process, including many of the original followers of Jesus. Others of his followers were scattered in various towns east of Israel. Thus they lost their leadership role in early Christianity, and that role was taken over by the churches outside of Israel founded by the Apostle Paul.

Though Paul's version of the faith was not the earliest version of what it meant to be a follower of Jesus, Paul's ideas became so persuasive they came to be viewed as the only authentic version of Christianity. This in itself does not mean Paul's version of the faith is either right or wrong. It does mean, however, his version was simply one version among a number of other versions of the Christian faith. What can rightly be said is that Paul founded the Gentile stream of Christianity and his version of the faith ultimately prevailed, becoming the accepted version of Christianity. It is wrong to assume his was the earliest version of the faith or the only version of early Christianity.

A CASE OF MISTAKEN IDENTITY?

Paul, of course, is entitled to his own beliefs or opinions about Jesus. And you, likewise, are entitled to agree or disagree with Paul's beliefs about Jesus. The question arises, though, as to whether Paul's understanding of Jesus leads us closer to or further away from Jesus of Nazareth. In other words, if we stop with Paul's understanding of Jesus, does that lead us to a case of mistaken identity?

As previously noted, Paul shows almost no interest in Jesus of Nazareth, either his words or his deeds. The reason is simple. In Paul's mind, Jesus doesn't become the universal savior of the world until God raises him from the dead. In his letter to the Romans, Paul writes that Jesus "was declared to be Son of God with power according to the spirit of holiness by resurrection from the dead" (1:3–4). For Paul, the pivotal events were Jesus's death upon the cross and his resurrection. About his life, Paul simply states Jesus "was descended from David according to the flesh" (1:3).

You may remember the Jesus People of Galilee who were with Jesus during his mission in Galilee. What was important to them was his words and deeds, what he taught them about how to live together in community. They wrote nothing of his death or his resurrection. Paul, on the other hand, wrote nothing of his words and deeds, and much about his death and resurrection.

You may also remember James the brother of Jesus and his Jerusalem community, who knew Jesus as the founder of sharing communities and emulated him by establishing an urban share-community in Jerusalem. They saw Jesus as a human Jewish Messiah.

Paul took their understanding of Jesus one step further, proclaiming Jesus as the universal Messiah ("Christ" in Greek) of the world. What this means for us is this: if you are searching for the missing person Jesus of

Nazareth, and you simply stop at what Paul believes about Jesus Christ, you will end up with a case of mistaken identity. This is not to say Paul's understanding of Jesus is right or wrong. He is entitled to his own beliefs about Jesus. It is to say, however, that his beliefs are of limited value in finding the missing person for whom we are looking. Don't make the mistake of assuming you have found Jesus of Nazareth when you know what Paul believes about Jesus. To find the missing Jesus of Nazareth we must go back beyond Paul to those who were with Jesus on his travels in Galilee, namely, the Jesus People of Galilee and his brother James. If we stop with Paul's beliefs about Jesus, we may very well end up with a case of mistaken identity.

PAUL AS CORROBORATING EVIDENCE

In spite of the limitations already mentioned, Paul can still serve as corroborating evidence for the essential message and mission of Jesus. Though Paul was in many ways a freelance maverick with his own unique understanding of the Christian faith, he did capture the spirit of community and equality taught by Jesus. Like Jesus, Paul understood the vital importance of a community of equals. In his own way, therefore, Paul serves as corroborating evidence of the original purpose of Jesus's mission in Galilee. When he visited the leaders of the church in Jerusalem, Paul saw the urban expression of the sharing community led by James the brother of Jesus. Though Paul never met Jesus, he did have the opportunity to learn of the communal arrangements Jesus had established in Galilee. As can be seen through the letters he wrote to the churches he founded, Paul evidently sought to replicate the sharing community concept in those churches. In his own way, therefore, Paul confirms the fact it was communities of shared resources Jesus (and James) had established.

In the letters to his churches, Paul proclaimed the core message of a community of equals: "There is no longer Jew or Greek, there is no longer slave or free, there is no longer male and female; for all of you are one in Jesus Christ" (Gal 3:29).

Paul also used the image of the human body to describe the equality of all in Christ: "For as in one body we have many members, and not all the members have the same function, so we, who are many, are one body in Christ, and individually we are members of one another" (Rom 12:4–5). In the twelfth chapter of First Corinthians Paul expands on his theme of the church as the body of Christ, stating that all are members of one body, each having a different function, yet each being equally vital to the well-being of the whole body.

Following up on the idea of the church as the body of Christ, Paul reminds the Christians in Rome what this means in their behavior toward one another:

> Let love be genuine. . . . Love one another with mutual affection; outdo one another in showing honor. . . . extend hospitality to strangers. . . . Live in harmony with one another; do not be haughty, but associate with the lowly. . . . Do not repay anyone evil for evil, but take thought for what is noble in the sight of all. . . . live peaceably with all. (Rom 12:9, 10, 13, 16, 18)

In addition, in his letter to the Colossians, Paul urges the members of his churches to exhibit these qualities:

> Clothe yourselves with compassion, kindness, humility, meekness, and patience. Bear with one another and, if anyone has a complaint against another, forgive each other. . . . Above all, clothe yourselves with love, which binds everything together in perfect harmony. And let the peace of Christ rule in your hearts, to which indeed you were called in one body. (3:12–15)

In his letter to the church in Philippi, Paul called on the members of the congregation to "do nothing from selfish ambition or conceit, but in humility regard others as better than yourselves. Let each of you look not to your own interests, but to the interests of others" (2:3–4).

Finally, Paul established a communal meal in his churches after the pattern of the communal meals of the Jerusalem church and the Jesus followers in Galilee. In the eleventh chapter of 1 Corinthians (vv. 17–22), he writes about this evening meal. He criticizes the wealthier members of the church, who did not work and therefore could arrive early for the meal, for going ahead of the poor at the meal and taking the majority of the food and drink. The result, Paul writes, is "one goes hungry and another becomes drunk" (11:21). In this selfish way, the wealthier members of the church "show contempt for the church of God and humiliate those who have nothing" (11:22). Paul ends his comments about the way the rich were ruining the communal meal by noting, "What should I say to you? Should I commend you? In this matter I do not commend you!" (11:23).

Paul understood the church to be a community of equals and the evening communal meal as a sharing of resources among equals.

In his various letters to the churches, Paul emphasizes the importance of the church as a community. His letters deal with issues such as how Jews and Gentiles should act toward one another, leadership in the group, what belonging to the group means, and relationships within the community. These letters reveal Paul's strong conviction that the character of community life matters greatly. For Paul and the early Christians, being a follower of Jesus was not simply an individual matter, but meant being a member of the community of followers.

CONCLUSION

In his theology, Paul added a number of elements to his understanding of Jesus that were not a part of Jesus's original mission in Galilee, nor were they a part of the understanding of Jesus held by his earliest followers in Galilee and in Jerusalem. If we ended our search for the missing person Jesus of Nazareth with Paul's viewpoint, we will have a case of mistaken identity. We will have Paul's understanding of Jesus, but we will not have discovered Jesus the man.

Paul did, however, capture the spirit of Jesus's communal sharing of resources in the Beloved Community. Thus Paul joins James from the earliest years of Christianity as corroborating evidence confirming Jesus's original purpose to establish sharing communities in the villages of Galilee, and thus helping us to find the missing person Jesus of Nazareth.

10

Wrapping Up the Case

IN EXAMINING BOTH THE primary and secondary evidence regarding the original intention of Jesus, the goal has been to get as close as possible to the Jesus who lived and taught in first-century Galilee. What did he say? What did he do? Like a detective, I have endeavored to follow the empirical evidence and to restrict myself to rational deductions or conclusions based on that evidence. I have sought to discover the human story of Jesus, free of theological interpretations that developed later. As stated earlier, everyone is entitled to his or her own opinion (or belief), but no one is entitled to his or her own facts. My goal has been to put aside beliefs about Jesus and simply analyze the available factual information related to Jesus.

After examining the evidence regarding Jesus's original intention in his mission in Galilee, what are the most plausible conclusions we can draw? Do we have reliable evidence upon which to make a determination about the missing person Jesus of Nazareth? Can we know his aim and purpose as he saw it? I believe we do have a sizable amount of reliable evidence about his message and his mission. We can know who he was, what he said, what he did, and why he died. We can also understand why he made such an impact on his first followers in Galilee, why their understanding of Jesus was lost to history for many centuries, and how that original viewpoint has been recovered in our day. By carefully examining that evidence, we can know enough to have a trustworthy picture of Jesus and his original purpose as he traveled throughout the villages of Galilee.

It is now time to wrap up the case. I will review the considerable amount of evidence leading to the conclusion we have found the missing person Jesus of Nazareth.

A. THE WORLD OF JESUS

We began with a summary of the evidence regarding the world of Jesus. If we do not find him in his own world, we will not find him at all. In his world, five basic historical facts should be kept in mind.

1. The Dominance of the Roman Empire

During Jesus's lifetime the Roman Empire was in its heyday, controlling most of the known world. Israel was a vassal state of the Roman Empire. The Romans ruled with an iron fist and demanded tribute from the various nations under their rule. The governor of each province within a nation was expected to collect tribute money from the populace and to keep the peace within the territory under his jurisdiction. These governors treated their territories as little fiefdoms through which they could accumulate as much wealth for themselves in as short a time as possible. Therefore, they imposed heavy taxes upon the people under their rule.

2. The Temple Tithe and Tax

Each adult male Jew in Israel was expected to pay an annual tithe (10 percent) of his income to the temple in Jerusalem. In addition, the aristocratic priests who ran the temple in Jerusalem imposed an annual temple tax of one-half shekel on each adult male in Israel. The temple authorities sent individuals out to the cities and villages of Israel to collect the annual tithe and tax from each household. The combination of Roman tribute and taxes, the tithe, and the temple tax created an onerous burden upon the Jewish people, especially the poor.

3. The Rich and the Poor

There were only two classes of people in Israel, the poor, who comprised about ninety-five percent of the population, and the wealthy elite, who composed the other five percent. The wealthy included the Roman bureaucrats, aristocratic Jewish collaborators, and the priests of the temple in Jerusalem. The rich elite lived primarily in the cities. The poor lived in the small villages. This pattern was especially prevalent in the farming province of Galilee, where Jesus conducted his mission. There is no record of Jesus ever conducting his mission in any of the cities, only in the villages.

4. The Plight of the Poor

During the lifetime of Jesus the plight of the poor in the Galilean villages was worsening dramatically. The farmers had small plots of land on which they could barely raise enough crops to feed their own family. They had difficulty paying the huge Roman and temple obligations and often had to borrow money from each other to survive. When that money ran out, they had to go to the wealthy elite to borrow funds (at high interest rates) for the next crop. Often they were unable to repay these loans, and as a result they lost their farms. They then became sharecroppers on land they had once owned, or even worse, day laborers who never knew when there might be work enough to take care of their own family's needs. Some became beggars or were even forced to sell themselves or members of their family into slavery in order to survive.

5. The Deteriorating Village Life

Village life in Galilee was deteriorating rapidly during this time. It was a desperate situation for the peasants, as they began competing against each other for scarce resources. They were also turning against each other, demanding repayment of the small loans they made to one another and doing almost anything they could to survive. As suspicions among the villagers grew, village life was falling apart, and the traditional Hebrew sense of community was being lost.

Jesus himself grew up among the poor of Galilee in the small village of Nazareth. We do not know how poor Jesus was, but we do know he understood the desperate plight of the poor in Galilee. He would have also seen the deteriorating village life and the loss of a sense of community among the villagers. This provided the setting for what he sought to accomplish in his mission in Galilee.

B. JESUS'S STATED PURPOSE

It is clear Jesus had a purpose in mind for his mission in Galilee. He did not wander aimlessly through the villages. But what was his intent? What was he trying to accomplish with his life? What was his own self-understanding? How did he see himself?

It is unfair to Jesus for us to impose our own understanding of his purpose without at least paying attention to his purpose as he understood it. According to the Gospel of Luke, Jesus saw himself as called by God to fulfill a specific purpose: to bring good news to the poor (4:18). It should be noted the term "the poor" is plural. Jesus saw himself bringing good news not just to individuals who are poor, but to the poor as a group. All the evidence related to Jesus of Nazareth indicates he purposely set about to accomplish this very specific purpose. He saw himself as the one who would inaugurate the kingdom of God in a very practical way in the villages of Galilee. With his words and deeds he would establish kingdom communities among the poor, people living as God intended them to live in relationship with one another.

C. JESUS'S VISION AND PROGRAM

By examining carefully the available written evidence—what Jesus taught and what he did as he went from village to village in Galilee—it becomes obvious he had a clear vision and program for what he wanted to accomplish. Jesus advocated an egalitarian, cooperative way of organizing the village life of the peasants of Galilee. The evidence supports the conclusion that Jesus had both a vision and a program of communal sharing of resources, which he called "the kingdom of God."

Jesus was a Jew, born to Jewish parents. He grew up in a Jewish village and lived all of his life in the Jewish nation of Israel. It is reasonable to assume he learned the Hebrew Scriptures as he matured, especially the Torah and the social prophets of Israel. His vision and program, therefore, would have emerged from his understanding of a basic truth found in the Torah and the Prophets: individual growth and development arises out of community. Wholesome communities tend to produce wholesome individuals. Community precedes individuality, and communities are at their best when there is a spirit of cooperation and sharing. Jesus's vision and program was built on that ancient truth. Jesus believed he had been called by God to teach the peasants of Galilee the way God wanted people to live and how a community of shared resources could be established in their villages. In short, Jesus was a community organizer.

It may be difficult for some to recognize that Jesus came primarily to organize the villages of Galilee into sharing communities. The modern emphasis on personal salvation and individual decisions may lead some to assume this was the purpose of Jesus's life. This emphasis on individual decisions, however, is not the only way to understand Jesus. The historical and biblical evidence indicates Jesus's mission was aimed primarily at communities, not just individuals.

In Jesus's teaching there is far less emphasis on individual private ownership of property and far more emphasis on the communal sharing of resources. This did not mean each person had to sell what he or she had and live in a socialistic community. Nor did it mean there was no room for individual accomplishment. In his plan, not everyone would have exactly the same amount of food and other necessities, but there would be enough for each person. Jesus knew that, in a community of sharing where no one seeks to become wealthy at the expense of other community members, each person will have his or her needs met.

D. JESUS'S STRATEGY

Another important piece of evidence helping us find Jesus of Nazareth and his purpose is his strategy of traveling from village to village throughout Galilee. The evidence is clear: Jesus was a wandering Jew, an itinerant. This was in stark contrast to other Jewish teachers, healers, and religious authorities (such as John the Baptist), who established a headquarters and encouraged individuals to come to them for teaching and healing. If Jesus had simply wanted to reach individuals, he could have followed that familiar pattern. Jesus, however, was intent on transforming the village life of the peasants of Galilee, so he went with his entourage from village to village to fulfill his mission "to bring good news to the poor." His strategy of going to the various villages of Galilee confirms he was indeed a community organizer.

E. JESUS'S PLAN

Jesus's strategy is also evident in his carefully developed plan to send out his disciples two by two into the villages he himself would not be able to visit. He gave his followers very specific instructions about what to take with them as they traveled to the villages, how to behave in the village, what to say and do while there, and even what to do if a village rejected them. His words about handling rejection are especially pertinent. He told them that if a village rejects them they are to shake the dust of the village off their feet, tell the villagers they have missed out on the kingdom of God, and then leave. From this guidance of Jesus to his disciples, it is obvious Jesus had in mind a mission to the village as a village, not just individuals within the village. Otherwise, Jesus would have told them to focus on receptive individuals in the village. Jesus, however, said that if a village rejected their plan of communal sharing, they were to "shake the dust from their feet" and go on to the next village.

F. JESUS'S STRATEGY IN THE VILLAGE

Jesus's first followers, those who were with him in the villages of Galilee, remembered what he said, and they wrote down a number of his teachings, preserved in the first editions of the Sayings Gospel Q, as well as the *Gospel of Thomas*. His words meant everything to them, and they remembered him beginning his visit to a village with these words:

> Blessed are you who are poor,
>   for yours is the kingdom of God.
> Blessed are you who are hungry now,
>   for you will be filled.
> Blessed are you who weep now,
>   for you will laugh. (Luke 6:20–21)

These are not pious, spiritual words. They are bold promises spoken directly to those who are poor, hungry, and sad. Jesus better have some plan to back up those promises or he will soon be run out of town. Jesus did indeed have a plan, a new way of organizing their village life that would enable them to withstand the harsh rule of the Roman government and their elite Jewish collaborators. Instead of competing with each other for scarce resources, Jesus taught them the ancient Hebrew value of communal sharing.

While in the village, Jesus also provided free healing for the peasants in exchange for free hospitality for himself and his entourage. Jesus did not come to the village as a superior or an inferior person. His vision was a community of equals, no matter who you were. He accepted everyone as they were, and all were included in his new community, the kingdom of God.

A third leg of Jesus's strategy in the village was his table fellowship of communal meals. It was here at the evening village meals that the villagers experienced what sharing really meant. Each one would bring something to share in the meal, and the amazing result was there would be enough for everyone. In this relaxed, joyful setting, through his one-liners and his parables, Jesus could teach the villagers how to conduct their communal life together.

It is clear from the biblical evidence that Jesus had a specific strategy for the time he spent in a village. He used teaching, healing, and communal meals as his way of establishing the Beloved Community within the villages of Galilee.

G. HIS INSTRUCTIONS TO THE VILLAGERS

As previously mentioned, we have a substantial number of Jesus's one-liners and parables preserved by his first followers in Galilee, those who were with him in the villages and who knew him personally. We also have additional teachings of his scattered throughout the Gospels of Mark, Matthew, and Luke. Further, we now have the scholarly tools to discern which of those teachings in the Gospels originated with Jesus and which were attributed to him by later authors. As we explore his original teachings, we see those teachings forming a coherent pattern. They fit together, especially when we view them from the perspective of first-century Galilean peasants, struggling under the oppressive rule of the Roman government.

His teachings revolve around instructions for the village peasants in their new life together, living as God would have them live (your will be done, on earth as it is in heaven). As we move beyond our modern tendency to interpret Jesus's teachings in an individualistic manner, and we begin to pay attention to the community aspects of his words, they make much more sense to that day and, consequently, to our day. When viewed from the perspective of Jesus as a community organizer, his one-liners and parables come alive in a fresh new way. We see the brilliance of Jesus as a teacher, for he was seeking to accomplish a very challenging task—teach people how to change their whole way of organizing their village life. People do not accept change readily, and for Jesus to be successful he would have to be a superb teacher and organizer. From the evidence, we can say he was both.

H. JESUS'S BROTHER JAMES

In addition to the evidence already presented, there is the socialistic community of shared resources in Jerusalem led by James the brother of Jesus. Following the death of Jesus, a group of his followers stayed in Jerusalem.

According to the book of Acts, they developed a radical style community of shared property and resources. It was an urban expression of the rural sharing communities Jesus established in Galilee. It is evident James got the idea for this type of sharing community from his brother Jesus.

What kind of share-community did Jesus establish? If the Jerusalem commune led by Jesus's brother James was indeed patterned after the Galilean village communities, it does not appear they sold the houses in which they lived. The book of Acts declares that the Jerusalem followers of Jesus ate their shared meals in one another's homes. They did not all live under one roof. Nor is it likely the Galilean villagers sold their homes, or sold absolutely everything they owned. They must have kept their own furniture and household items. Since they were a sharing community, they may have sold some items each individual did not need to possess, items they could share with one another, such as farm equipment. What they certainly shared was the income they gained and the food they produced. They probably also contributed clothing and food to a central supply for use by anyone in need. Thus they could be described as an intentional sharing community.

We should also note the New Testament letter attributed to James is very similar in content to the teachings in the gospels that originated with Jesus. They both emphasize the importance of ethics over beliefs and action over faith. As with James, beliefs were not Jesus's main concern. What mattered most was behavior, not just of individuals, but of the community and how it was organized for the common good of everyone in the village. Thus, in both the communal arrangement James established in Jerusalem and the New Testament letter attributed to him, James serves as corroborating evidence for Jesus as a community organizer.

I. PAUL AS EVIDENCE

As we have noted, Paul never met Jesus and his writings show very little interest in the life and teachings of Jesus. His focus was on the death and resurrection of Jesus, as he saw it. Paul, therefore, does not provide much help in getting to know Jesus of Nazareth. However, his letters to the churches do give us a glimpse of the communal relationships in his churches. He makes it clear that in Christ all the walls of separation between humans (male and female, Jew and Greek, etc.) have been broken down. His churches were egalitarian in nature, open to everyone, just as Jesus's village share-communities were egalitarian and open to all. So Paul, in his own way, does provide some additional evidence of the nature of the village communities Jesus established in Galilee.

J. JESUS'S CENTRAL THEME

The central theme of Jesus's teaching was the kingdom of God. When Jesus mentioned the kingdom of God, he thought of something very down to earth and real, the Beloved Community in the villages of Galilee. The kingdom of God was not a reality God would establish sometime in the future through divine intervention. Neither was it a complicated theological concept nor a utopian ideal in the mind of Jesus. It was a practical social-economic reality in the here and now, one the peasants could readily understand and put into practice in their villages. As such it serves as further evidence that Jesus was a community organizer in the villages of first-century Galilee. The kingdom of God he was establishing was designed to meet basic human needs. Jesus lived out the kingdom of cooperation and compassion in his own life and urged others to live in that way.

What we see in Jesus is the beginning of the establishment of the kingdom of God here on earth in a specific time and place, the villages of Galilee. It is the beginning of a new era in the way people can learn to live together in this world. Jesus's teachings were completely this-worldly. Sadly, a world-renouncing strain quickly developed in early Gentile Christianity, as seen in 1 John 2:15–16:

> Do not love the world or the things in the world. The love of the Father is not in those who love the world; for all that is in the world—the desire of the flesh, the desire of the eyes, the pride in riches—comes not from the Father but from the world.

This passage is tragically wrong in its emphasis on turning away from the world and renouncing the things of this world. Jesus's concern was for people in this world and how they could live together in a mutually beneficial way.

This kingdom (or realm) is characterized by a village living together in the way God intended, according to the will of God. As a Jew, Jesus saw God's will as revealed in the Hebrew Scriptures, building on ancient traditional Jewish roots. For Jesus, the practice of communal sharing of resources in the villages of first-century Galilee could be the beginning of the kingdom of God on earth: the place where God's will is done on earth as it is in heaven, people living together in the way God wants them to live. His message was not directed toward a supernatural kingdom in life after death, but a kingdom of social justice and equality here and now.

Jesus had a single-minded devotion to helping the peasants establish this new social-economic system in the villages of Galilee. The Gospels portray the strategy of Jesus as traveling from village to village with a sense of urgency, and then sending his disciples to the villages he would be unable to visit. His goal was to enable each village to develop and adopt his vision and program of the kingdom of God as a way of surviving and even thriving under the oppressive rule of the Roman Empire.

Jesus had a vision of the kingdom of God (communal sharing of resources) and a program to establish the kingdom in the villages of Galilee. He lived and taught an alternative lifestyle to each village willing to accept it. His compassion for the peasants went beyond almsgiving to a plan to rebuild and revitalize the peasant villages through a radical redistribution of resources.

K. JESUS'S DEATH AND THE ROMAN EMPIRE

Jesus was not trying to change the Roman Empire at large or to change governmental policy within Israel. That was not within the realm of possibility for a Jewish peasant from Galilee. He was also not seeking to overthrow the political authorities or drive the Roman rulers out of Galilee. Jesus realized the futility of trying to dislodge the entrenched power of the Romans. He did not, therefore, advocate armed resistance to Roman rule.

It was a social revolution Jesus inaugurated, not a military revolution. His aim was to change the behavior of each Jewish village in Galilee living under the rule of the Roman Empire. And this is exactly what he sought to do. He instituted a social change from the bottom up rather than from the top down. He taught the villagers a better way to live, one that did not depend upon the attitudes or actions of the ruling class. The peasants could live as healthy individuals in a healthy community no matter what their rulers said or did. Jesus's goal was to reorganize and revitalize life in the villages, upholding the traditional Hebraic values of community, empowering the villagers living under Roman rule. The most common view of Jesus is that he came to teach individuals about salvation and how to enter into heaven. If Jesus had confined his activities to that purpose he most likely could have lived to a ripe old age. In fact, if that is all he did, why would anyone want to kill him? Especially, why would the Roman government want to execute him? Jesus, however, was not just a religious teacher, confining himself to spiritual matters. He didn't just talk about the kingdom of God, he organized the villagers into sharing communes. This got the attention of both the Roman authorities and the Jewish religious elite in the temple in Jerusalem. They rightly viewed him as a revolutionary figure, upsetting the status quo and threatening the established way of life. The Roman governor of Galilee, Herod Antipas, and the temple leadership in Jerusalem, therefore, would have monitored Jesus's activities very closely.

Two people were mainly responsible for the death of Jesus. One was Caiaphas, the corrupt high priest of the Jerusalem temple from 18–37 CE. The other was Pontius Pilate, the cruel Roman ruler of Judea (the southern province of Israel) from 26–37 CE. They knew each other well and were long-time collaborators.

Here is what happened. Jesus and some of his male and female followers (including members of his family) decided to make a pilgrimage from Galilee to Jerusalem for the annual Passover festival. This festival was a dangerous situation related to possible insurrection against the Roman rulers. Each year large numbers of Jewish pilgrims came to the city of Jerusalem. The seven-day Passover festival commemorated Israel's escape from slavery in Egypt. It stirred up strong feelings regarding the lack of freedom the Jews were experiencing under Roman imperial power. The Roman authorities were always ready to deal with any signs of trouble that might arise during the Passover celebration.

When Jesus came to Jerusalem for the annual Passover celebration, he entered the center of Jewish worship, the Jerusalem temple. He saw the exploitation of the poor by the temple elite. His understanding of the kingdom of God as cooperation and sharing was very different from the oppression of the poor by the temple hierarchy. He began to drive out those who sold and bought in the temple. He overturned the tables of the moneychangers who exchanged Roman money for the Hebrew money required for use in the temple. They were cheating the people as they exchanged the money. Jesus also drove out those who sold pigeons to the poor for the required sacrifices, for they were charging exorbitant prices. This action confirmed the suspicions of the high priest of the temple, Caiaphas, and the Roman governor, Pilate, about Jesus. Though his actions of establishing communal sharing villages in Galilee could have gotten Jesus arrested at any moment, his behavior in the temple provided the opportunity for Caiaphas and Pilate to act. They both had been in power in Israel for many years, and these two long-time collaborators, therefore, had Jesus arrested.

Jesus was regarded as a threat to the Roman order, and he was executed by crucifixion under the Roman authority. Crucifixion was the punishment reserved for slaves and for those who threatened the social order of the Roman Empire. Such a painful public and humiliating death was meant to intimidate anyone who might seek to undermine Roman authority. In fact, thousands of Jews were crucified under Roman rule.

Jesus died because of his vision and program for the kingdom of God, the Beloved Community of equality and compassion. His death by crucifixion at the hands of the Romans is the final piece of evidence indicating Jesus was a social reformer, a community organizer who was a threat to the established order of the Empire. Jesus must have known his words and deeds as a community organizer would put his own life in jeopardy. Jesus had the courage and selflessness to remain true to his vision to the very end. His death, therefore, was not viewed by his followers as an embarrassing defeat, but as the death of a martyr who stood firm in his devotion to the cause of establishing the kingdom of God in the villages of Galilee.

His death, however, did not end the Jesus Movement in Galilee. What he started in the villages of Galilee continued on substantially as it had before his death. We know this to be the case because the Jesus People of Galilee continued the movement and wrote down his instructions of how their village life should be organized into share-communities, the kingdom of God on earth.

SOCIALIST OR CAPITALIST? LIBERAL OR CONSERVATIVE?

In summing up what we can know about Jesus, how would we describe him? What terms fit the evidence? Was Jesus a socialist or a capitalist, a liberal or a conservative? Though none of these labels would have been known to Jesus, the evidence points to the conclusion Jesus was a mixture of these designations. In his communities, individuals still owned their own property and maintained their own individual employment. Yet they also shared their resources in a communal manner. Jesus, therefore, could be said to be a mixture of a socialist and a capitalist. He was also a mixture of a liberal and a conservative. There were certain values from his Jewish heritage he wanted to conserve, such as the economic principles from the Torah and the Hebrew social prophets. There were also some radical new changes he wanted to inaugurate in the villages of Galilee. Jesus was introducing a new approach to community life, balancing competition with compassion, individualism with cooperation. The new economic plan Jesus inaugurated was a mixed economy, combining the best elements of capitalism and socialism. It balanced self-interest with the interests of others. It was a daring transformation of economic and social life of truly momentous proportions.

We might also ask if Jesus was a utopian, hoping to start some perfect society here on earth. The answer is that Jesus was pragtopian, a pragmatist seeking to change human behavior by first changing human communities. His approach was practical, requiring action. He was an activist, not just a theoretical thinker or talker. His goal was to build compassionate sharing communities. He was seeking to accomplish something practical for the people in the villages of Galilee, a sample of the kingdom of God for others to observe and emulate.

All of the evidence points to the conclusion that Jesus was a communitarian, a community organizer, who knew a wholesome community is necessary in creating wholesome individuals. For Jesus, the kingdom of God was a collective concept. It is not simply a matter of changing individuals, but of transforming communities.

The tendency today is to think of being a Christian as something a person does alone. The focus is on individual commitment to Jesus Christ, and living in such a way that you as an individual will enter into heaven after you die. Most Christian books are about self-improvement and an individual relationship with God. The focus is on individual and personal happiness, on what you as an individual must do to live a Christian life. Almost all of the Christian communication through magazines, books, the pulpit, and television is directed to the individual and his or her personal journey. There is little or nothing addressing the communal aspects of the Christian faith. This is in stark contrast to Jesus's focus on the quality of community life as central to the welfare of each person in the community.

It is my hope this examination of the evidence has enabled you, the reader, to find the missing person Jesus of Nazareth, and having found him, discover his original intention, what he was trying to accomplish with his life. It is also my hope you will honor Jesus's purpose and intention by focusing not just on one's personal religious life, but the common good of everyone in the community. In addition, I hope any religious community wanting to follow Jesus will seek to emulate what Jesus was seeking to establish in the villages of Galilee, not by replicating the pattern appropriate to that situation, but by applying the truths Jesus taught and practiced to today's world. That will be the subject of part 2.

And this wraps up the case of the most famous missing person in history, Jesus of Nazareth. By following the evidence, we have found the person who has been missing from the creeds of the church and most of the New Testament, and who has been hidden all these centuries within the four New Testament gospels. He may be a surprise to you, and he may even upset your comfortable way of thinking about him. Like a detective on the case, it has been my goal to take an honest look at the evidence regarding the missing person Jesus of Nazareth and draw the best conclusions possible from that evidence.

Part Two

Building the Beloved Community

11

Following Jesus

In addition to the five standard questions reporters are instructed to ask (who, what, where, when, and why), there is also the additional question, so what? Does it make any difference today for us to find the missing Jesus of Nazareth of 2,000 years ago? Does it matter what his original purpose was, what he was trying to accomplish with his mission in Galilee? If this quest for Jesus the man is just an intellectual exercise, then it is nothing more than a curiosity. If, however, we can take what we learn and apply it to today's world, then the quest has great significance for us. The quest is always carried out in light of the vital issues of our day.

It is my conviction Jesus and his teachings do matter in our world today. He had profound insights into the human dilemma. The basic human problem is the human tendency to look out for ourselves at the expense of everyone else. This self-centered way of life creates division between people, pitting individuals against one another in a frantic race to get ahead of other people. The result is a breakdown in caring and supportive relationships, with one group seeking to exploit other groups for their own enrichment. Jesus had an answer for the human dilemma. He knew how to transform communities and how to create responsible human beings within communities. Those insights are very much needed today.

The challenge for individuals as well as faith communities is how to translate the words and deeds of Jesus from his situation in first-century rural Galilee to our modern world today. This means we must be aware of the human dilemma of the peasants of that world, as well as the solutions he offered to them. We must then translate those solutions into our own world today. It is the purpose of part 2 of this book to offer guidance for that endeavor.

"FOLLOW ME"

As one reads the Gospels of Mark, Matthew and Luke, it becomes clear the call of Jesus is "follow me" (Mark 2:14; 10:21; Matt 4:19; 4:22; 9:9; 16:24; 19:21; Luke 5:27; 9:23; 9:59; 18:22). *Follow* is an action word. Jesus could have meant the word literally, as he was continually on the go in his travels to the various villages of Galilee during his mission. He also could have meant the word to be a call to emulate what he stood for and what he was doing. Either way, he issued the call over and over to "follow" him. What would it mean today for an individual, congregation, or denomination to follow Jesus?

In the teachings considered by the scholars to have originated with Jesus, he never said, "Believe in me." Nor did he say, "Worship me." The difference between following and believing or worshiping is significant. Believing and worshiping are passive activities. Each can be done without any real change in one's lifestyle or behavior. Christianity as a set of beliefs or as a way to worship requires nothing but conformity and assent. In a very real sense, Christians are not called to be believers at all, not in the sense of simply assenting to a certain set of beliefs. The invitation of Jesus was not to believe in him or to worship him, but to follow him, a much more exciting and fulfilling endeavor.

The church missed its calling to follow Jesus when it decided to emphasize a set of beliefs about Jesus as the criteria for being a Christian. The church began to focus on the death of Jesus, with the result that his words and his deeds came to mean little or nothing at all. As we saw in chapter 1, for example, the Apostles' Creed proclaims Jesus was "born of the Virgin Mary, suffered under Pontius Pilate, was crucified, dead, and buried." The missing element in that statement is his life. There is not one word in the creed about what he said or did.

It is time to seriously follow Jesus the person, paying attention to his words and deeds. It means to be passionate about the things about which he was passionate, and Jesus was passionate about establishing the kingdom of God, his Beloved Communities, here on earth. To follow Jesus is not to subscribe to a set of beliefs or doctrines, but to be involved in doing the kind of thing today that Jesus was doing 2,000 years ago.

Among Christians today, there are many different beliefs about Jesus, often conflicting with one another. Whatever those beliefs may be, however, one thing should be clear: the call of Jesus is to follow him, catching the vision he had and implementing that vision as much as possible. Those who claim to believe in Jesus ought to, at a minimum, seek to follow what Jesus taught and the way he lived.

Following Jesus begins as he began, with compassion for the poor and for those who are considered outcasts by the rest of society. Faith in Jesus without respect and compassion for humanity is a lie, as his brother James pointed out (Jas 2:14–26). Unless belief in Jesus leads to compassionate acts of caring, those beliefs are hollow and empty. To identify with Jesus is to see the worth and dignity of each human being.

To follow Jesus is also to understand, as Jesus did, that goodness can and will triumph over evil. He sought to build a better world for the peasants of Galilee, calling on them to resist the oppression of the Roman Empire by establishing cooperative communities of shared resources. He read the signs of the times of his day and knew what needed to be done. Jesus had an answer to the problems the peasants were facing in that situation.

It would be foolish to try to emulate today exactly what Jesus did in Galilee almost 2,000 years ago. What he did then would likely be unworkable on a large scale. What we can do, however, is begin to analyze our times in the same spirit he analyzed his. We can catch the bold and courageous vision he had and apply it to today's world. An important first step is to better understand the situation Jesus faced and the answer he provided, as seen in part 1 of this book. and then challenge faith communities to follow in his footsteps. Today, to follow Jesus means to be about the business of building a better world, one community at a time, a world where everyone has a better opportunity to have their basic needs met and to live life to the fullest.

Arguing over beliefs only divides us, as can be seen in the many denominations and churches found throughout Christianity. Perhaps, though, liberal and conservative Christians could come together now by allowing each one to have their own beliefs or opinions about Jesus Christ, and deciding to work together to follow Jesus in making this a better world for each person, one community at a time.

If individuals and congregations and denominations want to truly follow Jesus, they will be about the task of creating a better world right here, right now, meeting basic needs, ensuring equal rights, leaving no one out. When that is the goal, then the details of what to do and how to accomplish the goal will become clear.

A KINGDOM OF THIS WORLD

The kingdom of God Jesus envisioned is purely of this world: it is a new way of relating to one another in communities of compassion and cooperation. The new life Jesus offered was not an escape from this world to some other place where a person will live forever. The call of Jesus was to make this world a better place, here and now. As we noted earlier, Jesus's sayings and parables were completely this-worldly. The kingdom of God is not a belief system; it is simply lived day by day in relationship to others, with justice and empathy. When we look around our modern world it is clear the great need today is not new creeds, but a new basis for relationships among human beings.

Unfortunately, instead of following Jesus, through the centuries the church built its theology around the goal of individual personal salvation, with the promise of guaranteed entrance into a heaven in the life to come. This approach ignored the communal aspect of Jesus's words and deeds, making faith a private matter, often resulting in an exclusive focus on one's personal life, with minimal amount of concern for this world. The emphasis on personal salvation and eternal life, however, is out of step with Jesus's teaching of the kingdom of God as a cooperative endeavor in this life. It forgets or ignores the plural nature of the "you" in his teachings. Following Jesus is not about saving one's soul for eternity (a self-centered endeavor indeed), but about losing oneself in building Jesus's Beloved Community through compassion and care for others.

The goal for faith communities seeking to follow Jesus is to establish a more harmonious and equitable world, one community at a time. That is the great work to which they have been called, becoming more concerned with how we humans live together than debating the truth of various doctrines and beliefs. It is time for the churches to forget about their doctrinal differences with each other and begin to work together for the common good, especially for those with the greatest need.

Too often in the past the church has not truly involved itself in the human situation. It became strangely separated from what is going on in the world, content to create a little island of religiosity in the midst of the problems people are facing. The church must become consistently involved in working for the common good or face the prospect of becoming increasingly irrelevant to the world. To follow Jesus, the church will become more this-worldly and less other-worldly. In fact, without realizing it, the church has already begun this transformation. This can be seen, for example, in the funeral practices of the churches. In the past, the funeral message focused on the eternal destiny of the deceased. Today, this has given way to a celebration of the life of the person. In most denominations the funeral now puts less emphasis on the hope of heaven or the threat of hell and more emphasis on the quality of the life lived here on earth.

The good news is that the overall movement of the church today is toward a more this-worldly, humanitarian emphasis. The church is beginning to bring out its "better side," the side of compassion and concern for the people, the planet, and all God's creatures. It is not just focusing on converting individuals so they might live in heaven in some future world. It is working to transform the lives of people in this world. In doing so, the church is following in the footsteps of Jesus, as he proclaimed and implemented the Beloved Communities, the kingdom of God, on this earth.

The church is joining in the movement to heal the hurts of the world. It is happening in small corners of mainline denominations, evangelical churches, and the Roman Catholic Church. One of the most hopeful signs today is the emerging generation of evangelical pastors and laity who work toward peace, anti-oppression, and relief of poverty. The church is moving from the narrow religious agenda of the Religious Right, which was often used to divide people rather than bring them together. It is moving toward a broader and deeper compassion for people, bringing faith communities together around a wide variety of social issues, including poverty, peace, and the environment. On these issues, it is possible to find common ground around the common good, and to do it in a way that draws people together rather than dividing them from one another. There is a profound hunger for a new kind of spirituality, one that can speak to the major issues of the day facing our world.

THE DREAM OF JESUS

Jesus had a dream of people living together in a spirit of community and cooperation. His dream arose out of the heart of Judaism, which proclaimed a dream of a nation of economic fairness and equality, a nation that would be a light unto the world, an example of how God wants people to live in this world.

According to Luke, in Jesus's first sermon he proclaimed he was sent by God to preach good news to the poor, liberty to the imprisoned, recovery of sight to the blind, and liberation to the oppressed. In his mission in Galilee, he fulfilled that calling by forming share-communities.

Thus it is clear from the Hebrew Scriptures, as well as the deeds and teachings of Jesus, that God's major concern is the situation of the poor. It is obvious God expects people to be involved in changing the circumstances of the poor. We are to treat the poor as we would want to be treated if we were in their shoes. Jesus had both a vision and a plan to accomplish that task, the Beloved Community of shared resources to replace the selfishness and greed that were tearing the village communities apart.

For many people, however, the dream of Jesus is seen as a naive utopian fantasy. A prevailing idea today is that humanity is, and always will be, driven by divisive tribalism, competition for natural resources, and the quest for power. There will always be, it is said, an "us" and a "them," and the purpose of our nation is to protect "us" from "them." This concept presents itself as fatalistic rhetoric, proclaiming that humanity and human society is fundamentally unchangeable. In this view, humans will always be exclusively concerned with their own narrow self-interests.

Whatever partial truths there may be in these ideas, the tragic result is too many people either don't want to or have forgotten how to dream about a better world. More than that, they are afraid to dream because they do not feel empowered to dream the great dream. Thus the mentality insisting there is no alternative to greed and competition becomes a self-fulfilling prophecy.

However, scientists who study brain function have discovered the human brain is actually wired to reward cooperation, service, and caring. If our brains were not wired for life in community, we could not have survived as a species through the ages. We have an instinctual desire, also seen in the animal kingdom, to protect the group, especially the weakest and most vulnerable members, including the young.

These findings from neurological scientists are confirmed by social scientists who report that membership in a caring, cooperative community is a strong predictor of happiness and emotional health, far more than the amount of money or material consumption one has. Science from every corner corroborates this truth: biology, anthropology, psychology, and so forth.

All this confirms the dream of Jesus is not a pipedream. Those who choose to cooperate rather than ruthlessly compete are not fighting human nature. Those who learn to care and cooperate in a community setting discover this path not only provides the best chance for survival but also for happiness.

THE CALL TO THE CHURCH

A great task of the church is to recover the dream of Jesus, not by looking nostalgically at past eras of human history, but by committing itself to creating hope for a better world. Jesus asserted that God's essential nature is caring, compassionate, peace loving, forgiving, and generous. God wants us to care not only for ourselves, but also for others. We can learn to once again dream the dream of Jesus, then work to create a world of justice and peace, human dignity and respect, human community and love. The primary challenge is to truly believe in the possibility and to begin now to help make it happen. Our willingness to dream the dream of Jesus and make it our own is the call to the faith communities of today. We can stand up and declare, *yes*, we will actually take the teachings of Jesus seriously, and we will work to make them a reality in our world today.

The church must always remember that the gospel Jesus proclaimed was "good news for the *poor*." This means the contemporary church is called to make itself and its message similarly good news for the poor. What was that good news? It was that life could be different for the poor right now through the redistribution of their resources as they learned a new way of cooperation with one another, rather than wearing themselves out in fruitless competition with one another.

We should note that Jesus never asked the poor what brought them to their state of poverty or whose fault it was. Evidently, to Jesus it didn't matter *why* a person was poor. This is in stark contrast to our modern tendency to blame the poor for their poverty, to shame them for the resulting cultural traits, style of dress, tastes, language, and activities associated with poverty. Jesus never did this, nor should the church.

The church is our communal way of developing dreams and visions of how our communities—indeed our world—might be made better, and how we can work together to make that happen. The joy of religion is to dream and plan ways we can make our world a better place, one community at a time, for all human beings and all creatures on our earth.

This call to make our world a better place is not a call to a utopian delusion. The kingdom Jesus envisioned is not perfection on this earth, but a call to growth toward perfection. We will never have a perfect neighborhood, town, city, country, or world, yet we must seek a "more perfect union" on all these levels of society. Every step toward a more perfect world is worthwhile. Here we can follow the principle of Alcoholics Anonymous: progress, not perfection.

This call to the church is not a conservative or a liberal idea. The church can find common ground with both by calling each to a higher ground. The church can affirm the best of both liberal and conservative ideas and rise above the old conflicts. No matter what our differences may be, do we not all share the vision of a better world? Is it not a world of balance, one rewarding individual initiative while at the same time seeking communal well-being? Do we not all benefit from a world respecting diversity while celebrating our unifying ideals? And isn't the church in the most advantageous position to call out the best from both the liberal and conservative traditions?

It is difficult to know exactly what the future of the churches will be and how they will be organized to fulfill the calling to be about the task of making this a better world for everyone. We do know the process will be democratic. There is no one leader to unveil the mysteries or guide the mass of people in a spiritual direction. Today there are no more religious giants. We have outgrown the old teacher/disciple relationship and have become democratized. This is true in the secular world and must continue to become true in the churches. There is no one blueprint fitting every church or every community. Each religious tradition must be left free to work out the most effective means to share in the building of the Beloved Communities of Jesus.

Jesus had the wisdom to know a basic truth: good communities help make good people. He didn't waste his time and energy trying to determine whether humans are inherently good or evil, or arguing over other philosophical issues. He concentrated on the conditions making it possible for the good to emerge and the evil to be curtailed. For that reason, he became a community organizer in the villages of Galilee, setting the pattern for the church to be about the business of community organizing in the world today. If churches want to follow Jesus, they will come together in organizing our communities into healthy, wholesome places producing healthy, wholesome individuals.

THE CHURCH AS COMMUNITY

The church must also *be* a community, a place where people can feel connected to one another. A major task of any congregation is helping people develop a sense of belonging, forming strong relationships with one another.

The church is meant to be an alternative community. The life of the church can demonstrate what Jesus stood for by living a different kind of life in the midst of an individualistic society. While there are many other meaningful forms of human community available, the church offers the possibility of relationships with deeper meaning and purpose. Jesus developed this strong sense of community in the villages by establishing share-communities. While the modern church cannot replicate Jesus's pattern exactly, it can be a place of shared resources for everyone, a place where people know they are being cared for and accepted as they are, a place where a person can turn for help in a time of need. The church is at its best not when it is constructing bigger and more beautiful buildings, but when it is caring for its own people while at the same time reaching out in genuine caring to the community around it.

A church of any size can be a place of community, a place where people can satisfy their need for a sense of belonging and connections. Many Americans today are feeling disconnected from one another. A key role of a church is to provide opportunities for people to feel connected. The recent success of the megachurches revolves around the fact they are a collection of small communities—hundreds of small groups meeting a variety of needs and interests, little congregations held together by common values and friendships.

Two of the great cravings in the heart of humanity are the hunger for belonging and the hunger for meaning in one's life. The church is in the unique position to meet both hungers by offering the combination of a sense of belonging and an opportunity to make a difference in the world. The two belong together, and combined they give a sense of spirituality to a person's life. Each person wants to feel connected to other people and wants to feel his or her life counts for something. So the healthy church provides opportunities for connectedness and for social action in the larger community.

The church can be a center of community within the larger community. Of all the institutions in our society, the church ought to be the most accepting, most nonjudgmental, most inclusive community of all. Just as Jesus's share-communities were open to all, including the outcasts of society, so the church must be an open community where each person is loved and accepted. The church, following in the footsteps of Jesus, can be a place where people feel connected to one another, while at the same time challenging and enabling people to be part of something bigger than themselves.

The church, like Jesus's Beloved Communities of Galilee, can be a "light unto the world," a sample of the product called "the kingdom of God." It can be a model of altruism, compassion, and empathy, teaching society the necessity of caring, sharing, cooperation, and love. The church ought to stand for the things Jesus stood for, being involved in making this world a better place, one community at a time. The church is to be a model of the kingdom of God, the Beloved Community, life lived together as God intends for live to be lived.

The good news is, in America and worldwide, there is a growing desire for community. People want to be a part of something bigger than themselves, helping to improve their neighborhoods and their communities. At a time when there is so much separation and fragmentation in our society, people have started to hunger for community. People long to belong and to make a difference in their community, so the time is ripe for the church to follow Jesus through the creation of Beloved Communities.

12

Individualism and Community in America

ONE OF THE MAJOR obstacles to building Beloved Communities within the communities of America is our nation's rampant individualism. Over the past fifteen years, authors such as Robert D. Putnam, Robert Wuthnow, and Robert N. Bellah have rightly noted that America has become the most individualistic society in our world, perhaps in all of human history. Along with a number of American historians and sociologists, they have examined the increasing lack of community in America and its resulting consequences. Using a variety of measures to determine the degree of individualism versus community, they have concluded that America tops all other nations when its comes to the focus on the individual instead of the community as the measure of all things. We suffer from an excess of individualism and a deficiency of a sense of community.

Despite our foundations as a predominantly Christian nation, we have lost the sense of the common good and the commonwealth characterizing this country in its founding years. In fact, five of the original thirteen states used the term *commonwealth* to identify who they were, such as the Commonwealth of Virginia and the Commonwealth of Massachusetts. It was understood the chief purpose of government was to use the common wealth of the community for the common good. The common wealth of the state would build the infrastructure enhancing the life of each individual in the state: firefighters, police, criminal justice system, highways, bridges, public transit, food inspections, public school system, banking system, public assistance for the needy, a social safety net, and much more.

Each village also had a "commons" at its center, a public space for the residents of the village to gather together. There was a balance between the individual and the community, with each enhancing the other. The genius of America's founders was the concept of pooling the common wealth for the common good, thus enabling individuals to achieve their own goals and welfare. The government's job was to administer the common wealth for the common good of everyone.

In modern America, the pendulum has swung radically to the side of individualism, creating a society of very isolated and lonely people, as well as dividing and separating individuals from one another. This has been devastating on family and community values. It has also fostered a system allowing the rich to become even wealthier, while the poor have become even poorer. In fact, the gap between the richest and the poorest of our nation is becoming more like the huge economic gap existing in Jesus's day.

This one-sided emphasis on individualism is built on an erroneous foundation. It fails to recognize the fact we are first and foremost social beings. Community precedes individuality. We are a part of the web of life. None of us exists in a vacuum. As John Donne expressed it, "No man is an island, entire of itself; every man is a piece of the continent, a part of the main" ("Meditation XVII").

We are dependent and interdependent human beings before we are independent individuals. Only in relationships do we develop the qualities making us human—in the family first, and then in the larger community through neighbors, friends, classmates, teachers, coaches, and many others. We are who we are primarily through the relationships we have with others. Individuality can develop and be experienced only in the context of relationships with other human beings.

The way our society is organized makes it easy to believe in the primacy of the individual over community. Those who are most successful in our society are especially prone to forget the interdependent nature of existence and the interrelated factors that enabled them to reach their level of success. There is a tendency to think they have made it on their own, ignoring the fact we are each held and supported by the web of life surrounding each person. It is also easy for the wealthy to become consumed by self-justifying greed, wanting to accumulate more and more for oneself. The truth, however, is no individual or business can function at all without the framework of the common wealth. Every successful person uses the common wealth of society for his or her own good. There are no self-made individuals. We are each interdependent as well as independent.

Individualism is not bad in and of itself. It provides a sense of personal identity and helps us define healthy boundaries. It can also affirm the worth and dignity of each person. Through it, we can, therefore, be more accepting of other individuals, letting each person live one's own life. Individualism allows us to take pride in our achievements, fosters innovation, creativity, and an experimental spirit. It allows us to choose our own lifestyle and enjoy our privacy. There are many healthy aspects to a sense of individualism.

Excessive individualism, however, harms both the individual and society. It leads to unhealthy self-indulgence, causing one to be more concerned about his or her own good than the common good. It creates loneliness and destroys the sense of connectedness every human being needs in order to be fully human. People become overly desirous of privacy and less involved in the public sphere or village commons. This creates a loss of that sense of tribe or social life so important to human development. If individuals lack connection, empathy, and compassion for others, social problems set in, such as racism, sexism, homophobia, etc. The result is more frequent homicide, thefts, health problems, environmental destruction, and mental/emotional problems. Countries emphasizing individualism over the common good often have a higher number of unhappy people, as well as high crime and suicide rates. Individualism can also undermine a concern for future generations, as seen in America's attitude toward the environment and climate change in recent years. The result is we all lose when we isolate ourselves from cooperation, community, and a commitment to the common good.

Rampant individualism also exacts a price in its destruction of communal well-being. Consider, for example, the problem of the pollution of our air, water, and land. An individualist might say, "It will cost me, or my company, lots of money to install pollution-control equipment. Anyway, my pollution is small compared to the larger problem." If everyone reasoned this way, the result would be polluted air, water, and land. Thus, choices made individually become collectively harmful when others make the same decision to keep polluting. This is but one example. The need is to balance individual rights with communal rights. The only institution in a position to enforce this balancing act is the legal apparatus of the government, functioning as the guarantor of the common good in relation to individualism.

Antigovernment radical individualism is fostered when politicians and political parties express negative attitudes toward the government. When they campaign for elected office by running against the government ("government is not the solution; government is the problem"), the result is a loss of the sense of community and the common good. This disdain for government breeds a destructive individualism and can even result in a negative attitude toward obedience to the law.

This extreme individualism can also be seen in negative attitudes toward taxation. Taxes are a primary way of expressing support for the common good through a variety of governmental activities serving the needs of society: schools, parks, roads, health care, social programs, defense, police, and so on. Taxes are a way in which individuals express their concern for the common good. Through taxes, individuals pool their resources and receive benefits far greater than their individual tax money could accomplish on its own. The purpose of taxes is to use the common wealth to provide and maintain the common infrastructure that enables each person to follow their individual dreams. The common good is served when the common wealth (through taxes) is used to benefit everyone in society. To treat taxes as if they are evil is to undermine the sense of community and the common good so important to the functioning of a healthy society.

Rampant individualism is also seen in what some call our YOYO economy: You're On Your Own. When it is every person for himself or herself, a sense of anxiety and insecurity about one's economic future is inevitable. In reality, the daily operations of our capitalistic society give people justifiable reasons to be fearful. The YOYO economy is deeply oriented toward economic insecurity and fear. This economic fear breeds greed. People fear that the loss of one's job or a catastrophic illness will put them in extreme financial jeopardy. The basic fear is a scarcity of resources, the feeling there won't be enough to go around, so the desire to hold on to what one has becomes paramount. Surrounded by selfishness, individuals feel foolish if they do not look out for themselves, even at the expense of others, and certainly at the expense of the common good. In a YOYO economy, the primary feeling is everyone else is looking out for their own self-interest, so I will be a loser unless I look after my own self-interest, accumulating as much as I can for myself to protect against an unknown and uncertain future.

In the last few decades, as America has become more of an individualistic society, economic insecurity has increased greatly. The middle class feels squeezed financially in a way once felt only by the poor. With the exception of the rich, whether the government reports the economy is going up or going down, the average American feels anxious about his or her economic future. Guaranteed pensions and health insurance have virtually disappeared, especially for low-income wage earners. Prices for goods have increased while wages for workers have remained stagnant. In this situation, Jesus's words to "be not anxious" about food and clothing. fall on deaf ears, for each person knows his or her economic situation can change in an instant as a factory closes, or a company downsizes, or a corporation moves out of the country, or a family member encounters a serious illness. Understandably, Jesus's words to "take no thought for tomorrow" are ignored when everyone is on their own regarding their economic future. The individual or family may be only one or two paychecks away from economic ruin or losing their home. The way our economy operates gives people considerable reason to be anxious and fearful.

Much like the situation Jesus encountered in the villages of Galilee, there is a lack in the sense of community and commonality to undergird individual basic needs and security. Just as social, governmental, political, military, and economic forces at work in Jesus's time had combined to create a quality of life that left basic needs unmet, so these same forces have come together in our own time, with similar negative results. In that situation Jesus could rightly advise the villagers to "take no thought for tomorrow" because he taught them to become a community of shared resources where there would always be enough for each person. This is not to say it was easy for them to trust in the power of community. Yet villagers did trust in the power of communal sharing to enable them to develop Beloved Communities in their villages.

Jesus knew the problem with people is not just individual greed and selfishness. The way a community or society is organized either enhances or inhibits the qualities of compassion, community, and concern for the common good. A highly individualistic and capitalistic society creates personal anxiety and fear, undermining the humane qualities of generosity and kindness. People feel they have to look out primarily for themselves, even at the expense of others.

On the other hand, an emphasis on the common good creates healthier communities, societies, and individuals. Such places tend to have less crime, higher academic achievement, lower mortality rates, better health care, and more efficient and effective government. This is true regardless of the wealth or educational level of the community or the society.

According to the United Nations Human Development Report of 2005, countries having a blend of individualism and community, capitalism and socialism, such as Norway, Sweden, Denmark, Germany, Japan, Iceland, Australia, Canada, Switzerland, Belgium, France, and the United Kingdom are also the healthiest and the happiest. They have higher life expectancy, per capita income, educational achievement, and gender equality. They also have lower crime rates, infant mortality, abortion, sexually transmitted diseases, and teen pregnancy. The evidence is clear: it makes a difference how a nation organizes its society and the emphasis it places on the common good.

Fortunately, America's one-sided emphasis on individualism and capitalism is not fixed in concrete. There can again be a balance between individualism and community, between capitalism and compassion. The task of the church is to be the conscience of society and call our nation back to its roots of the common good. Sadly, the one-sided emphasis in America on individualism has often been fostered by the church with its focus on individual salvation and individual success, rather than the building of the Beloved Community. We now have the opportunity to refocus our churches and our nation on the true message of Jesus, reaching back to his message about the importance of community building.

THE COMMON GOOD

A great need in America is to recover the concept of the common good as a counterbalance to the rampant individualism permeating our society. This means seeing ourselves as a community, not just a collection of individuals with narrow interests.

The common good does not ignore the individual, but places the individual within the context of society as a whole. The common good means each person has what is needed to live a full human life: food, clothing, housing, health care, education, and work. These are basic to being human, and the idea of the common good brings these needs to the forefront of the national agenda.

The common good has its original roots in the Torah, the Hebrew prophets, and the life and teachings of Jesus. The Torah sets forth instructions for shared prosperity within the community. When Israel strayed from those instructions, the social prophets of Israel called the nation back to this vision of the common good. In his Beloved Communities Jesus sought the common good of everyone in the village, calling the people back to this ancient vision of economic and social equality. Today the church will be faithful to the biblical vision when it seeks the common good in our society. Based on its own religious tradition, the church must continually raise the question, Whatever became of the common good? The church is called on to challenge our government to be a government "of the people, by the people, and for the people." When people feel there is fairness in the economy and a basic fairness in the tax structure, the result is an improvement in the sense of community, as well as an increased commitment to one another. When there is a sense of shared prosperity and shared responsibility, people feel connected to the whole, and human behavior changes for the better.

In addition to it biblical roots, the common good is also rooted in the United States Constitution. The Preamble to the Constitution states:

> We, the People of the United States, in order to form a more perfect union, establish justice, insure domestic tranquility, provide for the common defense, promote the general welfare, and secure the blessings of liberty to ourselves and our posterity, do ordain and establish this Constitution for the United States of America.

In this Preamble four purposes are listed for which our government exists:

A. *To establish justice* means a basic fairness within the nation, especially regarding the laws of the land. No one is above the law and everyone is to be treated justly and fairly before the law.

B. *To insure domestic tranquility* refers to the need for government to provide a means for people within the nation to live together in a lawful and orderly manner.

C. *To provide for the common defense* means a united defense is needed to withstand enemy threats. Each state on its own would be unable to defend itself against an attacking enemy.

D. *To promote the general welfare* reflects the concept of the common good. The government is charged with promoting the welfare of all of its citizens.

The fourth purpose of government "to promote the general welfare" reflects the concept of the common good. The common good, therefore, has both religious and constitutional roots in America. The church must be in the forefront of reminding Americans of this dual heritage of the common good, reclaiming the balance between individualism and the common good, a balance that creates the best conditions in which the human spirit can flourish. Writing of the interconnectedness of all of life, Martin Luther King Jr. proclaimed, "Injustice anywhere is a threat to justice everywhere. We are caught in an inescapable network of mutuality, tied in a single garment of destiny" ("Letter from Birmingham City Jail").

Today the pendulum has swung dramatically away from community toward individualism. The exaggerated emphasis on free market capitalism and self-interest at the expense of the common good needs to be replaced with an emphasis on compassion, cooperation, and our common bonds. Many of America's current problems (the economy, high crime rates, poverty, loneliness, anxiety, insecurity) arise out of the failure to honor and respect the common good. We have forgotten the ancient religious truth: good communities help create good individuals.

The church today has a call to a great mission: to offer America a clear and compelling vision for our nation's future by calling it back to its religious and secular roots of the common good. For the church, a commitment to Jesus of Nazareth and his understanding of the kingdom of God mandates that we seek the common good for our society. The challenge is for clergy, lay leaders, seminaries, theologians, and ordinary worshipers to lead a movement to recover the concept of the common good. In doing so, we will discover we really do need each other. As in the Beloved Communities of Jesus, each person has something to give and something to receive. When we recover the idea of the common good, we can then find common ground on many of the issues currently dividing us from one another.

Let's make the common good common again.

13

How to Start a Beloved Community

MARGARET MEAD ONCE SAID, "Never doubt that a small group of thoughtful, committed citizens can change the world. Indeed, it is the only thing that ever has."

Jesus demonstrated the truth of Margaret Mead's observation. He did not operate as a solitary individual seeking to change the situation of the Jewish peasants in Galilee. He was not a Lone Ranger. Jesus was aware of the inability of one human being acting alone to accomplish the purpose of community development. He enlisted, therefore, a group of followers, "a small group of thoughtful, committed citizens," to work with him. He taught and empowered his disciples to do what he was doing: change people's lives by changing their communities.

The modern faith community is a cooperative enterprise of thoughtful committed followers of Jesus that could likewise work to change the world for the good of all people. The advantage the church has is that it is already a community of committed people. Through the church, people work together, not simply as individuals, but as members of a larger community. Working as part of a faith community is essential, for each person alone is unable to see all that must be seen, and alone, each person lacks the strength to accomplish all that must be done.

As I use the term *church* in this context, I mean a wide variety of congregations and denominations: mainline Protestant, evangelical, Pentecostal, Roman Catholic, Unitarian Universalist, and any other faith community that wishes to be a part of the process of establishing the Beloved Community in our cities and towns. The building of the Beloved Community need not be restricted to Christianity. Though this was Jesus's vision, we can work together with the Jewish, Muslim, and Asian faiths in the task of community development. The word *church* is, therefore, meant to be an inclusive rather than exclusive term.

It should be noted at the outset that community organizing is not easy. In fact, the history of community organizing in America is not encouraging. There have been many questions raised about the effectiveness of efforts to help the poor. For decades, well-intentioned individuals and groups have tried and failed to solve the many problems facing the poor in our country. Many programs were begun through President Lyndon Johnson's War on Poverty. They were often unsuccessful because they were handed down from the top, did not involve the indigenous population in the planning, were too short-term, and were not well managed. These failures led to a backlash against community development.

More recently, however, there has been a new effort by government, foundations, social workers, nonprofits, and religious groups to address poverty and social problems. Learning from past mistakes, these efforts are showing encouraging signs of progress and change. The time is ripe for faith communities to follow in the footsteps of Jesus by being involved in the process of community transformation.

To address the practical question of how to start a Beloved Community, I want to address a series of questions. This will provide the necessary basic practical information for an individual or congregation to take the steps toward establishing a local expression of the Beloved Community.

A. WHAT IN THE WORLD CAN WE DO?

There is much the church can do. It is important to recognize that there are several different levels of social action steps available to be taken in forming the Beloved Community. Each step is valuable in the process, and each successive step becomes more challenging and difficult.

1. Service. Acts of social service include the establishment of a food pantry, a clothing closet, a meal program, tutoring, child care, youth clubs, scouts, programs for senior citizens, a free medical clinic, or counseling services of various kinds. This is the traditional way by which churches and nonprofit organizations respond to a need. It is a way to do something immediately, and is the way local residents often experience the initial steps of community organizing. Relieving the symptoms, however, does not always solve the underlying social problems causing them. Little impact is made on the larger public policy issues, which may keep producing far more problems related to poverty, such as crime, substance abuse, and gang activities. Service, though, is often a good starting point, and its value should not be minimized. It is this first step felt most immediately and directly by those with the greatest need.

2. *Education.* The purpose of social education is to help people learn about the causes and cures of social issues. The goal is to inform people about the various aspects of the issues and to look at the issues in the context of our religious values. Education may take place through public meetings and forums, workshops, home discussion groups, public worship, and meal events. Through this process, people become informed about the issues and acquainted with one another, further facilitating a sense of community-building.

3. *Advocacy.* The purpose of advocacy is to work through governmental structures to affect public policy. This can include visiting elected officials, meeting with governmental agencies, writing letters to the newspaper, and giving testimony at public hearings. Through these efforts, public policy can be affected.

4. *Community Organizing.* This approach is the ultimate step in establishing the Beloved Community. It is based on the recognition that individuals have much less power to change their situations without the strength of groups who know how to organize and influence power. It is also often true that those with the greatest need have fewer skills to fight against their own oppression. Such is the nature of oppression at its roots. Poverty is disenfranchising. People in need frequently don't have the social ties, connections, resources, knowledge base, or leadership skills required to effect change. Those social facts make community organizing a challenging step indeed. It's also a potential stumbling block in that those who have the skills, knowledge, and resources may appear paternalistic or even condescending to those who do not, but who have the greatest need. These are the trappings. Jesus overcame this problem because he came to a village as neither a superior or inferior person. He came as an equal who could identify with those he wished to help.

Faith communities serving the local population, therefore, must be involved in the process of community organizing. When only outsiders are seeking to create new communities, plans and programs are often imposed on the local residents. This is counterproductive. Later in this chapter, I will highlight the details of community organizing, which includes developing a strong organization and empowering people so they can achieve self-determination. Through this endeavor, community transformation can occur, one step at a time.

B. WHERE IS A BELOVED COMMUNITY ESTABLISHED?

The quick answer is wherever there is a need. America has developed a permanent underclass, with poverty being passed down from generation to generation. The poor have largely calcified into low-income communities where the neighborhood is rife with crime, substandard housing, inadequate schools, a sense of hopelessness, and a feeling that there is no way out. All this combines to create dangerous social alienation. These low-income areas concentrate the pathologies of poverty, such as family breakdown, substance abuse, poor education, rampant crime, and a lack of social services or opportunity.

It is in these zones, relegated to poverty and despair, the faith communities need to work together for transformation to create Beloved Communities. Working with nonprofits, government, private enterprise, and the indigenous population, the faith communities can lead the way in the process of changing the climate of these impoverished areas.

An early step in building the Beloved Community is to identify a manageable geographical area. The Beloved Community can be like an oasis in a desert. The entire process works best when a particular area is identified and becomes the point of focus.

C. HOW LARGE WILL THE BELOVED COMMUNITY BE?

One of America's great jurists and thinkers, Louis Brandeis, once said there could be no true community "save that built upon the personal acquaintance of each with each." Aristotle commented that in order for a city to function properly, all its citizens should be within the range of a single man's voice. With the development of modern means of communication, today that definition is greatly expanded. The principle, however, remains valid. There must be opportunity for communication of shared values and shared hopes. There is great value in being visible to one another, seeing each other, and having live interaction with one another.

There is, however, no one size or shape of the Beloved Community that fits every situation. There will be a variety of types of Beloved Communities, each developed by the local indigenous population. The geographical area, therefore, of the Beloved Community can be a single block, four square blocks, one square mile, an urban neighborhood, one zip code, a town, a village, or some other configuration.

D. WHY ESTABLISH A BELOVED COMMUNITY?

There are two basic reasons faith communities should be involved in establishing Beloved Communities in impoverished zones. First, the Bible tells me so. As we have seen, in his first sermon, Jesus proclaimed that he was sent to preach good news to the poor, release to the captives, recovery of sight to the blind, and liberation to the oppressed (Luke 4:18). This was his mission statement, indicating what he saw as his purpose in life.

As a Jew growing up in a Jewish home in a Jewish village in a Jewish country, Jesus knew the economic principles of historic Judaism related to the practices of Sabbath and Jubilee, which recognized that a free market economy, left to itself, would end up with the poor being exploited and harmed. When ancient Israel failed to live up to these economic principles, the social prophets (Isaiah, Jeremiah, Micah, Amos, etc.) called the nation to return to its economic roots. They roundly condemned the rich for exploiting the poor, calling for radical social justice to be restored.

Jesus put the teachings of the Torah and the Prophets into practice by becoming a community developer in the villages of Galilee. He called people back to those basic principles of fairness and equality. He reached out to the poor and the outcasts of his society and taught them a new way to live in relationship to one another. He empowered them to move from selfish competition with one another for scarce resources to communal sharing of those resources.

The Bible contains thousands of verses dealing with the issue of poverty. In the Hebrew Scriptures (the Old Testament), it is the second most prominent theme, right after idolatry. In the New Testament, one out of every sixteen verses refers explicitly to the poor; while in the four Gospels, about one in ten verses is directly related to the poor and the issue of poverty. The Bible makes it clear that God has a special concern for the poor and expects his people to show compassion for the poor by actively seeking to empower them.

Second, we all live downstream. This slogan is usually applied to environmental issues, and rightly so. In a very real sense, however, the slogan applies to all of us, wherever we live. That is to say, we are all affected by what happens around us.

The prophet Jeremiah proclaimed this basic truth. About five hundred years before the time of Jesus, the nation of Israel was decimated by the Babylonians. Thousands of men, women, and children of Israel were taken into captivity and exiled to the city of Babylon. They were now captives within an enemy city. The prophet Jeremiah wrote a letter to the Israelites who were in exile in the foreign city of Babylon. Speaking for God, Jeremiah said, "seek the welfare of the city where I have sent you into exile, and pray to the LORD on its behalf, for in its welfare you will find your welfare" (Jer 29:7). For their own good, while they were in exile, God wanted them to be actively working to make the city where they were being held a better place.

Jeremiah proclaimed the basic truth that your personal welfare is directly related to the welfare of the city in which you live. In other words, we all live downstream. If you have an impoverished community in your area where people have grown accustomed to inadequate schools, inaccessible health care, prison as an alternative lifestyle, single-parent homes, and long-term unemployment, everyone in the larger surrounding community will be impacted. An impoverished community produces hopeless and desperate people around you, and you will be living in fear and anxiety. The results of compacted poverty cannot be contained, and no one benefits from the consequences. Crime, drugs, and gangs quickly become everyone's problem. Each person will pay more for police protection, the criminal justice system, prisons, plus many other social costs arising from an ongoing impoverished area within the larger community.

The ancient wisdom of the religious traditions applies here: Love your neighbor as (or while) you are loving yourself. This is enlightened self-interest that should appeal to everyone, not just those who are religious. It is the better part of wisdom to look out for yourself by looking out for your neighbor, wherever that neighbor may live. If your neighbor is hopeless and sees no way out of a bad situation, then your own safety and welfare is at risk. You will be fearful and you will live behind locked doors, high fences, and perhaps in a walled-off community. Seek the welfare of the city, for in its welfare you will find your own.

It has been said, *poverty is a weapon of mass destruction.* Poverty destroys everything in its path: individuals, families, neighborhoods, communities, and nations. Thus there are both biblical and practical reasons for faith communities to have a strong commitment to building a Beloved Community in their midst. Everyone's life will be enhanced when a Beloved Community is established within the larger community.

E. WHO ESTABLISHES A BELOVED COMMUNITY?

The term most often used is a Congregation-Based, Community-Organizing Group, or as it is often referred to, a CBCO. It is a collection of faith communities, schools, civic leaders, and nonprofit groups using their collective power to bring about change in an urban community. The vision of the Beloved Community is congregations and their partners working together to create holistic communities.

Government programs alone are not sufficient to provide the new kind of urban communities that are needed. Government must do its part, but government can be inefficient, bureaucratic, and slow. Nor can the business sector be expected to transform low-income areas into Beloved Communities. Businesses can be helpful, but their primary motivation is to make a profit. The nonprofit organizations can also be a vital component in developing the Beloved Community, but each one rightly tends to focus on one specific problem area.

The faith-based communities must pave the way. Lasting systemic social changes do not usually take place without the active involvement of communities of faith. The church, through the CBCO group, can provide the unifying glue to bring the various sectors together to work for the common good of the community. Through their collective efforts, they are much more effective than if they separately try to effect change in the community. As these various sectors intersect, they can celebrate each other's endeavors, while at the same time remaining aware of the challenges and even disagreements that will inevitably arise.

The issues CBCOs tend to focus on are affordable housing, access to health care, transportation, a living wage, criminal justice reform, education, and jobs programs.

The involvement of congregations in CBCOs gives members of the faith communities opportunities to be involved in the city dealing with some tough issues. It connects the congregation more deeply with the city. An important benefit of involvement with a CBCO is that members get to know other groups' members while working to improve their communities. Familiarity with the other creates comfort, social ease, and trust. The result will be a quite remarkable convergence of efforts from the governmental sector, the business community, and the nonprofit organizations.

F. WHAT IS THE ROLE OF THE CHURCH?

The role of the church is the same role Jesus played: to be a catalyst in helping people form their own Beloved Communities. One thing that made Jesus special was he did not claim to be special. From the evidence, we see that Jesus always pointed away from himself to others. In his compassionate healing ministry, he never claimed credit for the healing of an individual. He is reported to have repeatedly said to the person healed, "Your faith has made you whole." When he spoke about himself, he did so in humble terms. Mark 10:17–22 reports that a man came up to Jesus, addressing him by the term "Good Teacher." Jesus responded by saying, "Why do you call me good; there is no one good but God alone." He also once remarked, "foxes have holes, and birds of the air have nests," but as for himself, he said he had "nowhere to lay his head" (Luke 9:58). In other words, he was homeless. Further, Jesus deflected attention away from himself to his followers when he said to them, "You are the salt of the earth. . . . You are the light of the world" (Matt 5:13, 14).

When Jesus came to a village he did not come to promote himself. He came as a catalyst to empower the village people to organize their village life in a way benefiting each resident of the village. He stayed only a brief time, long enough to enable them to implement the plan for a community of shared resources. He did not even leave a team of leaders behind to oversee the implementation of his program. Evidently he believed that within each village existed the resources and assets needed to build the Beloved Community. He worked in solidarity and identification with the local village population. He did not see the villagers as clients to be ministered to but as a resource to be empowered.

Jesus's meal ministry was an example of his inclusiveness and belief that each person was an important asset. Long-term benefits could be realized when everyone had a place at the table. He included prostitutes, tax collectors, lepers, the ill, and other outcasts at the table. For that, he was roundly criticized by the religious leaders and the aristocrats of his society. In spite of that criticism, he made sure everyone was included and everyone was affirmed.

Likewise, the church must not come to a community to promote its own interests. The church serves best when it follows Jesus's example and serves as a catalyst to empower the community residents to build a healthy and holistic community. The resources and assets needed to accomplish this task are already in the community. Those resources include governmental agencies at work in the community, businesses within the community, nonprofit organizations, and most of all the indigenous population itself.

As with Jesus, there are no clients in the Beloved Community. The residents are not seen as clients to be taken care of, but as capable people to be empowered. The need is for interdependence, affirming each of the community components as an important asset capable of being integrated into a community's vision for change.

G. WHAT IS COMMUNITY ORGANIZING AND HOW DO WE DO IT?

The great calling of the church is to follow in the footsteps of Jesus, the community organizer par excellence, by being about the process of community organizing today. This means the church is to be involved in helping to establish the Beloved Community wherever possible. Where do we begin?

1. Congregational Conversations. Community organizing always begins with conversations: conversations among friends and strangers about what is important to them, best done in the setting of a meal. From the biblical evidence, we know communal meals were an important part of Jesus's ministry. When Jesus and his entourage came to a village, we can imagine the first thing that happened was communal meals and conversation.

The Beloved Communities of today must begin, as with Jesus, with conversations between friends and strangers in the setting of a meal. It starts with one person—a pastor, a lay leader, an ordinary worshiper—catching the vision of Jesus and wanting to help make that vision become a reality in the world today. It then expands within the congregation, built around many conversations where congregants connect and share their dreams and visions for community building. People talk about the Beloved Community and why building that community in their neighborhood is important to them.

Out of these conversations emerges a common vision. People learn to envision a transformed community, imagining what that community can become. They allow themselves to develop a grandiose dream for the future—not just for next year, or five years from now, but of twenty-five or even fifty years from now. They can dream of what their community can be for their children and grandchildren. The common vision that emerges becomes the standard against which they measure and determine the practical steps that they can take today.

2. Inclusion of Other Faith Communities. The organizing process expands by drawing together other faith-based organizations in the neighborhood or community to share and discuss what it would mean to follow Jesus in forming a Beloved Community in that setting. No one church has the resources or people to do this by itself, nor should it try. We need each other to develop the Beloved Community, and we make a stronger impact by working together for the good of the community.

It may seem that diverse groups of faith communities would have difficulty reaching consensus on the social issues of the day. The extremists have controlled the agenda for so long that the more moderate voices have been silenced. When committed people of faith start talking to each other, however, they find they have much more in common than they had previously thought. When their common desire is to make this a better world for people, one community at a time, they discover they can reach consensus or near-consensus on almost any issue. When they have a great goal in mind, they do not waste time and energy arguing about beliefs or fighting with each other over theological issues. They have a larger commitment to the ideal of people united in helping one another. When this occurs, no opposition exists that would undermine the endeavor to establish the Beloved Community.

Already there is a new spirit developing within many religious communities. As people interact with one another, they learn to be comfortable with their own religious understanding alongside other faith traditions. They do not feel the need to see themselves as superior to other faith expressions or even to those with no religious faith. People learn they can have their own beliefs without judging or rejecting anyone else's positions as wrong. They can let their faith be the right thing for themselves, without it having to be the right thing for everyone. This spirit of humility and acceptance opens the door for a wide range of partnerships and genuine cooperation for the good of the poor of the community. This cooperation for the common good will increase the effectiveness of the faith communities and expand their influence in the larger community.

The church is at its best when it is forgetting itself and focusing on meeting the needs of others. Often churches send out the message that what is important to them is the conversion of people to their particular faith tradition and the increase in the number of church members. People can see through this subterfuge. They realize the church is not seeking the good of the people but its own good. However, when the church surrenders its desire to convert and convince people to join, it becomes a true servant community making a difference in the world. When the church gives itself away in compassionate service to others, it is following Jesus in a very practical and positive way.

3. *Inclusion of the Nonprofits.* The circle then expands to include the nonprofit organizations already working in the targeted geographical area. These nonprofits are made up of many volunteers. Most of these nonprofits wisely focus on a single issue: housing, food, health care, income fairness, the environment, workers' rights, poverty amelioration. In every community there are nonprofits engaged in addressing these and a myriad of other social issues.

One of the most effective ways the faith communities can make a difference in a community is by forming coalitions, not only with each other, but also with the nonprofit agencies already at work in the community. There is strength in numbers, and as these coalitions form, there is a great opportunity to make a significant impact on a community. By working together, we demonstrate our interdependence and our cooperative spirit. We will work with others who have different perspectives, but who share the same concern for the mission of helping the poor, the oppressed, and the powerless. We can work alongside those who do not share our exact faith commitment, but who are motivated by an ethical concern for others.

A faith community, however, must come with the right spirit to the endeavor as it joins with the work already being done. The temptation is for the faith community to see itself as the primary or superior means through which social action can take place. It may seek to keep the effort to help others under its own control, or to see itself as the one having the "right" answers for the community. It may also be inclined to use its involvement in the community for its own gain, at the expense of the community. To be truly following in the footsteps of Jesus, faith communities must approach the task humbly, with a cooperative spirit, working alongside those who are already compassionately involved in making the community a better place for everyone.

4. Inclusion of the Local Population. The circle grows wider by drawing in the indigenous population and getting them involved in the community-building process. Meals and conversations will again be the basic means by which this can be accomplished. People will be talking to each other, sharing ideas, information, and resources.

The local residents will define the neighborhood problems needing attention, and that will determine the appropriate steps needed to address those problems. The cookie-cutter approach, which attempts to impose the same solutions everywhere, will not work. If outsiders seek to create their own answers to the local problems, the plans and strategies will be imposed on the residents of the community, and this will be counterproductive. The local population must be involved in analyzing both the needs and assets of the neighborhood, helping to develop plans and strategies for addressing the problems.

This expanding step-by-step process is a simple and effective way to get things done. As each person takes in new information, he or she synthesizes it and comes up with other, new ideas, and momentum is gained. People share these newly forged thoughts and ideas with one another. Each new thought is integrated into the next new thought, producing a cumulative awareness of the problems and the solutions. The most important thing about this process is that each individual is valued for his or her insights and contributions.

Within this process, information is the great equalizer. The Beloved Community is not egalitarian just because every member is equal. What occurs in the building of the community is members treat one another as equals because each person has access to information. There are no secrets; there is no inside information giving some people power over others. Full access to information empowers each individual. This results in people in the Beloved Community tending to trust and nurture one another.

5. Other Groups. Two other groups need to be included in the building of the Beloved Community: the private sector of business and markets and the public sector of government on all levels: local, state, and national. In reality, a healthy community is like a three-legged stool. It is composed of three important segments: (1) the nonprofit sector, both secular and religious; (2) the private business and market sector; (3) the governmental sector. All three sectors need to be functioning well together for the common good of everyone in the community. Each has a role to play as they interact with one another, and each does what it does best, not trying to control or compete with the other sectors. As they each work for the common good, the community functions in a way that is good for everyone.

The goal of the Beloved Community is holistic community transformation. It is not content with Band-Aids of relief. Piecemeal, tentative attempts to address only the symptoms of community needs are not enough. It requires the slow, hard work of broad-based community organizing and sustainable community development. Building the Beloved Community means being about the task of systemic, sustainable change, focused on asset-based community development, working together with every sector of the community for the health and wholeness of the community. This involves analysis and identification of needs, as well as an appropriate plan for the utilization of people and resources to address those needs.

Following Jesus in changing the world one community at a time has the power to lift both individuals and congregations out of the pursuit of the trivial. The goal, however, is not simply to make one's individual life more fulfilling, nor is it the enhancement of the life of a congregation. The goal is bigger than that. The ultimate goal is to transform communities into holistic communities of shared resources, as Jesus did in his ministry in Galilee. The Beloved Community can be initiated by the local churches, but it is not focused on the growth and development of the churches; it is focused on the health and welfare of the entire community.

The faith communities are really in a unique position to lead the way in community organizing. There are individual congregations located within the geographic zone where the Beloved Community is to be developed. Most of the members of those faith communities live within the neighborhood. These congregations can join with congregations outside the community to form a cooperative coalition. This prevents the endeavor from becoming a situation where outsiders are coming in to do things *for* people rather than *with* people.

Faith communities can lead the way in the forming of a cooperative coalition in the targeted neighborhood. The problem with much of the social work being done is that the groups and agencies have different agendas and different priorities. One group is working on economic issues, another on health care, another on housing, and so forth. The various groups seldom interact with one another, even when they are working in the same neighborhood. The need is for a single, in-the-neighborhood broker to bring the various groups and agencies, as well as the local population, together to work in a holistic manner. This comprehensive approach to community development may seem obvious, but social service endeavors are often piecemeal in their practice. The faith communities, both those outside and within the targeted area, are in an ideal position to serve as a catalyst for a truly cooperative spirit in the community, one that leads to the establishment of the Beloved Community. Approached in the right spirit, the church can form a coalition of community agencies, schools, corporations, governments, and local residents who will work for the common good of everyone in the community. The resulting community transformation will then be greater than the sum of its individual parts.

H. WHAT ARE THE KEYS TO BUILDING A BELOVED COMMUNITY?

There are five important keys to keep in mind in establishing a Beloved Community:

1. Clear Purpose. The members of the Beloved Community know why they are together and they have agreed on the way in which they will be together. They have founded their community not on directives, doctrines, and a multitude of rules, but on their desire to build a healthy community. As they know their reason for being together, the diversity of gifts among the people becomes a contribution to the community rather than a problem. Everyone feels included when they are clear on the purpose of the community and are willing to see others as helpful contributors to what the community is trying to create.

2. Egalitarian Decision-making. The Beloved Community has a process of dialogue and deliberation for finding common ground. If solutions to problems are to be found, there must be a process for talking, deciding, and moving to action. The process of deciding together is critical to the Beloved Community. Involving people in the decisions affecting their lives results in better decisions and decisions that are implemented faster.

3. Organization to Accomplish Tasks. The Beloved Community will need to have the ability to address and implement the means to get the work done to build a healthy community. The focus will not be on the form of the organization but on the work to be done. The architectural wisdom applies here: Form follows function.

4. Openness and Accessibility. The Beloved Community is inclusive, accessible, and open to everyone. A healthy community has a large enough space for a diversity of races, ages, income levels, beliefs, and ideas. The Beloved Community will give much attention and direction to finding avenues for engaging people in the complete life of the community.

5. Leadership. The Beloved Community broadens the circles of leadership to create a system of leadership that is not centralized or hierarchical. Decisions are not made by only a few people. Leaders will be servant leaders rather than authoritarian figures telling people what to do and how to do it. The large-scale challenges of community building will require people to ask themselves: what will work and what can we do? These practical questions will be answered as channels and vehicles for leadership are expanded to allow the work to be approached collaboratively through teams, involving multiple efforts and multiple leaders.

I. WHERE CAN I GET HELP?

Community organizing is a daunting task. Most clergy, lay leaders, and ordinary worshipers are not trained and equipped to fulfill the role of community organizers. Fortunately, however, there are several national organizations providing excellent information and training needed to be involved in community organizing and development. Help is available. Here is a brief description of several places an individual or congregation may turn for guidance in starting a local Beloved Community:

1. Communities of Shalom is a grassroots, faith-based community development network of congregations and community members working together for healing, health, and wholeness in their communities. In this effort, local congregations work with different sectors of a community toward transformation of the individual, the community, and the environment. Its focus is on systemic and sustainable change. Communities of Shalom seeks to engage congregations to build a future together, re-weave the fabric of community life, and transform the world, one community at a time. Its approach includes asset-based community development, organizing for direct action, and multicultural, multifaith collaboration. The Resource Center, located at Drew University in Madison, New Jersey, provides ongoing training, technical assistance, and regional support to Shalom sites. The Web site is www.communitiesofshalom.org.

2. *Industrial Areas Foundation* (IAF), based in Chicago, is a secular model of community development. It calls itself nonideological and nonpartisan. One basis of IAF organizing is the "face-to-face" individual meetings in neighborhood homes for the purpose of initiating relationships and healing the broken social fabric of the community. These meetings are based on the solid premise that individuals and communities define their own needs far more capably than outsiders. The IAF works with congregations as well as secular groups such as civic associations, labor unions, and neighborhood groups and clubs. Contact IAF at www.industrialareasfoundation.org.

3. *Gamaliel Foundation*, also based in Chicago, is a network of some fifty-five faith-based community organizations. The foundation aims to create grassroots, interfaith, interracial, multi-issue organizations that work to empower people to participate in the political, environmental, social, and economic issues affecting their lives. Their Web site is www.gamaliel.org.

4. *The Pacific Institute of Community Organizing* (PICO) national network builds community organizations based on religious congregations, schools, and community centers, which are often the only stable civic gathering place in many neighborhoods. PICO helps congregations identify and solve local neighborhood issues and is deeply rooted in local communities. It aims to bring people together based on faith and values, not just issues or anger. The process PICO utilizes involves listening to the concerns and ideas of the indigenous population through individual one-on-one meetings, house meetings, and listening campaigns. As a result, PICO federations establish a broad following and choose issues that matter most to their communities. PICO also encourages meeting with public officials and policy experts to research how things work and who really has the power to make changes. Their Web site is www.piconetwork.org.

5. *The Direct Action and Research Training Center* (DART) in Miami has a deliberate process for bringing religious congregations together around shared concerns and values to challenge the economic, political, and social systems to act justly. DART trains leaders to conduct a series of one-on-one or small community meetings to surface problems and build internal networks of relationships. It provides guidance in researching problems and determining long-term, systemic solutions to problems. It

focuses on selecting issues locally by having members vote to determine the problems they wish to resolve. Their Web site is www.thedartcenter.org.

6. *Beloved Communities* has as its goal to foster and model a spirit of community based on Dr. Martin Luther King Jr.'s vision of a "Beloved Community." In this spirit, they envision and work toward social and economic relations that affirm and realize the equality, dignity, worth, and potential of every person. It pursues its mission of building an inclusive, egalitarian community through involvement in community organizing, public meetings and other forms of advocacy, as well as training and coalition building. Their Web site is www.belovedcommunities.org.

Each of these six national community-organizing groups provides training and assistance in the process of community organizing. They indicate places where successful faith-based community organizing has occurred so one can see examples of what can be accomplished. The good news for pastors, lay leaders, and ordinary worshipers is that help is available.

14

Systemic Issues in Building the Beloved Community

In building the Beloved Community, the goal is not charity or piecemeal rescue efforts, but a sustainable holistic approach that deals with the systemic problems in a community. There are a variety of areas to be addressed in this process, and each area will need a team of individuals who care about the issue and will be committed to long-term investment of time and energy in dealing with the issue. Developing the team approach to each of these systemic issues is an important part of the process of building the Beloved Community. Six systemic issues need to be addressed.

A. POVERTY

In an advanced country like the United States, poverty should be seen as both an embarrassment and an aberration. Poverty, however, is still prevalent in our country. The United States has a population of 300 million. Out of that number, 37 million, including 13 million children, live in poverty. Over 60 million additional people are classified as near-poor, living just above the poverty line. This means that nearly a third of our population are poor or near-poor.

It is time for the faith communities to insist that widespread poverty in the midst of plenty is morally unacceptable. The problem of poverty, however, can seem so big, so complicated, and so entrenched that many people are tempted to give up before they get started. The truth is that there are many things available to be done, if we are willing to think about poverty and its cures.

The first step is to rid ourselves of the idea that poverty is inevitable. The fact that we accept the idea of poverty is the very reason it continues to exist. If we firmly believe poverty is not acceptable—that it should not exist in a society like ours—then we will come together to create a poverty-free community. Poverty is not natural to human beings, so we can dedicate ourselves to bringing an end to it as soon as possible. It simply takes a few committed individuals to say, "Let's work together to eliminate poverty in our Beloved Community."

Traditionally, the poor have been seen as a social problem, as hopeless and helpless people. As a result, the innate capacity of the poor to use their creative energy and skill has been overlooked. What is needed to get poor people out of poverty is for the Beloved Community to create an environment where the poor can make productive contributions on their own behalf and be a benefit to the entire community. In building the Beloved Community, three major steps can be taken to empower people to escape the bonds of poverty:

1. Living Wage. The alarming fact is that most of the poor and near-poor work—and work hard—in jobs with low wages, no retirement benefits, and inadequate health insurance, if they have any at all. While their wages remain low, the cost of living continues to increase, and they still fall below the poverty line.

Work should be a pathway out of poverty. A living wage for good work is a religious value. We must focus our efforts on making work a way out of poverty for low-income families. This means being involved in the struggle for a "living wage" for America's working people. In many cities and states across America, voters have approved measures to raise their minimum wage above the federal level. In many cities a Living Wage Coalition is already active, ensuring good work is acknowledged through a pay scale that enables a family to live above the poverty line.

In the past, the Horatio Alger dream of getting out of poverty by pulling yourself up by your bootstraps was a part of the American culture. The American ideal was a classless society where children from different family economic levels had a similar chance of success. The belief was that the United States was a land of opportunity where you could start out poor and become rich through hard work.

Today that ideal has essentially become a myth. The truth is that Horatio Alger stories are rare anecdotes, and stories of people trapped by their parents' poverty in a permanent underclass are common. In fact, the best predictor of a child's economic success now is the income level of his or her parents. Children born to parents who are in a poverty situation are very likely to remain in a poverty situation as adults.

None of this is inevitable. The great need is to establish a system ensuring that work is a route out of poverty. In addition to a minimum living wage, there is a need for benefits that include access to affordable health care and retirement income security. In the past, when work provided adequate health and pension benefits, a serious illness or the loss of a job wasn't necessarily devastating. Now such a turn of events is more than likely to place a family in severe economic peril.

No one who works a full-time job should have to live in poverty. A living wage is an important step in empowering people to be lifted out of poverty.

2. *Work Cooperatives.* A growing movement in the United States is the formation of work cooperatives, where each participant is both a worker and an owner of the venture, sharing the costs and profits equally. Cooperatives give more people access to business ownership. Workers and managers are the same people. They don't need to make huge profits for shareholders, and there is no pressure to keep wages low.

Another advantage of work cooperatives is that as people pool their resources and skills, only a small amount of capital is needed to get started. This enables the poor and the near-poor to have the resources to start a business together.

The United States Federation of Work Cooperatives is a grassroots organization of and for worker cooperatives and the organizations that support the growth and continued development of worker cooperatives. The mission of the Federation is to create stable and empowering jobs and worker-ownership. It advances workplaces owned, managed, and governed by workers through cooperative education, advocacy, and development. For more information, visit the Web site of the United States Federation of Work Cooperatives at www.usworker.coop.

3. *Microcredit.* A recent development, spearheaded by Muhammad Yunus, is microcredit for the poor. Known as the banker to the poor, he has written several books about creating a world without poverty. Professor Yunus established the Grameen Bank, which has dared to give the poor bank credit. In the past, financial institutions asked the question, Are the poor credit worthy? The answer was always *no*. The poor, therefore, were left out of the financial system. Muhammad Yunus realized that if the poor are to get the chance to lift themselves out of poverty, the barrier to credit must be removed. He believed giving credit to the poor allowed

people to have a chance to make a living through self-employment, using their creativity to develop goods or services that they sell directly to those who need them. Credit for the poor can create self-employment and generate income for them.

The basic principle of this approach is that each person has an innate but generally unrecognized skill: the survival skill. The goal of microcredit is to empower individuals to use the engine of creativity within themselves. Thus, the Grameen Bank offers the poor not handouts or grants, but credit, like any other respected businessperson gets—loans they must repay with simple interest (not the compound interest charged by conventional banks), through their own productive work. Microcredit is a loan offered with no collateral, with the goal of supporting income-producing businesses aimed at lifting the poor out of poverty.

A key element in the process is that each person who borrows from Grameen Bank belongs to a self-made group of five friends, no two of whom may be closely related. The group functions as a small social network providing encouragement and support for the borrower. This community-oriented dynamic of Grameen Bank is an important reason for the success of the program. When Grameen members were asked about why they repay their loans, the most common answer was, "I would feel terrible to let down the other members of my group."

The microcredit approach to dealing with poverty will appeal to many members of the congregations involved in building the Beloved Community. Funding for the program could be supplied by persons with wealth who will find microcredit for the poor an attractive investment opportunity to pursue. The big advantage for donors is that when they invest in a credit bank, they get their money back. It is not charity or philanthropy. The donor is not required to keep giving more and more each year to the program. It is thus a sustainable enterprise.

Everyone understands that money is important. The unique problem of the poor is there is no one to bring money to them. Microcredit solves that problem in a businesslike way. The fact is there is plenty of money to lend to the poor. It is simply a question of mobilizing it and making it available to the poor.

For more information about the microcredit program, contact Professor Yunus and the Grameen Bank at the Web site www.grameen.com.

B. AFFORDABLE HOUSING

The Hebrew social prophets knew that the dream of God for humanity included each person having one's own place upon which to build a life for oneself and his or her family. They spoke directly to their understanding of what God wanted to happen:

> They shall build houses and inhabit them;
> they shall plant vineyards and eat their fruit. (Isa 65:21)

> Build houses and live in them; plant gardens and eat what they produce. (Jer 29:5)

> They shall all sit under their own vines and under their own fig trees,
> and no one shall make them afraid;
> for the mouth of the LORD of hosts has spoken. (Mic 4:4)

Home ownership is not only a major part of the American dream, it is also vital to the building of the Beloved Community. A person who owns his or her own home becomes a stakeholder in the community. Studies have shown that people who are asset holders behave more responsibly and are more civic minded than those without any property. After all, they have a stake in the future of their community.

Rudolph Giuliani promoted the "Broken Windows" theory of urban development. The idea was that if a broken window goes unrepaired, the tendency is for vandals to break more windows, and then break into the building itself in a downward spiral of crime and urban decay that spreads to more buildings and entire neighborhoods.

The theory has its critics, but it is hard to argue with the common sense of it. The same concept applies to home ownership. If a renter lives in a building owned by someone else, there is less interest in maintaining the facility. If, however, a person is a homeowner, there is a strong incentive to take care of one's home and property and to care about the surrounding neighborhood and community.

An important factor in building a safe and healthy neighborhood is to expand the number of homeowners in that neighborhood. Everyone needs to have at least a small stake in the community, their own place of security for themselves and their family. However, safe and affordable housing is increasingly scarce in America, even for many working families. So congregations seeking to establish the Beloved Community will want to work in the area of affordable housing for everyone.

In many communities there are organizations working in the area of providing affordable housing. Churches can become a part of the process, serving as conduits to help people fulfill the dream of home ownership. This can include pre- and post-purchase counseling for potential home owners regarding loan and banking processes, mortgages, expectations about care and maintenance of property, and the building of owner equity. It could also mean searching for vacant property and abandoned buildings suitable as potential housing sites.

Until the 1980s the federal government provided major funding for affordable housing, often working with churches as partners. As federal funds have diminished, the need for affordable housing has increased. There are, however, hopeful signs of renewed interest in this area. One is NeighborWorks, a federally funded network of more than 240 member organizations who share a common mission: to promote affordable housing opportunities. NeighborWorks has set standards in education, community development, and lending to preserve and create sustainable, affordable home ownership.

Another hopeful sign is the Community Housing Trust (CHT). A local housing trust acquires parcels of land through purchase, foreclosure, tax abatements, or donation. If a housing unit does not already exist on a parcel of land, the trust arranges for one to be built, then sells the building but retains ownership of the land beneath. The new homeowner leases the land for a nominal fee (perhaps $25 a month), generally for 99 years or until the house is sold.

This approach enhances affordable housing in several different ways. First, homeowners have to be in a low-income category. Second, the buying price of the home is reduced because it does not include the price of the land. Third, the trust works with lenders to reduce mortgage costs by using the equity of the land as part of the calculation of the mortgage. This reduces the amount of the down payment and other closing costs, and it eliminates the need for private mortgage insurance.

The Community Housing Trust keeps the property affordable by restricting the profit that buyers are able to take when they sell the house. Homeowners get back all of their equity, plus the market value of any capital improvements they made to the property. However, they retain only 25 percent of any increase in the value of the house, and none of the increase in the value of the land. This approach gives the buyer access to the benefits of home ownership, including tax deductions, accumulated equity, and stable housing costs. In return, the buyer gives up the chance at any windfall profits. The buyer can make a modest profit as the house is sold, but the reality is that most CHT homeowners would never have been able to buy the home in the first place. Thus they are able to finally enter the world of home ownership and end up in a better position than when they started.

The tenants and owners of the CHT vote for and serve on its governing board, along with government officials and other city residents with technical expertise, such as attorneys, architects, and urban planners. This promotes community involvement, making it a democratic, self-governing entity as well as an affordable housing program.

There are over two hundred Community Housing Trusts in the United States today. Half of those trusts have started within the last ten years. You can get information about the Community Housing Trust at their Web site: www.mycht.org.

Another example of cooperative efforts to enhance community and economic health is the Community Land Trust (CLT) movement. By holding land as a community asset that can be leased to individuals to provide permanent affordable access to land for housing, farming, and small businesses, CLTs help create a foundation for healthy, stable, and diverse communities. For more information, visit www.community-landtrust.org.

There is a growing belief that housing is a fundamental human right rather than simply a commodity. Making home ownership a reality for the poor is an area where churches can join with local affordable housing coalitions and governmental agencies. Creating stakeholders through home ownership is an important step in building the Beloved Community.

C. SOCIAL CAPITAL

A healthy and vibrant Beloved Community needs social capital, which includes publicly owned space such as parks, playgrounds, urban gardens, green belts, town squares, common areas, sidewalks, streets, and other public spaces. These open public places are where people go to meet, play, debate, and celebrate. Social capital also includes adequate sources of income, satisfaction with employment, home ownership, good medical care, financial security, cultural events and public gatherings, a sense of safety, low crime rates, adequate police protection, good schools, as well as a friendly, nurturing, supportive community. Building social capital is an important part of developing the Beloved Community.

If you build social capital, you can raise the level of the quality of life and individual happiness. Lack of social capital breaks down the overall quality of life in a community. Thus, increasing the social capital of a community is a way of preventing social problems too.

Social capital is the part of life involving the "we" side of human nature. To build social capital as a source of well-being, those developing the Beloved Community will want to start with things that are a part of everyday life.

Community gardens, for example, are a community-based endeavor designed for use rather than for financial gain. They are located on land the gardeners themselves do not own. Community gardens represent real production meeting real needs, and are a healthy source of social capital. Community gardens can be the start of a genuine sense of community.

There are a variety of types of community gardens: vegetable, flower, tree, or a combination. Churches can serve as sponsors of community gardens. Contributions of land, tools, seeds, fencing, soil improvement, or money are all vital to a successful community garden. The American Community Gardening Association has excellent information on their Web site for starting a community garden; visit them at www.communitygarden.org.

There are thousands of parcels of vacant and empty land in the cities of the United States. This land could become an important part of the Beloved Community for use as an urban commons, helping ordinary people survive and even thrive. A productive commons is vital to the well-being of a community. In a society that places great emphasis on "private" property, it is healthy to work together toward what we have in common, not just what we keep apart from one another.

D. CITY PARKS

Every community needs parks, especially in urban areas. Parks are comforting and calming places. Every child knows the importance of a patch of green grass. In urban areas where people live together in tight spaces, a park provides open space as a respite from the crowded conditions.

Parks are healthy places, especially in an urban environment. A growing body of research indicates that open spaces consisting of leafy vegetation filter pollution and trap particles of soot and dirt. Tree leaves also serve as cooling islands in the midst of heat generated by concrete city surfaces.

Parks show us at our best, providing space for the soul. Parks and gardens are essential to human social and psychological well-being. The October 2006 issue of *National Geographic* cites recent studies in Chicago concluding that "people living in buildings near green areas had a strong sense of community and coped better with everyday stress and hardship. They were less aggressive and less violent, they performed better on tests of concentration, they managed their problems more effectively."[1]

Researchers have also found that green space helps to reduce the crime rate. In and around buildings, the greener the surroundings, the lower the crime rate against people and property. The research team also found less litter and graffiti in natural landscapes.

National Geographic also reported that a national study of 450 children with Attention Deficit Disorders revealed reduced symptoms when they were exposed to natural environments. "After play in green spaces, parents reported that the children's ability to concentrate, complete tasks, and follow directions improved dramatically—in all age groups in all parts of the country."[2]

Grass and trees provide a welcoming place for people to gather. In the crowded core areas of cities, people need the welcoming atmosphere of a park. They need big open green spaces where they can play together, even in suburban sprawl neighborhoods.

This means that a vital ingredient in constructing the Beloved Community in an urban environment is the presence of a large, green city park, or even several smaller ones throughout various neighborhoods. They need to re-create the kind of spaces that provide opportunities for people of all ages to gather for talking, walking, playing, relaxing, and discovering.

1. Ackerman, "Space for the Soul," 112.

2. Ibid., referring to a study conducted by Frances Kuo and her colleagues at the Landscape and Human Health Laboratory of the University of Illinois. The study focused on residents of the Robert Taylor Homes, a housing project of 28 identical high-rise buildings in Chicago.

If there is not already such a park in the area where a Beloved Community is being developed, that should be one of the first orders of business. The city government can be petitioned to make an investment in the community through providing an appropriate city park. A park in a community represents a minor public investment with a huge payoff. Parks help people take care of themselves so the city government doesn't have to spend so much on social, medical, and safety services trying to fix their problems.

The builders of the Beloved Community could "adopt a park," providing a staff person to be present in the park to help develop recreational, social, and educational activities for all ages. This could be a cooperative venture in conjunction with other nonprofits as well as the local city government.

A Beloved Community needs a central park, where people can easily and safely gather for a variety of community activities. A realistic goal is to have a park within a half-mile of every resident in the Beloved Community.

E. EDUCATION

Our country's founders were well aware of the importance of education. Thomas Jefferson said, "Every government degenerates when trusted to rulers of the people alone. The people themselves are the only safe depositories. . . . to render them safe, their minds must be improved to a certain degree. An amendment to our Constitution must here come in aid of public education."

Another of the founders, John Adams, wrote, "Laws for the liberal education of youth . . . are so extremely wise and useful that to a humane and generous mind, no expense for this purpose should be thought extravagant."

Contrary to these lofty ideals, in many low-income areas, inadequate schools are the rule rather than the exception. For those working to establish the Beloved Community, developing high quality schools within the community is an important goal.

For children to succeed in school, we need to focus not just on their academic achievement, but also on their social and emotional well-being. It is shortsighted to save money by cutting school counselors and psychologists and then to spend millions of dollars later on combating crime, prisons, unemployment, and welfare. Urban schools often lack adequate resources, forcing students to learn in substandard facilities and overcrowded classrooms. People vote to cut support for public education, then complain about how many police we need on the street. Yet there is a direct correlation between the quality of education we provide for our children and the results of that education, or lack thereof, in their adult lives.

A focus on high-stakes testing has narrowed the range of the content of education and pushed teachers into a test-driven curriculum. Children have the right to a quality education focusing on their full potential, not an education that limits their ability to learn and fails to graduate one-fourth of our children. By focusing on raising test scores and policing hallways instead of supporting the full development of children in a holistic fashion, we rob the students of the quality education they deserve.

We should be aware of the individualistic nature of the American educational system and its consequences for students in American schools. From the first days of school, we learn that some students will be rewarded and recognized for their achievements, while others will be judged as failures and will even become invisible. Since so much of our education is focused on individual achievement, it is easy to overlook the more profound and lasting consequences of the school system on the inner psyches of children. While children may quickly forget the academics, the effect on their psyche will stay with them for the rest of their lives.

This becomes a major issue in high school and college. School violence (Columbine, Virginia Tech, etc.) is a major issue in educational circles. This violence has been linked to the deep sense of isolation and invalidation felt by the perpetrators. In our society, schools are an arena of constant struggle for recognition and validation of a student's worth. Especially in high school and college, the "you're on your own" approach to education can leave a student feeling ostracized and excluded. This individualistic approach to education creates many social problems in our society. It takes a serious toll on the emotional life of young people who are extremely vulnerable at this time of life. It should be no surprise that being treated poorly on a social level can serve as a catalyst for an angry response.

There is an alternative to the "you're on your own" approach to education. Jesus taught that the old competition approach to life does not work as well as cooperation—a sense of shared responsibility and mutual respect. The lessons of trust, cooperation, and partnerships have a wider importance for our society, helping to move us from a preoccupation with divisions toward a focus on our common humanity and common ground.

Perhaps nowhere in the world do elementary schools intentionally draw children into mutual social relationships and establish a spirit of cooperation and participation than in Japan. In the Japanese school system, the children study and learn in groups, where they develop a sense of cooperation. The small group is the basic building block of education.

The Japanese school system recognizes classmates are a resource. In fact, they are a more crucial resource than books, pencils, and laptops. Peers are teachers in their own right. What the children are learning from one another in groups is as important as what they learn from the teachers.

In fact, in Japan the teacher serves more as a guide or a coach. The teacher oversees the groups in the classroom, rather than dispensing truth from the front of the room. Knowledge emerges from the group rather than being absorbed from on high. Gifted children as not singled out for special learning opportunities, and slower learners are not consigned to a watered-down curriculum. The faster learners help the slower learners. As every teacher knows, when one teaches a subject to students, the teacher learns far more than the students. Thus, the faster learners absorb the material more completely and retain it more fully, because they feel the responsibility to teach it to the slower learners in their group. The slower learners also learn more quickly and easily when they have the support of the group. Everyone is a member of the team, and the team is everything. The Japanese school system is built on the principle of cooperation and inclusion, rather than competition and exclusion.

Does it work? International tests show that in terms of basic academic skills, Japanese students have consistently outperformed American students, and the Japanese students feel a greater sense of belonging as opposed to a sense of isolation and rejection often found in American students. This means that the principles of cooperation and community Jesus taught can be included in the educational approach of the Beloved Community.

One step to consider in starting the Beloved Community is developing a *charter school*, using the cooperative principles of Jesus (and Japan) in the school. Charter schools are

- publicly funded, and are not vouchers for private schools;
- open to *all* students;
- pioneers and innovators in public education;

- meeting parents' needs;
- appealing places for teachers to work;
- committed to improving public education;
- operated by an array of nonprofit groups;
- playing an important part in school reform;
- demonstrating a record of student achievement.

In 2008, there were over one million students enrolled in more than 3,500 charter schools in forty states plus the District of Columbia and Puerto Rico. A majority of these new schools have been launched since state legislatures began passing charter legislation in the 1990s. Chartering is a radical educational innovation that is moving states beyond reforming existing schools to creating something entirely new. Chartering is at the center of a growing movement to challenge traditional notions of what public education means.

Chartering allows schools to run independently of the traditional public school system and to tailor their programs to community needs. Policymakers, parents, and educators are looking at chartering as a way to increase educational choice and innovation within the public school system.

A good starting place for a charter school is an elementary school. It is less expensive because there is not a need for athletic fields or other advanced facilities required in a middle school or high school. Also, since the steepest learning curve for a child is before the age of five, preschool is an important feature of the charter school program and must be included in the Beloved Community educational system.

For more information about charter schools and steps to take to start a charter school, visit US Charter Schools at www.UScharterschools.org.

The Beloved Community can include a cooperative coalition to join together to start a charter school or other educational options to meet the community needs. The goal should include high expectations, higher-quality teachers, a cooperative learning curriculum, more motivated students, and greater parental involvement. In short, all of the conditions educators identify as important ingredients of good schools.

F. CRIME AND PUNISHMENT

More than 2 million Americans are in prison, by far the highest number of prisoners in the world. The United States has less than 5 percent of the world's population and almost 25 percent of the world's prison population.

As a point of comparison, the International Center for Prison Studies at King's College in London issued a report indicating that Germany imprisons 88 out of every 100,000 people. The comparable number in the United States is 751 out of 100,000, roughly eight times that number.[3]

In the United States incarceration tends to be a common response to crime. Being "tough on crime" is an easy approach to take and is popular among politicians. Get-tough sentencing guidelines imposed by state legislatures tend to lock up many people who do not need to be in prison.

There is an important point related to crime: the United States has, by far, the highest rate of childhood poverty of any industrialized country—almost twenty percent. Other major countries, like Canada and Western European countries, have social programs in place that result in a very small population of poverty, especially among families. Unlike other industrialized countries, in the United States affordable quality childcare is usually not available to low and moderate income families. In addition, many of these low-income children attend inadequate schools and drop out of high school at very high rates. In fact, among First-World countries, the United States rates nineteenth in high school graduation rates. It is no surprise many of these ignored, jobless, and poorly educated children then engage in destructive and criminal behavior as adults.

If we adequately invested in low-income children in this country, we could produce more children who work and pay taxes, rather than producing criminals who cost over $50,000 a year to incarcerate.

The cost to incarcerated individuals, their families, and whole communities is very high, while the return on our investment in imprisonment is very low. Incarcerated people usually debilitate, becoming worse criminals. The only way to reduce the high crime rate in the United States is to address the real causes of crime: gaping educational disparities, pervasive poverty, mental illness, drug addiction, and broken relationships. Most criminal behavior is an act of desperation, mental illness, drug-related problems, or a combination of all three.

3. Cited in Liptak, "U.S. Prison Population."

One response to the enormity of the crime problem in our country is the well-known Prison Fellowship program begun by Charles Colson. He, his staff, and over 40,000 volunteers take part in a Christian ministry to the prison population in this and over one hundred countries. They have also addressed poor prison conditions and certain problems in the way our society approaches criminal justice. He is due much credit for his work in this area, and churches working to build the Beloved Community can be involved with Prison Fellowship.

However, the Prison Fellowship program does not deal with the structural issues leading so many people into a life of crime. The building of the Beloved Community will seek to address the root causes of criminal behavior and change the social conditions in such a way as to help keep people from becoming prisoners in the first place.

There are alternatives to prison—many prisoners are incarcerated for nonviolent crimes. In the Beloved Community, we can be smart about nonviolent offenders. We can help establish drug treatment programs and encourage revisions to parole practices.

A major part of the problem is the fact that "recycled prisoners" make up a large percentage of the prison population. In fact, the Justice Department reports two-thirds of the approximately 650,000 prisoners released each year return to prison within a few years (recidivism).

One problem for the formerly incarcerated is the difficulty of finding a job. The hardest thing to do when a person is released from prison is to find employment, usually due to gaps in work histories, lack of skills, and the stigma of a criminal record. This often leads to desperation and, in many instances, more criminal behavior and recidivism.

There are initiatives that can reduce or even end the problem of recidivism. Studies have shown that work-based reentry programs keep newly released prisoners from recommitting crimes. This improves public safety and reduces the cost to taxpayers of prosecution and incarceration.

One such program is the Doe Fund in New York, which operates a successful work-based program in New York. The results of this program are impressive: only 4.8 percent of the program graduates are rearrested within a year of their release, compared to 44 percent nationally. In addition, the cost of the program is about half that of incarceration. The mission of the Doe Fund is to develop and implement cost-effective, holistic programs to break the cycle of homelessness, addiction, and criminal recidivism. The programs ultimately strive to help homeless and formerly incarcerated individuals achieve permanent self-sufficiency.

To get more information and discover how this program can be replicated in your community, contact the Doe Fund at their Web site: www.doe.org.

The churches can also be involved in existing support programs for families of incarcerated men and women. Studies have proven that the combination of full-time paid work, stable housing, and comprehensive support services brings about the best results for formerly incarcerated individuals. Reentry programs are the only thing ever proven to keep people out of jail after incarceration. Churches can help released and paroled persons get back into the work force and into society.

A FINAL WORD

The evidence in the first part of this book leads to the conclusion that Jesus's original goal in his mission was to establish kingdom-of-God communities among the poor in the villages of Galilee, his Beloved Communities. In other words, Jesus was a community organizer. To follow Jesus today means that the church must be about the business of community organizing, especially in low-income areas. It is a grand and noble enterprise that will give the church a lofty reason for its existence in this new era.

Building the Beloved Community will enable the church to call out the best in its members. It will move people toward the part in each human being that really wants a world of kindness, generosity, peace, social justice, environmental sanity, and love. People care about their world and about one another. Humans have an inborn desire to make life better for their fellow humans, if they can. Some never get a chance to put this instinctive, natural desire into practice. The building of the Beloved Community gives individuals the opportunity to contribute to increasing the well-being of others in very practical ways, making a difference in the lives of people. This is a gift the church can offer to its members.

Building the Beloved Community can unite people of faith in a great common cause. Doctrines and beliefs often divide faith communities from one another. However, as Francis David once said, "We don't have to think alike to love alike." Neither do we have to believe alike to love alike. We can let love be our doctrine, as we work with one another in building a Beloved Community that will include good housing, good jobs, and good schools—things we all want for ourselves and our children. It will be a sacred community, based on the belief that God's intention is for each person to be seen as a person of dignity and worth. It will be, as someone put it, the kin-dom of God, where we are each a brother or sister to one another.

The following closing thoughts are based on notes from a commencement address given by David W. Orr, professor of Environmental Studies and Politics, Oberlin College, on May 10, 2008, at Duke University. Building a Beloved Community is not an easy task, yet it is not an impossible task, either. Thus we face the task with neither optimism nor pessimism. Optimism says that the cards are stacked in our favor, so we don't need to work very hard at the task. We can sail right past any problems facing us. Pessimism, on the other hand, says the cards are stacked against us, so there is no use working at the task. The problems are too big for us.

Neither optimism nor pessimism is the way to face the work at hand. Rather, we face the task with hope. What gives hope its power is the release of human energy generated by the longing for something better. The capacity for hope is the most significant feature of the human race. It provides human beings with the energy to get started at working to make our world a better place, one community at a time. Hope realistically acknowledges the problems we face, but is confident that we can work together to accomplish what everyone really wants—a better world for everyone. So hope rolls up its sleeves and gets to work doing what Jesus did: building the kingdom of God, the Beloved Community, one community at a time.

Appendix

The Sources of Sayings Considered to Have Originated with Jesus of Nazareth

1. Twenty-four sayings whose source is both the Sayings Gospel Q and the *Gospel of Thomas:*

Saying	Q Gospel in Luke	Gospel of Thomas
Prophet without Honor	4:24	31
Blessings on You Poor	6:20	54
Blessings on You Hungry	6:22	69
Hidden and Revealed	6:31	6:5
Lend without Return	6:34–35	95
Speck and Log	6:41	26
Grapes, Thorns, Figs, and Thistles	6:43–45	45
John the Baptist in the Wilderness	7:24–25	78
Hidden and Revealed	8:17	5:1
To Have and Have Not	8:18	41
Nowhere to Lay His Head	9:58	86
Eat What Is Served	10:8–9	14:4
Seek and Find	11:9	2:1
Seek and Knock	11:9–10	92

A Strong Man	11:21–22	35
Placement of the Lamp	11:33	33:2–3
Inside and Outside of the Cup	11:39–41	89
Do Not Fret	12:22–24	36
Parable of the Mustard Seed	13:18–19	20
Parable of the Leaven	13:20–21	96
Parable of the Dinner Party	14:16–24	64
Parable of the Lost Sheep	15:4–7	107:1–3
Serving Two Masters	16:13	47:2
Coming of the Kingdom	17:20–21	113

2. Thirty-three sayings whose source is the Sayings Gospel Q:

Saying	Found in Luke
Love Your Enemies	6:27, 35
No Merit in Loving Those Who Love You	6:32
Turn the Other Cheek	6:29
Coat and Shirt	6:29
Give to Beggars	6:30
Forgive, and You Will Be Forgiven	6:37
Let the Dead Bury the Dead	9:60
Stay at One House	10:7
Entering a Town	10:8
The Peasants' Prayer	11:2–4
Government and House Divided	11:17
Satan Divided	11:18–19
By the Finger of God	11:20
Parable of the Unclean Spirit	11:24
Condemnation of the Pharisees	11:43

Veiled and Unveiled	12:2a
God and Sparrows	12:6
Hairs on Your Head	12:7
God's Care for the Sparrows	12:24
Adding an Hour to One's Life	12:25
God's Care for the Lilies	12:27–28
Settle Outside of the Court	12:57
The Narrow Door	13:24
Hating One's Family	14:26
Salt without Flavor	14:34
Saving One's Life	17:33
Parable of Money Held in Trust	19:12–27
Be on Guard against Prideful Scholars	20:45–46

Saying	**Found in Matthew**
Sun and Rain on the Just and Unjust	5:45
The Compassion of God	5:48
The Peasants' Prayer	6:9–13
God and Sparrows	10:29, 31
First and Last	20:16

3. THREE SAYINGS WHOSE ONLY SOURCE IS THE *GOSPEL OF THOMAS*:

Saying	**Found in Thomas**
The Rich Investor	63:1–3
The Empty Jar	97
The Assassin	98

4. **Fourteen sayings whose source is the *Gospel of Thomas* and a parallel saying:**

Saying	Found in Thomas	Parallel Saying
Parable of the Sower and the Seeds	9:1–5	Mark 4:3–8
Fire on Earth	10	Luke 12:49
What Defiles a Person	14:5	Mark 7:14–15
Prophet without Honor	31:1	Mark 5:4
City on a Mountain	32	Matthew 5:14
Sly as a Snake	39	Matthew 10:16
Aged Wine	47:3	Luke 5:39
Wine and Wineskins	47:4	Mark 2:22
Left Hand and Right Hand	62:2	Matthew 6:3
Parable of the Leased Vineyard	65:1–7	Mark 12:1–8
Parable of the Precious Pearl	76:1–2	Matthew 13:45–46
True Relatives	99:2	Mark 3:31–35
The Emperor and God	100:2	Mark 12:13–17
Parable of the Treasure in a Field	109:1–3	Matthew 13:44

5. **Seven sayings whose source is Mark:**

Saying	Found in Mark
The Healthy Do Not Need a Doctor	2:17
Fasting and Wedding	2:19
Lord of the Sabbath	2:27–28
Parable of the Seed and the Harvest	4:26–29
Children in the Kingdom	10:14
Difficult for the Rich	10:23
Camel through the Eye of a Needle	10:25

6. THREE SAYINGS WHOSE SOURCE IS MATTHEW:

Saying	**Found in Matthew**
Parable of the Unforgiving Slave	18:23–35
Castration for Heaven	19:11–12
Parable of the Vineyard Laborers	20:1–15

7. TEN SAYINGS WHOSE SOURCE IS LUKE:

Saying	**Found in Luke**
Satan Falls Like Lightning	10:18
Parable of the Good Samaritan	10:30–35
Parable of the Friend at Midnight	11:5–8
Parable of the Rich Farmer	12:16–21
Parable of the Barren Fig Tree	13:6–9
Parable of the Lost Coin	15:8–10
Parable of the Prodigal Son	15:11–32
Parable of the Shrewd Manager	16:1–8a
Parable of the Widow and the Judge	18:2–8
Parable of the Pharisee and the Tax Collector	18:9–14

Note: A total of 94 sayings and parables are considered by the Jesus Seminar to have originated with Jesus of Nazareth. The rest of the sayings and parables attributed to Jesus in the gospels of Matthew, Mark, Luke, John, and Thomas are considered to be a product of the early church and/or the writer's imagination.

Bibliography

Ackerman, Jennifer. "Space for the Soul." *National Geographic*, October 2006, 110–15.

Bellah, Robert N., Richard Madson, William M. Sullivan, Ann Swindler, and Seven M. Tipton. *The Good Society*. New York: Alfred A. Knopf, 1991.

———. *Habits of the Heart*. Berkeley and Los Angles: University of California Press, 1985.

Borg, Marcus. *Jesus: Uncovering the Life, Teachings, and Relevance of a Religious Revolutionary*. New York: HarperCollins, 2006.

———. *Jesus in Contemporary Scholarship*. Valley Forge, PA: Trinity Press International, 1994.

———. *Meeting Jesus Again for the First Time*. New York: HarperCollins, 1994.

Boyte, Harry. *Commonwealth: A Return of Citizen Politics*. New York: The Free Press, 1989.

Butz, Jeffrey J. *The Brother of Jesus and the Lost Teachings of Christianity*. Rochester, VT: Inner Traditions, 2005.

Cain, Marvin. *Jesus the Man*. Santa Rosa, CA: Polebridge Press, 1999.

Charlesworth, James H. *Jesus within Judaism: New Light from Exciting Archaeological Discoveries*. New York: Bantam Doubleday, 1988.

Chilton, Bruce. *Rabbi Jesus: An Intimate Biography*. New York: Doubleday, 2000.

Chilton, Bruce, and Jacob Neusner. *The Brother of Jesus: James the Just and His Mission*. Louisville: Westminster John Knox, 2001.

Christianson, Michael. *Equipping the Saints: Mobilizing Laity for Ministry*. Nashville: Abingdon, 2000.

Crossan, John Dominic. *The Birth of Christianity*. San Francisco: HarperSanFrancisco, 1998.

———. *The Historical Jesus: The Life of a Mediterranean Jewish Peasant*. San Francisco: HarperSanFrancisco, 1991.

———. *Jesus: A Revolutionary Biography*. San Francisco: HarperSanFrancisco, 1994.

Crossan, John Dominic, and Jonathan L. Reed. *In Search of Paul*. San Francisco: HarperSanFrancisco, 2004.

Ehrman, Bart D. *Jesus Interrupted: Revealing the Hidden Contradictions in the Bible*. New York: HarperOne, 2009.

Eisenman, Robert. *James the Brother of Jesus*. New York: Penguin Books, 1997.

Freke, Timothy, and Peter Gandy. *The Laughing Jesus*. New York: Three Rivers Press, 2005.

Funk, Robert W. *A Credible Jesus: Fragments of a Vision*. Santa Rosa, CA: Polebridge Press, 2002.

———. *Honest to Jesus: Jesus for a New Millennium*. San Francisco: HarperSanFrancisco, 1996.

———. *New Gospel Parallels*. Santa Rosa, CA: Polebridge Press, 1990.

Funk, Robert W., Roy W. Hoover, and the Jesus Seminar. *The Five Gospels: The Search for the Authentic Words of Jesus*. Santa Rosa, CA: Polebridge Press, 1993.

Funk, Robert W., and the Jesus Seminar. *The Acts of Jesus: The Search for the Authentic Deeds of Jesus*. Santa Rosa, CA: Polebridge Press, 1998.

Hedrick, Charles W. *Many Things in Parables*. Louisville: Westminster John Knox, 2004.

———. *Parables as Poetic Fictions: The Creative Voice of Jesus*. Peabody, MA: Hendrickson, 1994.

Herzog, William R. *Parables as Subversive Speech: Jesus as Pedagogue of the Oppressed*. Louisville: Westminster John Knox, 2004.

Horsley, Richard A. *Jesus and Empire: The Kingdom of God and the New World Disorder*. Minneapolis: Fortress, 2003.

Horsley, Richard A., and Neil Asher Silberman. *The Message and the Kingdom*. Minneapolis: Fortress, 1997.

Josephus. *The Essential Writings: A Condensation of Jewish Antiquities and The Jewish War*. Translated and edited by Paul L. Maier. Grand Rapids, MI: Kregel Publications, 1998.

Keller, Suzanne. *Community: Pursuing the Dream, Living the Reality*. Princeton: Princeton University Press, 2003.

Kloppenborg, John S. *Q Thomas Reader*. Santa Rosa, CA: Polebridge Press, 1990.

Kraybill, Donald B. *The Upside Down Kingdom*. Scottsdale, PA: Herald Press, 1978.

Laughlin, Paul Allen. *Remedial Christianity*. Santa Rosa, CA: Polebridge Press, 2000.

Lerner, Michael. *The Left Hand of God: Taking Back Our Country from the Religious Right*. San Francisco: HarperSanFrancisco, 2006.

Liptak, Adam. "U.S. Prison Population Dwarfs that of Other Nations." *New York Times*, April 23, 2008. Online: http://www.nytimes.com/2008/04/23/world/americas/23iht-23 prison.12253738.html?scp=3&sq=april%2023,%202008&st=cse.

Loehr, Davidson. *America, Fascism, and God*. White River Junction, VT: Chelsea Green Publishers, 2005.

Mack, Burton L. *The Lost Gospel: The Book of Q and Christian Origins*. San Francisco: HarperSanFrancisco, 1993.

McLennan, Rev. Scotty. *Jesus Was a Liberal: Reclaiming Christianity for All*. New York: Palgrave Macmillan, 2009.

Meyers, Robin R. *Saving Jesus: How to Stop Worshiping Christ and Start Following Jesus*. New York: HarperOne, 2009.

Miller, Robert J., ed. *The Complete Gospels*. Santa Rosa, CA: Polebridge Press, 1992.

Mitchell, Stephen. *The Gospel According to Jesus*. New York: HarperCollins, 1991.

Naisbitt, John. *Megatrends*. New York: Warner Books, 1982.

Patterson, Stephen J., and James Robinson. *The Fifth Gospel: The Gospel of Thomas Comes of Age*. Harrisburg, PA: Trinity Press International, 1998.

Peter F. Drucker Foundation. *Community of the Future*. Drucker Foundation Future Series. San Francisco: Jossey-Bass, 1998.

———. *Organization of the Future*. Drucker Foundation Future Series. San Francisco: Jossey-Bass, 1997.

Putnam, Robert D. *Bowling Alone: The Collapse and Revival of American Community*. New York: Touchstone, 2000.

Reich, Robert B. *I'll Be Short: Essentials for a Decent Working Society*. Boston: Beacon Press, 2002.

Robinson, James M. *The Gospel of Jesus: In Search of the Original Good News*. New York: HarperCollins, 2005.

Sheehan, Thomas. *The First Coming: How the Kingdom of God Became Christianity*. New York: Vintage Books, 1986.

Sosnik, Douglas B., Matthew J. Dowd, and Ron Fournier. *Applebee's America*. New York: Simon & Schuster, 2006.

Spong, John Shelby. *Jesus for the Nonreligious*. San Francisco: HarperSanFrancisco, 2007.

Taussig, Hal. *Jesus before God: The Prayer Life of the Historical Jesus*. Santa Rosa, CA: Polebridge Press, 1999.

Vaage, Leif E. *Galilean Upstarts: Jesus' First Followers According to Q*. Valley Forge, PA: Trinity Press International, 1994.

Wallis, Jim. *God and Politics: Why the Right Gets It Wrong and the Left Doesn't Get It*. San Francisco: HarperSanFrancisco, 2005.

———. *The Great Awakening: Reviving Faith and Politics in a Post-Religious Right America*. New York: HarperCollins, 2008.

Yunus, Muhammad. *Creating a World without Poverty: Social Business and the Future of Capitalism*. Philadelphia: Public Affairs Books, 2007.